D0409873

JEREMY SEABROOK

Orphans

A History

HURST & COMPANY, LONDON

First published in the United Kingdom in 2018 by
C. Hurst & Co. (Publishers) Ltd.,
41 Great Russell Street, London, WC1B 3PL
© Jeremy Seabrook, 2018
All rights reserved.
Printed in the United Kingdom by Bell & Bain Ltd, Glasgow

Distributed in the United States, Canada and Latin America by
Oxford University Press, 198 Madison Avenue, New York,
NY 10016, United States of America.

A Cataloguing-in-Publication data record for this book
is available from the British Library.

ISBN: 9781849049429

This book is printed using paper from registered sustainable
and managed sources.

www.hurstpublishers.com

In memory of Jane Bradbury, 1942–2016, with love

CONTENTS

INTRODUCTION

Orphans through the ages have been—like widows—objects of conspicuous religious piety, and beneficiaries of much charitable enterprise. In view of their exalted place in the practice of human virtue, it is, perhaps, surprising that they have been treated with far less compassion than this would suggest. Frequently they have been subjected to violence, abuse and punishment.

We often think of orphans as those who have lost their parents through sickness, accident or early death. Yet it is important not to forget that orphans have also been created by ruling entities and governments, at times of war and civil strife. Equally it should be appreciated that certain orphans have been artificially made—not through the death of their parents—but by the forcible separation of children from their families. This may have been officially declared to be 'in the interests of the children themselves'. A great mission of 'rescue' took place in the nineteenth century by charitable institutions—Barnardo's and the Church of England Society, for instance—in which children were separated from depraved or drunken parents. This was sometimes referred to as 'philanthropic abduction.' Beyond this, from the seventeenth to the twentieth century, about 150,000 children were sent to the 'dominions', which not only saved considerable sums to payers of the poor rate, but also peopled apparently unpopulated lands with a new, raw citizenry of Empire.

1

Although orphan heirs to great fortunes became wards of the Crown or of local boroughs, the majority remained subject to the unmerciful Poor Laws. It is not known how many were unofficially adopted or simply taken in without ceremony by kin or neighbours. There is no doubt that love and duty did indeed save great numbers of forsaken or bereaved children. Their fate has been less thoroughly recorded than that of those who found their way into institutions—workhouses, reformatories, bridewells and penitentiaries run by the state, charity or private entrepreneurs.

Some biographies of orphans paint a picture of those who were impelled to make their own way in the world, to achieve success, fame and wealth by whatever talents they possessed. But many more simply perished, wasted away or indeed, in the eighteenth century, drew their last breath as soon as they saw the light of day. Many survivors were subjected to harsh and punitive regimes. This book explores the paradox of attitudes of piety and punishment towards the orphaned.

For beyond inspiring charitable sentiments, orphans also provoke fear. Those with no known antecedents, not rooted in secure families, who must make of themselves what they can, are potentially dangerous. They do not learn to mouth prayers at their mother's knee. They are not schooled to the disciplines necessary for a well-ordered life. For this reason, they must be compelled to labour; a penitential atonement for guilty or sinful parents, the product of whose union they are often believed to be.

I have drawn upon primary and secondary historical material. Interviews with the living as well as published memories of the long dead have aided my attempt to reach some of the ambivalences of orphanage (the abstract noun, not the receptacle in which so many found a cheerless refuge). It also looks at the orphan as metaphor, since we recognise orphanings that are not just literal in our world of perpetual upheaval and unchosen change. An orphan can be cultural, spiritual or linguistic, as well as being an outright outcast, orphaned through a state of exile and loss of identity.

INTRODUCTION

The first part of the book deals with the existential experience of being an orphan—through direct testimony, literary examples and the stories of well-known orphans. But at the centre of the book is the history of orphans, principally in Britain, with references to contemporary examples elsewhere. It concludes with an essay on orphaning as metaphor.

I am grateful to scholars, writers and researchers who have dealt with the stories of orphans in greater depth than I can hope to achieve. These include Ivy Pinchbeck and Margaret Hewitt for their book *Children in English Society* and Joanna Penglase for *Orphans of the Living*. I would also like to thank A. L. Beier for *Masterless Men*, Sue Elliott for *Love Child* and Lawrence Stone for *The Family Sex and Marriage in England 1500—1800*. Hugh Cunningham provided inspiration with *The Children of the Poor*, as did Lydia Murdoch with *Imagined Orphans* and Laura Peters with *Orphan Texts*. Nicholas Orme's work *Medieval Children* was invaluable as was Steve Hindle's *On the Parish*. The work of these scholars and many more informs this book, and if I have absorbed, and even reproduced, some of their ideas without acknowledgement, I apologise and beg their understanding.

I am indebted to the many individuals who shared their stories, discussed the issues involved, made observations, and in the case of Iqbal Hossein, conducted the interviews from Syria and Myanmar, especially on Myanmar and Syria. I gratefully acknowledge the help of Charlotte Bradbury, Anna Mottram, Paul Macey, Pandurang Hegde, Trevor Blackwell, Ivan and Wisia Ruff, Chris Guite and my dear, late friend, Barry Davis. I should also like to thank the staff of the British Library, especially in the Music and Rare Books reading room, for their courtesy and helpfulness.

Jeremy Seabrook
May 2018

PART ONE

ORPHANS

ORPHANS

Isolation of the orphan

In my primary school was a boy whose father 'ran away' and whose mother 'put her head in the gas oven'. This narrative was very graphic—the father running, perhaps stumbling, on his road to permanent disappearance, while it sounded to us as though his mother had removed her head before placing it, like any good housewife, tidily in the gas oven.

This overawed the whole class and made the orphaned child an object of fascinated revulsion. As the only remaining individual in the story, he must have been—in some way undiscernible to us—responsible for such shocking desertions. Our inability to confront bereavement reinforced his culpability: he was shunned.

We looked at him in wonder when he returned to school after a surprisingly brief absence. His clothing looked awkward, his hair unkempt, his shoes scuffed. This neglect seemed a proper expression of the condition of one whose father had not thought him worthy of his company, and of the mother who had preferred death to her child. He was to be avoided for fear of contagion. We knew how to value our own parents and wanted to know nothing of the mysterious art of matricide.

Before he returned to school, the teacher told us he needed special care and affection. We should not ask him questions, but should behave as though nothing had happened. One or two girls, recognising his loss, offered him small presents, but most of the class, their interest satisfied, soon fell into an excluding indifference.

For the rest of our time in that school he exuded an air of the sinister and the irregular. It would not be forgotten, although the tragedy faded, and he was more or less reintegrated into the class. He lived with an auntie and uncle, an object of charity. He could not take other children home to tea, and he forfeited friendship, since there was no one to judge whether or not there were suitable companions for him.

Meaning

The word 'orphan' clearly derives, via late Latin and Middle English, from the Greek *orphanos*, bereaved. Its earlier Indo-European provenance suggests a more violent experience. *Orbha* is to put asunder, and the root *reup* or *reub* means to snatch or seize. *Orbho* means one bereft of a father, and by association deprived of free status (Sanskrit has *arbha*, small, weak, or a child). The loss of freedom is reflected in Old Church Slavonic *rabu* slave, while *rabota* is servitude, like Gothic *arbya*, German *arbeit*. This indicates the subordinate condition of orphans, their unknown origin that compels them to work, in order to justify, not only their maintenance, but their very existence.

A long train of associations clings to words, and suppressed experience haunts the simplest expressions. Orphans, as well as objects of pity, can also be figures of fear, who must work to expiate their absence of known progenitors. If they appear in public discourse as pitiable, this also helps society ward off their semi-magical, and possibly criminal, ability to do away with their parents.

Children of the poor

The extension of concern to the children of the poor—whether in families or robbed of them—in Western society is very recent. Ruling castes have been indifferent to them, except insofar as they were likely to cause social disturbance or to question the wisdom of their betters. Their voices, always faint, have been stilled by time, their mouths stopped with the mould of forgotten burial-grounds. Some whisper of their experience still reaches us, chiefly from the annals of crime and madness, parliamentary investigations into the state of child labour, records of the Poor Law and, later, in the pages of social observers and researchers.

The last children embraced by official concern are those grown up as wards of the state, in a category now referred to as 'cared for' children. This, like so much in the lexicon of modernity, does not always mean what it says. The interest in their fate by authority has been stimulated by stories of children abused in institutions—run by state, charitable or religious establishments—and by scandals that have emerged from decaying industrial communities. Young girls have been 'groomed', often by men from other cultures who have recognised (correctly and opportunistically) a long tradition of coldness towards such children, who had freedom to be in the streets till late at night and to come and go as they chose. Their 'availability' suggested they were nobody's children, and unscrupulous males assumed they might therefore be anybody's. They offered presents, clothes, cosmetics, drink and drugs, before passing them from hand to hand in a disordered sub-culture of sexual exploitation, without regard for their youth or dignity. In Rotherham, Rochdale and elsewhere, South Asian men abused young girls with impunity, children whom even police described as 'prostitutes' and whose chaotic lives were an open secret, which agencies of the state did their best to deny or conceal. Jayne Senior, passionate campaigner on behalf of young girls abused and tortured in Rotherham, was silenced by police, social workers and council officials.[1] She was offered a secure email address to pass on information to the police, only to discover that it was a box for spam and none of the information she offered reached them. Many of the girls—some as young as eleven—were also living with their families. These could be described as victims, first of all of a kind of cultural orphaning, which I discuss later in the book, before they became prey to sexual predators. A significant number were also fostered or otherwise in care. One young girl was told by her abuser to accuse her stepfather of assaulting her, so she could 'go into a kids' home and come out whenever she wanted'.

When the story became public, the outrage expressed at disregard for this outcast—and cast out—youthful population was the more potent for the lateness of public recognition of the harm done to them. Whether they were in institutions or foster-homes, with relatives or even with the most loving parents, an absence of sufficient oversight or guidance meant that they could be viewed, to a certain degree, as orphaned. The ardour of those who now pursue their abusers shows, not only a desire for justice, but also guilt at long years of neglect.

Orphans and unbelonging

Peter Laslett describes the family as the supreme pre-industrial productive entity—a collection of people that included not only spouses and children, but also servants, dependants and employees.[2] Only paupers stood outside this unit, for they alone had no function. They, like the orphans (many of whom were of their number), not only depended upon charity for their maintenance, but, being without kin, were bereft of attachment to the dominant institution of the country.

Perhaps this is why the orphan is such a significant figure. Those without identity were to be pitied, as frequent biblical admonition shows. If women were once subsumed into the identity of husbands and fathers, orphans—even more radically—had no separate being at all. *Filius nullius* expresses a deeper illegitimacy than birth outside wedlock: it implies existence outside society. Orphans were placed high among the ranks of the deserving poor, since they were clearly not responsible for their plight. Yet at the same time their severance from belonging suggested a malevolent capacity for disruption.

The diversity of orphans

The definition of 'orphan' appears easy: a child whose parents have died. Historically, and in some patriarchal societies today, it refers to those who have no father. This is because the orphan's maintenance depended upon one capable of providing it; had lack of love defined orphans, the motherless would certainly have been perceived as the most forlorn. Circumstances and context make the concept more elastic than the clarity of the word suggests, and the simple formulation covers a great diversity of experience. Modifying Tolstoy's observation on families, orphans are all orphans, but each orphan is an orphan in her or his own way.

Orphans have also been made, rather than born, not only by their own parents, but also by the state, by ideology, by religion, by disease, war, civil strife and persecution. This introduces another ambiguity into the position of 'orphan', which can also affect the innocence of his or her position. We hear of people orphaned of more than parents, since other losses—cultural, national, spiritual—also contribute to a wider unbelonging. This mimics the status of 'orphanage' (that is, of being an orphan, not the stony receptacles which in recent centuries contained so many of them).

First of all, there are existential orphans, whose parents have died from disease or social violence, or as a result of accident or natural catastrophe—earthquakes, landslides, floods. The death of mothers in childbirth has also not infrequently led to the flight of the remaining parent. Secondly, orphans are made by human agency, direct or indirect. These, too can be categorised: first, parents who desert or abandon their children, whether for economic or social reasons (poverty and an inability to care for them); or shame because the child was born out of wedlock, or as a result of rape. Then come more indirect influences—social separation, the removal of children by the state from guardians considered unfit to raise them by virtue of neglect or incapacity. Lastly there are the children robbed of carers by conflict and social strife, especially war—always the most promiscuous generator of orphans. A particularly brutal example was that of Alex and Patrycia Klis, Polish girls of twenty and twelve, whose parents were killed by a terrorist bomb when they went to meet them from the concert given by Ariana Grande at the Manchester Arena in May 2017.

Living testimonies

Each of these factors will influence the nature of loss; loss which will also be modified by the manner of the bereavement, the age at which it occurs, and the circumstances which attend it. Zoe was given up at birth for adoption because of social pressure (the era of 'gymslip mothers', as pregnant schoolgirls were known in the 1960s), and has known only her subsequent carers. Renata saw her parents shot by the Nazis on the streets of Rome when she was five. Andrew's last sight of his widowed mother was in an ambulance that turned the street corner when he was eight. Daniel was fifteen when he was left at home to look after his three younger siblings while his mother went shopping. She never returned. Carla, whose mother was dead, knew her father had been dying of motor neurone disease for as long as she could remember. At the age of sixteen she took over management of the household until he died a year later.

Another major determinant is the quality of the care the child receives as a result of her or his bereavement. Eleanor was sent to a boarding school by her guardian—an uncle—when she was eleven, and remembers a cold and loveless adolescence and a guardian who had no interest in her at all. Chloe was the object of too much attention by her guardian, and narrowly avoided being abused by him. Deborah was cared for by the grandmother she always called mother—an inscription she placed on her gravestone when she died. Pandu's care was spread among the villagers of the South Indian village where he lived. Although historically, many children were taken in by relatives, friends and neighbours, in the industrial era most were consigned to institutional care. This ranged from bleak work-houses to the militaristic regimentation of orphanages of char-ity or the state, from 'cottage homes' superintended by bogus kin—house-mothers and fathers, aunties and uncles—to 'care homes' run by religious charities, the state or private interests. In some of these, children were abused physically, emotionally and sexually. Their stories are only now being heard.

The nature of the care such orphans received greatly influ-enced their ability to make adult relationships. Even those embraced by loving families were sometimes haunted by absences which undermined their sense of worth. They speak of envy of the unquestioning acceptance of children who lived with their biological families, where the question of their origins never arose.

Some feel they were 'thrown away' or 'rejected', and never learned why. Others, like Ariyo, resourceful and intuitive, sought figures in the landscape they could turn into surrogates to serve their need for parental love. When her mother became mentally ill, she transferred her affection to a neighbour she called 'mother':

> She [my birth-mother] behaved in a dangerous and erratic way. She heard voices. She used to write all over the wall and throw things out of the window. I dreaded going home from school, I was so anxious what I would find. She was afraid of demons and devils. It was part of the culture she had grown up in Nigeria. She was very religious. But belief in sorcery and black magic was strong... The woman on the floor above us fostered us even before my mother became ill. I called her Mum. Then when I was pregnant

with my little boy, I became very attached to another woman, who was from Sierra Leone. My first trip to Africa was to Freetown rather than Lagos—I absorbed more of the culture of my adoptive mother than of my own heritage.

Many children seek out an individual—a teacher, a member of staff in a children's home, a neighbour—to use as a compensatory source of missing affection; an absence that had to be filled out of their own need. Some persuaded themselves that they had indeed been loved, which helped them with their later relationships and parenting capacity.

Whatever the cause and circumstances of loss, patterns recur in the later life experience of orphans. The most familiar story is difficulty in establishing mature relationships with others; incomprehension of what is expected, the fragility of attachments, and the anger that comes when these break down. Many also speak of an inability to show even the deepest feelings which lie choked within, unable to find expression in the presence of the loved other. Colin never knew his father, a gunner, killed on D-Day. At the age of five, he was placed in orphanages, run by sisters of various abstract virtues like Mercy and Charity, and later, in a Salesian school, where he learned the value of security and discipline, but not of affection or sentiment. 'I wasn't taught how to love. I can't do it now. It isn't because I don't want to, it is because I can't. It always comes out as physical, sex. You don't need to learn how to be sexual, but you do have to learn to love. A relationship requires something more and that world is closed to you.'

Suzanne, now in her forties, brought up in care, was sexually active by the time she was fourteen:

We lived by numbers. We all had our own tasks. The day was structured, you went to school, you came home, you did housework, you watched TV for an hour then at nine it was turned off, whatever was on. Of course we were obsessed with sex—it was the only entertainment we had. Most girls I was with got pregnant. They thought it was love. Nobody taught us anything about relationships. We had sex education in school. It was clinical, didn't have much to do with sex and even less with education. We were a gift to the first man we met.

Frances, fostered by a woman motivated by Christian duty, acknowledges the care she was given, but knew it had nothing to do with emotion. When Frances married, her husband complained of her coldness:

> I used to say to him 'What do you want from me?' and he said, 'I want you to show you care.' I did care. We had terrible arguments, I would sob and cry and not know what I was doing wrong. I felt inadequate. I thought I wasn't worthy of him, because he knew things about life I didn't. He wasn't cleverer than I was. We separated after seven years. I know now what it was all about but when you are living it, you don't understand.

'Kindness to orphans is a killer.' Janice was aware of the special treatment she received from the aunt who brought her up, from the teachers at school, from the people she worked with when she started as a waitress at the age of fifteen:

> It makes you feel there is something special about you, but not in a good way. You feel people's pity, and you can't do anything with it. You get the sense you don't belong. When they tell you everything is going to be all right, you know it isn't and can't be. It made me angry. I always had a temper, and I lost friends and jobs through it. I still am angry. It isn't their fault, people who wanted to make it up to you for all you'd been through. I should resent my Mum and Dad who dumped me. But I never knew them. They emigrated to Australia. My auntie couldn't have children, so that's why she took me. She felt guilty and I treated her like shit.

When siblings are orphaned, their greatest consolation is each other. Hetty Day depended upon her older sister for surrogate mothering, and she provided comfort for her brother, even though they were separated within the orphanage.[3] Eileen Simpson and her sister Marie clung to each other throughout their time in convent, preventorium and during fostering by family members at war with each other.[4] Benny says that the presence of his brother in the care home kept him sane. 'We were so close, we felt each other's grief and pain. He was dearer to me than my wife ever was.'

Many speak of suppression of feelings and their later catastrophic outburst. Institutions and establishments set up for the reception of orphans taught concealment, assisted, no doubt, by the values handed down from a higher social class of the stiff upper lip, taking it on the chin, putting on a brave face. Colin says, 'I only really faced what had happened to me when I was thirty-three. I had a breakdown. I had decided not to think about it, for fear of what I might have to confront; until in the end, of course, it confronts you.'

Ariyo also learned to suppress what she knew:

> It took me a long time to get past my upbringing. I eventually had cognitive behaviour therapy. I learned there is a chain reaction to things that happened long ago. I had never thought of it like that. It comes back to me at sensitive moments. At such times, I don't like myself. I am strong and independent, but I also have a history of self-harm. When I was eight, I wanted to kill myself with a knife… I fear everyone is going to leave me—I suppose that is the fear of the orphan, I am frightened of rejection.

Thoughts of violence are often close to the surface. 'There are unresolved issues, feelings of rage,' she continued. 'One day at the bus stop I wanted to get a machete and just lay about me. I could not understand why I was unhappy.' Men often take refuge in the traditional cultural 'safe' haven of male invulnerability. Ryan, who left care at eighteen with no idea of the world into which he was entering, found an emotional home in a gang:

> We used to do stuff, nicking and taking cars, drugs, I never thought about it. I was hard, I mean hard, I didn't have any sympathy for anyone—snatch a bag from an old woman, knock an old boy over, take his wallet, even if you only got twenty quid out of it. It was like it wasn't me. My demons took over. I mean it, I was possessed. I never got caught. A lot of my mates are inside, they're homeless, some on the streets. I had girlfriends, so many girlfriends, I didn't

need to fuck the same one twice if I didn't want to. I just turned all the frustration I had outside. I knew it wasn't right. I thought it would stop one day. But I didn't know how. Kelly saved me. I never met anyone like her before. She made me look at myself. I broke down. I cried for a week, believe it or not. I was twenty-three.

There is, too, a haunting by loss, and strange recurrences down the generations. Antoine never knew his father. His mother, from Warsaw, had lived in Paris since the 1930s in a poor part of the city.[5] She had TB, was deported by the Nazis in 1944, and died in Auschwitz. Antoine was four. He was rescued just before his mother's deportation by an organisation that protected Jewish children. When the woman who rescued him married, her husband insisted the child be sent away. He grew up in the Pas de Calais, in a small village where German soldiers were billeted, and where two other Jewish orphans had also been taken in by a family. He grew up as a Catholic, first with a foster-mother, then in a boarding school and finally in the French navy. He had a half-sister he did not know existed until after the War:

> I became very hardened. I surrounded myself by a carapace, a thick shell. I used to joke a lot, but I had armour of steel to conceal my feelings. Whenever people talked of their family troubles—a father who was too strict or a mother too protective—I would say how lucky I was not to have a family and be burdened by such problems. I barricaded myself behind Jewish humour.

Antoine had a brief affair (*une aventure*) with a woman, as a result of which she became pregnant, and gave birth to a little boy. 'I would not deal with it. It made me feel only horror and revulsion. I didn't want to see either her or him. I fled.' The woman committed suicide when the child was four—exactly Antoine's age when his mother had been sent to Auschwitz:

> That was when I knew I had to do something about my emotional state. It was only as a result of psychotherapy that I was able to release some of my suppressed childhood memories. My therapist told me 'You have many flaws, but you also have strengths that

others do not have. You will find the father you never had within yourself.' And he was right. I discovered my son was living not far from where I had been brought up. I got to know him, and gradually built up a relationship with him, first as a father, and now as a grandfather to his child.

Colin also lived through a repeat of his mother's experience:

I asked my mother before she died why I had been rejected and placed in an orphanage. She never replied. I later discovered she was a twin: there had been a boy and a girl. She was farmed out at birth, and the son was kept. I think her jealousy of him affected me: I was rejected as revenge against the boy who had been favoured, because she had four daughters by different men; and they all remained with her.

Siobhan was abandoned to a convent in Dublin; and she also left her own children. She did not know how to mother them properly:

They were like creatures from another planet. Of course I loved them. But I was frightened. I thought I would do everything wrong. I got hold of a child-rearing book, but couldn't make head nor tail of it. In the end I told the child welfare officers I might harm them. I didn't mean that I would hit them but that I would not know how to comfort them or feed them properly. I could see myself in a tenth-storey flat, with two starving children, because I had no instinct for it. They say the mothering instinct comes naturally, but it didn't to me. I'd never known it. They call it instinct, but it's really giving out to your own children what you have received. I often wonder what happened to them. I hope against hope one day there will be a ring at the bell, and it will be them, and they'll say they forgive me. But it won't happen. I never forgave my mother, I don't even know who she was. I guess that is how they think of me.

Many orphans say 'I had to bring myself up'. They speak of 'scavenging for love, as foxes scavenge for food.' When he was fourteen and his mother was dying, Gerard hovered on the edge of his friends' families, 'looking for warmth, comfort, food'. Orphans have to make themselves, find within themselves an identity they do not receive from loving attachments. When

Antoine was told he would have to find 'the man you are within yourself', there were echoes of the psychology of eighteenth-century stories about orphans. But their picaresque tales provide salvation or rescue from external sources: they do not have to show the world who they inherently are. Antoine says:

> When I hear men call themselves 'self-made' they don't know what they're talking about. Most of them had secure families, even if they were poor. Sometimes people say—as they did of Ted Heath—'He came up from nowhere.' Nothing could be further from the truth. Nowhere means you have no idea where you belong, who gave you birth.

Mariam lost her father to cancer when she was eight. Her mother had taken him from Baghdad to Britain for treatment and he died there:

> I still dream that my father is in the UK, and that he comes back to us. I can see him in his navy-blue suit and tie. He tells us he is well, that he got held up by business... As a result of his loss, I married early, a first cousin. I wanted to keep the same name, as he was my father's sister's son. He was older than I, and because of this family closeness, I saw him as a second father. I was sixteen. It was a disaster. He used to beat me because I was 'ill-mannered'. I had become an independent woman and he had no concept of such a thing. His expectations and mine were quite divergent even though I was apparently only a girl of sixteen... I left him, but then went back. He had become very religious. He went to work in Libya. He was in a car accident, and was given a transfusion of polluted blood imported from France. It destroyed his liver. He died. I am now here as a refugee. Being orphaned has pervaded my whole life.

Ariyo, whose mother, mentally ill and fleeing her husband's violence, is not, in theory, an orphan, but she was effectively deprived of both parents, one by sickness and the other by absence. She also describes herself as a cultural orphan, since her Yoruba heritage was all but effaced in moving, first to France, and then to Britain. She was bullied at school and played truant all the time. At fifteen she was raped. No one supported her. The police lost all the evidence. When the case came to the Old Bailey, the jury acquitted the rapist:

> The police had been in possession of all my clothing, the torn bra, everything. All of it was missing. As a result, I suffer from endometriosis. The mental health charity MIND suggested I go to the Criminal Injuries Compensation Board. Compensation was denied, because no one had been proved guilty. There was an appeal and I went to a tribunal, where the police accused me of 'being only after money'. I was awarded compensation.

Unloved children are often reckless, feeling they have nothing to lose. Travis, whose parents had died before he was five, said:

> When I think of the loss of my parents, I'd rather be dead. When you are young, if you do something wrong, you think 'I might as well go the whole hog and push it to extremes'. That's how I feel. You stop thinking straight when you are hurt and insecure. You lash out because nothing can be worse than the situation you are in.

Many adults who live on the streets, in abandoned cars, in doorways and under bridges were orphaned. Jos never knew his parents and was moved from one children's home to another, 'slept rough', as he euphemistically calls it for twenty-five years. Alcohol dulled the cold and the pain. 'I've been spat at, kicked and pissed on where I slept.' Housed by a charity a year ago, he has had no significant adult relationships, but his dog, part collie, part Labrador, is his 'best friend.' He spoils her and feeds her better than he eats himself. 'She saved my life. If it wasn't for her, I wouldn't be here now. When you see people on the street with dogs, it's not for protection, it's not because they're pets. It's because it's the only creature they have to show them affection.'

Forsaken children try, in one way or another, to compensate for what is missing in their lives; and this yearning sometimes invents imaginary parents, relationships and rescuers. Eileen Simpson said her mother, 'had always been for me a celestial spirit, an angel rather than a flesh-and-blood woman.'[6] Hetty Day retained her mother's handkerchief in her institution for fatherless children, an object which became a precious means of evoking her presence. Arun, who never knew his mother, dreamed of an Indian princess, who would come one day and tell him there had been a terrible mistake and that she would take him from the children's home back to an India he had never seen, and which loomed in his fantasies as an earthly paradise.

Others lied about their parentage, which other children never believed. 'If your father is a diplomat, what are you doing here?' they would say to Kevin, who replied that his father was on secret government service and had placed him in the home temporarily. He was mocked and bullied. He says:

> I never learned to love. But I did learn to hate. I hated most of the other kids, and I hated the staff. The staff were not unkind. They were indifferent. They sat and talked about their own lives, where they were going on holiday, about their boy- and girlfriends, about their families. I wanted to say to them, 'Why are you going on about your families in front of a load of kids who don't have any?'

Suzanne didn't talk to other children about the mother she imagined:

> I did remember her, or I thought I did. I saw her as a model, slim and blonde and very glamorous. But that was my secret. Everything in the home was public, there was nothing you could call your own. So my dreams were my private space, and I never let anyone come anywhere near it.

Sadie also kept her feelings to herself. 'I have the clearest memories. I was more aware of emotions than adults gave us credit for. They think you don't understand, but that is not the same thing as understanding your feelings.'

As adults, many orphans want to remove themselves as far as they can from the memory of their pain. They may reinvent themselves, and in the process become very successful. One woman found an identity in her conversion to Islam:

> I was brought up an evangelical Christian, but I came discon-nected from them and left religion. But I needed to get back. A

friend talked to me about Islam, and under his influence I went to mosque one day. Before long I took *shahada*. It was a feeling in my heart. I saw a woman in a hijab—I didn't like it at first. It was a hard transition. What persuaded me is that Islam is very family-oriented. I thought at first, 'What have I done?' But now I feel it was meant to be. It has transformed my life.

Sadie, who had mothered her own chaotic mother, and nursed her through addictions to drink and drugs, has become a children's nanny. This prolonged a role familiar to her, but she now wants to leave it in quest of a self-determination that has so far eluded her:

I became a nanny at sixteen. It is easy to become trapped in what you know. I love my work, and the families I have lived with love me. This has been a form of healing. But now I know what loving families can be, I want to move on.

Orphans in literature

The fate of orphans in literature reveals much about popular social and emotional feelings towards them that often transcends the time of writing, and makes them recognisable today. Those who have known neither the affections nor the constraints of family life inspire a mixture of fear and admiration. They may be dangerously unstable, since they can invent a persona for themselves according to their imagination and choice. Yet many novels hinge upon ultimate reunion with their rightful—and usually socially redemptive—progenitors. Their detachment from social context permits exotic and picaresque story-telling. Cheryl Nixon observes that rich orphans have predominated in fiction, while orphans of the poor have inspired more factual and often polemical reporting.[7]

This is not to say that fictional orphans do not know misery and poverty. But unlike the great majority of real orphans, who rarely discover that they are the offspring of wealth and breeding, their literary counterparts usually find their true origins and are restored to their proper station. Henry Fielding's Tom Jones, for instance, believed to be the child of a servant and school-master, is finally found to be the love child of the Squire's sister. His lineage purified, he is able to claim the hand of Sophia, daughter of the local gentry. Caste is maintained. Esther, in Dickens' *Bleak House*, is revealed as the daughter of the cold, passionless Lady Dedlock, to whom she was born before she married Sir Lester. Saved from anonymity and shame, she mar-ries respectably, and lives in a house given by Mr Jarndyce, her guardian, one of Dickens' many providential rescuers of the shamed and oppressed. Oliver Twist also—one of the most celebrated literary orphans—is restored at the end to the benign guardianship of the loveable Mr Brownlow. Oliver Twist is one of the least convincing orphans. Published in 1837, Dickens' strength lies in his depiction of the workings of the newly enacted Poor Law Amendment Act: his evocation of the work-house, its pompous functionaries and oppressed inmates is acute and penetrating. But Oliver maintains his innocence and virtue, even as he passes through the foulest criminal dens in London. He never loses his fundamental gentility, a characteristic clearly inherited, since the other orphan in the book, Rose Maylie, with whom he has a strong affinity, is his aunt.

The interest in Dickens' orphans is, in the first place, social. They speak of the great scatterings and upheavals of early industrial Britain—the loss of kin, the separation of flesh and blood by migration, poverty and mortality. David Copperfield— escaping from a punishing stepfather and the unbending Miss Murdstone—remakes himself after the fashion of earlier eight-eenth-century picaresque hero-orphans. He runs away from the vintner's establishment, where his stepfather has placed him and walks to Dover in search of his only relative. David Copperfield makes use of his orphan vicissitudes to become a successful writer. The two female orphans—Little Em'ly and Martha—are both seduced and betrayed, Little Em'ly, his child-hood friend, by the man David idolised at school. Salvation for them comes in the form of emigration to Australia: the 'dominions'—to which many nineteenth-century orphans went, an emptiness where earlier experience lapses and new starts are, in theory, possible.

Dickens also captures recognisable personal features of the orphan experience. There is no chance that Pip's ancestry in *Great Expectations* will reveal high connections, since from the beginning he contemplates the churchyard where the graves of his parents leave no doubt of his complete dereliction. Both he and the haughty Estella are manipulated orphans, Pip by the escaped convict he helped as a child on the marshes, and Estella by the embittered Miss Havisham, deserted on her wedding day. Miss Havisham hardens the heart of her ward against men in revenge for her own abandonment, while Pip imagines his change of fortune to be due to the intervention of Miss Havisham. In fact his social ascent is created by the lowest personage, a convict, a discovery which shames him, since this devalues the gentlemanly estate to which he has risen.

Much orphan experience familiar to us is captured in the nineteenth-century novel. George Eliot's Dorothea Brooke was orphaned at twelve, and she and her sister went to live with their benevolent but ineffectual uncle. Dorothea, ardent and passionate, has little scope for her idealism and spiritual energy, until she meets and marries Mr Casaubon, who is engaged on a major work of research, *Key to All the Mythologies*. She subordinates her intelligence to what she sees as the profound life-purpose of a scholar who, already in middle age, sees in her a pliant assistant. Dorothea discovers he is an ineffectual and jealous pedant, and her search for a figure to whom she could offer the humble tribute of her orphanhood is doomed.

Daniel Deronda, George Eliot's other orphan, is also passionately idealistic, and his—at first unknown—parentage impels his effort to become a redemptive force for a lost and scattered Jewry. This is the orphan as man (more rarely woman) of destiny. He stands in contrast to the narrow and venal society of Britain, despite his adoption by a British aristocrat, to whom he owes his education, charm and courtesy. An exile, from both family and nation, he later learns that in spite of having been disowned by his mother as a child, his paternal origins lie in a tradition of Spanish Jews, which has produced many scholars and men of action. His mission is to 'awaken a movement in other minds, such as had been awakened in his own', a kind of proto-Zionism. He rejects the love of the shallow but tormented Gwendolen in favour of marriage with Mirah, a poor Jewish woman he has rescued from despair as she was about to drown herself in the Thames.

Charlotte Brontë's Jane Eyre, although of known—and respectable—parents who died in a typhus epidemic, becomes the ward of her uncle, on whose death she passes into the custody of his widow. In this hostile household, she is made aware of her dependent status, little more than a servant. She is perceived as wilful and passionate (the wildness of those without parents is a recurring theme, not only in fiction). Her outbursts at her aunt's injustices is characteristic of perceptions of orphans—they have ungovernable tempers, a strange, wild spirit; whether as a result of anger at their desertion or because they have never known parental tenderness. At the age of ten, she is sent to a punitive orphan school, where her reputation pursues her. When she goes to work as a governess, her moody, taciturn employer falls in love with her. Only when she agrees to marry him, is the existence of a mad wife confined to the attic revealed. When Jane recoils for his suggestion they should nevertheless live as husband and wife, Mr Rochester observes—in a familiar acknowledgement that there is no one to guide the moral behaviour of orphans,'You have neither relatives nor acquaintances whom you need fear to offend by living with me.' She runs away, and is taken in by a household of strangers, who later turn out to be close kin. Rescued from her outcast state, she is absorbed into a network of family belonging. This reassimilation into respectable society calms her tempestuous orphan temper. When she returns to seek out Mr Rochester, the house has been burned down, his wife dead, and he is injured and half-blind; conditions which sanction a renewal of her love. Observance of social and moral convention lies a thin integument covering the depth of the orphan experience.

Heathcliff in Emily Brontë's *Wuthering Heights* is an even more disordered example of the uncontrollable orphan. Rescued from the streets of Liverpool by the benign Mr Earnshaw as a boy, his swarthy and 'gypsy-like' appearance suggests he is of the lowest origins. He is brought into the home of his benefactor to be raised with his own children, Hindley and Catherine. Although the Earnshaws are known to be a volatile and passionate family—their lives shaped by the landscape of the wild, remote Yorkshire hills—nothing prepares them for the complex, tormented relationship between Catherine and Heathcliff, a profound, punitive compulsion that drives them together and apart. Both marry others to wound one another and themselves, with tragic consequences. Heathcliff, a man of capricious cruelty and indissoluble attachments, damages the lives of the intermingled Linton and Earnshaw families into the next generation. His sensibility is 'devilish', like a 'wild animal', not quite human. His origins remain unknown, but the absence of kindred—and of any other name than Heathcliff—makes of him a sombre, brooding mystery, the orphan wrecker of other people's lives. Such characteristics were widely attributed to outcast children in the nineteenth century.

Orphans are in moral and spiritual danger from the absence of parental care and guidance. When they are paragons of beauty, like Flora and Miles in Henry James' *The Turn of the Screw*, and Billy Budd in Melville's tale, they are particularly at risk from baleful influences, both earthly and supernatural. In Henry James' novel these influences are the ghostly Quint and Miss Jessel, while in Melville's story we witness the intense homoerotic hatred of the ships' master-at-arms Claggart. Budd, the 'Handsome Sailor', universally admired, says all he knows of his origins is 'that I was found in a pretty silk-lined basket hanging one morning from the knocker of a good man's door in Bristol.' Melville observes 'noble descent was as evident in him as in a blood horse'. Accused by the master-at-arms of being part of a mutinous conspiracy, Budd is so shocked he is unable to speak, and he delivers a blow that knocks his accuser to the ground and kills him. To maintain discipline, Budd is hanged and consigned to the waves. Reports of the event describe Budd as having stabbed Claggart in the heart with a knife, 'the deed and implement employed sufficiently suggest that though mustered in the service under an English name, the assassin was no Englishman, but one of those aliens adopting English cognomens whom the present necessities of the service have caused to be admitted into it in considerable numbers.' Budd's lack of family connections allows malice to write the obituary of his orphanhood.

The evil which threatens Flora and Miles, whose guardian is absent and wishes not to be disturbed by details of their upbringing, is of a different order. The governess who under-takes their education—and protection—is herself haunted by her predecessor, the dead Miss Jessel and her employer's former valet, Quint, in whose company the children had spent much time. Their illicit relationship and lack of moral values have exercised a baleful effect upon the children. The governess (unnamed) sees herself as their saviour, and tries to interpose herself between the seductive corruption of the dead and the innocence of the brother and sister, which she cannot distin-guish from possible guile. She ends by hugging Miles to herself so tightly in order to preserve him from the predatory vision of Quint that, 'his heart stopped.' Orphans are open, not only to contamination by example from beyond the grave, but may also be complicit in their own perdition.

The fatherless

The word 'orphan' is heard today in rich countries principally in requests for charitable donations. It is not that orphans have ceased to exist—although there are fewer of them—but if 'the orphan' has an archaic ring in English, this is because it is out of keeping with the duty of the modern state to care for them.

Historically, fatherless children were also considered orphans; a condition supported by biblical references (Deuteronomy 10:18, 'He executes justice for the fatherless and the widow and loves the sojourner, giving him food and clothing'; Psalms 68:5, 'A father to the fatherless, a defender of widows is God in his holy dwelling'; Jeremiah 49:11, 'Leave your fatherless children, I will keep them alive, and let your widows trust in me'). Perhaps unsurprisingly, it is in patriarchal cultures that the fatherless are still regarded as orphans.

The testimony of Hetty Day in chapter four tells the story. Reedham Asylum for Fatherless Children, in which she spent ten years in the 1930s, expected all its children to have mothers living. Whatever the institution was called—asylum, school, orphanage—the assumption was that any child whose father was absent, whether dead, deserted or unnamed, was parentally deprived. This is far from the contemporary experience, since women have proved highly capable of bringing up children without a male presence, and of earning a livelihood at the same time; although this has depended on the radical change associated with the welfare state.

Plato's words on those who care for orphans have lasting resonance. In *Laws*, Book 11, his Athenian stranger declares, 'They shall fear, first, the gods above who pay regard to the solitude of orphans, and secondly, the souls of the dead whose natural instinct is to care especially for their offspring.' The isolation of the orphan, and his or her relationship with vanished begetters, are disturbing—who can say what powers their dead may have endowed them with? They are a reproach to the unbereaved as well as emblems of universal mortality. It is inevitable that, in addition to the pity they inspire, they also stir more troubling feelings and are an irritant to those responsible for the administration of human societies. The child-witches on the streets of Kinshasa in the Democratic Republic of Congo embody this maleficent spirit. These, expelled from their families are—or have become in fact—orphans as a result of their condition. A Save the Children Report by Javier Aguilar Molina, 'The Invention of Child Witches in the DRC', 2003–2005, contains the following story of a 'prophetess': Three children had been bewitched by their maternal grandfather. Their father had fallen ill and died of tuberculosis. The mother had died of AIDS 'caused' by the children through witchcraft. Two of the children sought refuge with their maternal grandmother and one of the boys decided to look after himself. Basically, the family lived well, but since the mother had refused to give money to her parents, the grandfather decided to take revenge. The father's sister was angry with the children because she thought they should have warned her so that she could get them exorcised and thus break the circle of death. The conclusion of the informant was 'They are orphans through their own doing'.[8]

These psychological ambivalences pervade the treatment of orphans by government, by centuries-old Poor Laws, even by the welfare system. Despite scriptural adjurations and extensive charitable provision, they have been treated with hostility or at best carelessness. They are regarded as an encumbrance upon the parish, or unfortunates to be placed out of sight and out of mind in institutions, orphanages, with wet-nurses and baby-farmers, many of whom would expedite their departure from a world in which they were unwelcome.

2

THE CARE OF ORPHANS

Abuse of and indifference to orphans is a story that has become familiar. So it is important to remember that this has not, historically, been characteristic of all children bereft of parental love, however wanting in tenderness those in whose negligent care they often failed to thrive. It is easy to overlook children tended over the years, whether or not adopted, by near family, kin, neighbours or charitable strangers. Most of their stories go unheard, for whoever heard of a happy orphan or a joyful child who has lost her parents?

When life was more precarious than it is today, it was perhaps easier to read one's own possible destiny in the fate of others in a village or neighbourhood. But whatever moved people to absorb lost children into their own family, their compassion was doubtless influenced by the fragility of life and the omnipresence of death. Recognition of the common experience made it a matter of course, as well as a religious duty, to shelter the helpless. Many orphans were brought up without distinction of status from the children of agricultural labourers in cramped cottages, whether they had been orphaned by accidents in the fields or in the industrial mishaps of early industrialism. The scars of loss healed under the sometimes rough touch of duty.

They were helped too by the growth of bonds of affection between children who swam in the rivers, clambered through the trees, worked to draw water or help with hay-making, caught rabbits or harvested mice as they fled before the reapers' scythes. Who knew—or even cared to enquire—who belonged to whom, whose mother had drowned in the mill-pond or died in the smallpox epidemic, and whose father had, in defiance of his place of settlement, taken flight to the hovels around the city shambles, abandoning his children, not to parish or poor-house, but to the kindness of others?

Informal adoption of children was widespread. The Elizabethan Poor Law insisted the first provider of relief should be the immediate kin of those in need. Parents and grandparents were expected to look after their children and grandchildren, and children should take care of their parents before applying for help from the parish. (There was no demand that grandchildren should take responsibility for their grandparents.) Steve Hindle described this as part of the 'hidden world of informal expedients', whereby the poor survived.[1] 'Falling on the parish' was a vivid popular image, and it meant just that—a social, even moral, descent, to be avoided if possible. Given the spontaneous nature of caretaking arrangements of the forlorn, unprotected infants were certainly also exploited and abused. But this was also the experience of many children of the lawfully wedded, born, as they were, to labour, from before infancy. Far more orphaned children were probably absorbed into the household of kin or neighbours than were ever known to the parish; just as the people who received parish relief represented only a fraction of the poor. Hindle estimates that 20 per cent of people lived a hazardous existence, but only one quarter of these were relieved by the parish. The Puritan Philip Stubbs complained in 1583 that people relieved by the Poor Laws represented 'not one hundredth part of those in want'.[2]

If it is hard to capture the subjective experience of orphanhood, this is because, as Peter Laslett observes, 'the emotional pattern of that [pre-industrial] society has vanished for ever, and people may then have had a quite different attitude to sudden death, orphanage, widowhood and living with step-parents.'[3] This does not mean that people became inured to loss in a time when death was ubiquitous, but their consciousness of mortality was certainly not blunted. What saved people from being in a constant state of mourning was a combination of the human ability to live in the here-and-now and the imperative of labouring, contriving, begging or stealing for survival, as well as an awareness that another life awaited them after death. Such consolations were depicted in the painted walls of churches, in relics and images of saints, as well as in the small wisdom that passed, more or less unchanged until the industrial era, between the generations.

Stories of the inclusion of orphans into wider networks of kin are familiar in the industrial age. Richard Hoggart, who celebrated working class cultural tradition in his *The Uses of Literacy: Aspects of Working Class Life*, was orphaned at eight.[4] His father had fought in the Boer War and died in 1920 when he was two; six years later his mother succumbed to tuberculosis. He wrote of his relief when he, his older brother and younger sister learned they would not be consigned to an orphanage, but would be raised by the extended family in a household where his grandmother, two aunts, an uncle and an older cousin would be the significant figures of his childhood. This left him with a lasting sense of the importance of community, in which people shared their common sorrows and pain. This form of solidarity, embodied in webs of informal care by women in Britain, continued into the mid-twentieth century.

A remedy for the dereliction of the growing army of the poor in the early sixteenth century was embodied in the Elizabethan Poor Law. This was recreated at a later age, first of all spontaneously in response to the human-made desolation of industrial life as people, independently of scanty and unmerciful official provision, built their own network of protection and caregiving against an indifferent world. Later it would manifest itself in the now-strained apparatus of the welfare state.

Alan Johnson's memoir describes becoming an orphan at thirteen.[5] It commemorates the tenacity of his sixteen-year-old sister in maintaining the household after their mother's death. When Alan hears she has died, he is appalled by the enormity of it. He said, 'I knew that Lily deserved tears, but my eyes remained resolutely dry.' Linda, his sister arranged for the body to be collected from the mortuary. She visited Somerset House to apply for the birth certificate. She arranged the funeral. Everywhere officials asked 'Why haven't you got an adult with you?' Linda even persuaded the council to provide accommodation for them, since their lodgings were unfit for human habitation. It was illegal for a girl of sixteen to be a council tenant, but she managed it. Johnson writes, 'what mattered most to Linda and me was being together, free from any institution.'

The orphans of Easedale

In 1808, eight children were orphaned in a small village in the Lake District. One cold snowy day in March, George and Sarah Green left their cottage in Easedale on foot to go to a country sale in Langdale. They also wanted to find a new situation for George Green's illegitimate daughter, Mary, in service at an inn. Having failed to achieve this goal, they set off for home across the fells at five in the afternoon. They were never seen alive again. They were found, Sarah on rough ground above a waterfall, and her husband at the foot of a precipice. Confused by the mist that had descended, he had lost his footing and fell. She, trying to assist him, probably died of exposure.

In the cottage, their daughter Jane, aged eleven, was in charge of five younger children, the youngest, Hannah, still at the breast, and four boys, George, John, Thomas and William. The children waited until eleven o'clock and then went to bed, assuming their parents had remained in Langdale because of the weather. Jane milked the cow and looked after her siblings. By Monday noon, one of the boys went to borrow a cloak for Jane, so that she could go in search of their parents.

This raised the alarm. Fifty or sixty men formed a search party, while some village women went to the cottage. There they found no money, a few potatoes, some meal and legs of lean dried mutton. The family had concealed the depth of its poverty. They had lived by bartering from the home or the stable for potatoes and meal. George—who was 65 and had been married before—sold peat and did odd labouring jobs. The land had been mortgaged. Their cow was old and gave only a quart of milk a day.

The bodies of the couple were brought to the cottage on the Wednesday, and on the Friday were buried in Grasmere churchyard. The few effects were sold, the cottage left empty. The mortgage was paid and nothing remained.

Eight of the children were under sixteen. Mary was the eldest. The second girl, Sally, worked as a servant for the poet Wordsworth's family. After the funeral, George was taken in by his half-brother (George's eldest son by his first marriage). The other five children were left to the parish.

An Act of 1782 permitted boarding out orphaned children to respectable persons in or near the parish where they lived. The parish gave a weekly allowance with the agreement of the Visitor of the Poorhouse, until such time as the orphan could be apprenticed—around the age of ten.

Dorothy Wordsworth had observed the fate of a neighbouring orphan boarded with a family, who was employed nursing the children. She said he had, 'the face of a child who had none to love him.' By the age of sixteen, this boy 'does not know a letter in a book; nor can he say his prayers.' He was employed carrying slates to town, from where he returned intoxicated.

She wanted to preserve the newly orphaned from such a fate. It would be difficult to find them a home in their native place. She opened a subscription to assist the parish to place them with respectable families, to be maintained and to acquire some learning. The parish agreed to pay two shillings a week for each until they were fit for service or apprenticeship.

The plight of the orphans became known, and donations from the aristocracy and gentry were supplemented by contributions from writers. Walter Scott, Robert Southey, Walter Landor and Thomas de Quincey all gave; as did many local people of lesser means. More than £500 was raised from almost three hundred individuals. A committee formed to administer the charitable fund allowed each child an extra shilling above the parish allowance, and one shilling and six pence for Hannah, the baby. Foster homes were found—Jane and Hannah remained together, boarded with a blacksmith and his wife, who were childless and distantly related to George's first wife. There, the girls learned sewing and reading. William and Thomas stayed with a family who had recently lost a son aged twenty. John, seven, lived with a sheep-farmer, who was either a widower or a bachelor.

The money, carefully laid out for the twenty years until Hannah came of age, rose to five hundred and thirty-six pounds, nineteen shillings and sixpence, having been prudently invested; of which almost £400 was spent. The rest was distributed among the eight children.

There is little record of how the children fared in later life; but all survived.[6]

Orphans of Chicago

A cruel echo of this occurred in 2017. A car had plunged into a cold Illinois lake, and a paramedic dived into the freezing water. Inside the car, he found an infant, and administered CPR, swimming ashore with the child. This baby was one of seven children who all survived a tragedy that engulfed the family.

A fire had broken out in the early morning in the family home, in a village thirty miles east of St Louis. Six children under the age of fourteen escaped, but the estranged husband of the mother, the father of the children, died. The body in the car was that of the mother; the baby her youngest child. There had been a history of abuse before they were married. The man had been fined and sentenced to probation for beating her while she was pregnant. They later married, but the relationship was unstable; and the woman obtained an emergency protection order against her husband, and a divorce in 2013. It was reported that the children were with the Illinois authorities, 'and will be placed with relatives.'[7]

Orphans of the extended family

Spontaneous support offered to abandoned children in our past is common today in the assimilation of orphans into the families of kin, even quite distant 'cousin-brothers' and 'cousin-sisters', in the global South. Webs of kinship among the labouring poor (but not the destitute) of Victorian England served a function similar to that of the—now fraying—extended and joint families in South Asia.

When Pandurang's father died, responsibility for his upbringing was spread across a web of kinsfolk in the Karnataka countryside in south India:

> It was midnight in the rainy month of August. I was woken up and taken to the front veranda of our ancestral house. A few hundred metres away I saw a lantern beside someone sleeping under the *peepal* tree. It was the body of my father. My mother was weeping inconsolably. I was told my father was dead. It was like something in a dream, a surreal world, darkness all around, tall trees of jackfruit and mango, the faint light of a kerosene lantern. I wondered why my father was sleeping under the tree. The entire village was there to witness the death.
>
> My older sister held my hand and took me close to the body. I could hardly see his face, as it was dark, and the light from the lantern was very weak. I clearly remember my mother sobbing and my sisters joining her. It was strange for me, not knowing what death meant. I went back into the house and slept on the floor.

I witnessed for the first time the rituals of bathing the dead body and then taking it to the burning-ground as a six-year-old. As the youngest of six siblings, I had to be part of the ritual until the body was destroyed on the funeral pyre.

We hardly spent much time together as father and son: with so many cousins and children of all ages, we were in our own world. The family extended to the whole village community, so I did not immediately miss my father. He had been ill—my memory was of constant coughing, very weak, smoking *bidis*, pungent Indian cigarettes. But I soon realized that, as a widow, my mother lost her status. As wife of the head of joint family, she held a special position, which was lost. We had to adjust our relationships with others. At school most of my classmates talked about their fathers.

The joint family, cousins, older brothers and maternal uncles filled the role of father, always available for support or advice. The emotional bonding with my mother was my salvation. Although not literate, she gave me confidence. The rural upbringing also gave me comfort and I never felt lonely. Even the labourers were part of daily life and took care of me because I was an orphan. As joint families have dissolved, orphans have greater challenges in life: government-run orphanages cannot provide the security a child needs.

If I was never made aware of my orphaned status, credit goes to the family, the village and the whole network of rural life. In the present world, this sounds utopian. But it gave me a broader perspective—a journey from a small village of eight households to activist on a national and international stage for the preservation of the forests which nourished humanity and the value systems that depended on them.

The reservoir of compassion

Compassion is one of the most inexhaustible—and often undervalued—human resources. Hilda, in her late fifties, has cared for ten children over a period of twenty years in her south Yorkshire town:

> You do love them; some more than others. I always felt more for those who were less lovable, who were not pretty or had behaviour

problems. Those you could deal with were easy, they responded without reserve. But when a child came to you who had been ill-treated and didn't trust anyone, you waited to catch the first smile, the first gleam of affection and acceptance that she knew you were there for her. You can't describe the joy you feel. I don't go to church, but I do believe in something beyond this world that can transform people's lives.

Greta's mother died in childbirth, and her care was immediately assumed by her grandmother:

I was never told she was not my mother. She *was* my mother. I realised she was much older than the mothers of friends at school. Sometimes other children would say something, and I always leaped to her defence. The love she gave me was the most precious gift I received in life. She did tell me eventually, but by that time she was dying and I had my own family. It didn't matter what her real relationship was. The last thing I said to her was 'God bless you Mother', and I am as proud of her today as when I was small, even though she died more than forty years ago.

In the stories of surviving orphans, prominent is the mercy of neighbours and even strangers who offer shelter, often without reward. Charity—in the sense of a human quality, as opposed to an organisation with a head office and career-structure—is constantly replenished, and if the reservoirs of pity sometimes fall low, they never dry up.

The power of community

In fourteenth-century England it is estimated 1.5 million people—perhaps one-third of the population—died of the Black Death. It was believed the disease could be contracted from the breath, touch or even the gaze of victims. Perhaps the response of survivors was as it is today in poor countries beset by sickness and loss; particularly where AIDS and Ebola have recently provoked fears similar to those inspired by medieval pestilence.

In Tanzania in 2002 AIDS drugs were far beyond the reach of the poor. It was common to hear that, 'Whenever you go home, you find more people missing. You do not ask after them. You know their fate.' One woman buried all her seven adult children. Villages became the destination of returnees from the city: earlier migrations of hope in the other direction had yielded nothing but the sickness that would take their lives.

The elderly, resigned to seeing their children pre-decease them, saw a world turned upside down. Millennarian Christian sects and fundamentalist Islamic movements helped the old find strength to nurse their own adult children and take care of their orphaned descendants, some of whom were also HIV positive. A younger generation wasted away, while the elderly lived on, desperate to provide nutrition to prolong by a little the lives of those they loved. This called for courage in carers of the terminally ill, protectors of orphans of a malady few understood.

Asha Likele lived in Luis Mbeza just outside Dar es Salaam; a settlement created in the 1970s under Nyerere's programme of compulsory villagisation. Asha's family had to move only a few kilometres from her hillside *shamba* (field), which she could cultivate in the time left over from duties on communal land.

In 2002, in her sixties, she was looking after six children orphaned by AIDS, four boys and two girls aged between five and sixteen, children of three families, six dead parents. Asha's older brother had taken some of the children, but when he, too, died, she assumed responsibility for all of them:

> Allah did not bless me with children of my own. It was natural I should look after them. They call me mother, since all but the eldest came to me very young. Other children tell them I am not their mother, but they do not believe them.

> I am not rich. I live by farming, so the income is small. I have ten acres inherited from my father, enough to feed the seven of us and to sell something in the market. I have income from renting a room in my house. One younger sister helps me with the *shamba*.

> Young boys are not active or helpful. Salehe, my eldest, finished school. I gave him money to fry chips for an income, but he found a job in the town. He wants to mend cars. The garage owner says if

I provide him with spanners and tools, he will teach him. He is a very energetic boy. For three days he went missing. Sick with worry, I thought he was in mischief. He had gone with a man who taught him to drive and was teaching him electricity. I said, 'If you misbehave, I will chase you from the house, even though I love you.'

My husband does not live here. He has other wives. He stays about forty kilometres away, in an old slave town on the coast. He sends money sometimes.

We were forced to move here in 1974. We were not happy, because we had to leave our orange and coconut trees. Fortunately our land was not given to anyone else, so I can still use it. The government introduced poultry-keeping, tailoring, chickens and cows, and set aside fifteen acres for communal farming. Some people removed from good land were resentful and angry. The intention was to sell everything that was harvested and to distribute the rewards according to the amount of work done. But the money disappeared. We were given a ten-ton truck but it was sold. The most powerful people took the land for their own use.

Asha works from early morning until dark:

Young people do not want to work on the *shamba*. They know only money. They think the produce of the earth is worth nothing, because there is nothing to show for many months. Money as wages comes daily into your hands. Farming brings a different kind of wealth.

Asha stands with her orphans between rural and urban life. These are no longer spatial differences: the spirit of urbanism, technology, communications, reaches the furthest corners of the earth; and few are untouched by urban life, even if they still live in places ostensibly 'rural.' All Asha's children will be absorbed by the occupations of the modern world. She feels something more powerful than her love has insinuated itself between her teachings and her children's perception of the world:

I wake at five o'clock in the morning and after prayers I cook breakfast. In the busiest farming season I prepare food for the whole day before leaving the house. At other seasons I walk home

41

and make a mid-day meal. I grow maize and rice. I don't have livestock and cannot afford fertiliser.

Asha never went to school. She can read a little Arabic, having spent a short time in a madrasa. She does not know how old she was when she married. 'In those days, parents watched the development of a girl, and when she began to menstruate they sought out a husband for her.'

At bedtime, Asha tells her children stories she heard from her parents. She tells of a man who had two wives, and brought up two families, one loved and one not loved. The children of the unloved family went to another woman to be cared for. This is their favourite story.

She communicates her humane version of Islam: to love others, respect elders, lead honest lives, not 'to run here and there'—her euphemism for sexual promiscuity:

I am sorry for young people today. There are temptations we never had—alcohol, drugs and bhang. Marijuana was always there. It grows wild. We ate it as a vegetable because it is very nutritious. Now they pick it and sell it for smoking. Our elders used to drink beer only at festival times. Now young people want stimulus all the time. They drink *gongo*, fermented and filtered from papaya, cassava and sugar-cane. It is cheap and strong. People drink to pass on their pain to another day.

Asha is thankful to have someone to look after:

I weep when I see children without parents, and there are too many of them. They did not choose for their parents to die. I find happiness in the love I can give. What I pray for is to live long enough to see them reach adulthood and become good people; to develop their skills and respect all human beings. They all go to school; and the authorities, knowing how I am placed, do not charge fees.

When I met her it was Ramadan. Asha was preparing the *iftar* snack, to break their fast after sundown. The youngest children do not fast, but the older ones must observe the religion she has taught them.

The November rains are late; but a vigorous shower falls noisily on the metal rooftops of the huts, dripping off the plantains and acacias and scattering the children who are playing in the dirt yards.

When the crisis swept Africa, it was not government or international agencies that held society together, certainly not financial institutions or pharmaceutical companies. Rather it was the uncelebrated humanity of millions of people who did not need instruction to keep alive the orphaned and abandoned.

Asha's story arouses memories of different epidemics in Britain in the nineteenth century, cholera, typhus and consumption, which orphaned many then. Although some of the poorest found themselves in orphanages, in most communities, relatives or neighbours took on the care of bereaved children who were spared the shame and humiliation of institution or workhouse.

3

ORPHANS OF THE RICH

It should not be thought that orphans, in a society as hierarchical and class-ridden as Britain, have been exempt, historically, from the privileges and disadvantages associated with their social status. Although this book addresses principally the story of poor orphans, we should also look briefly at the very different destiny of those of more elevated status.

Orphans destined to inherit fortunes have naturally inspired greater solicitude than those who expect nothing. It was, in Britain, a feudal seigneurial right to take possession of the revenues of any children of a deceased tenant-in-chief until they reached majority—twenty-one for a male, fourteen for a female. The Crown assumed the right to sell such wardships to the highest bidder, or to offer them to privileged courtiers, who would enjoy the yield of the estate until the ward came of age. By this point he or she was often married to someone in the family administering the wardship.

There was considerable commerce in orphan heirs to property. In 1540, Henry VIII, for whom wardships were one source of replenishment for his treasury, replaced the Master of the King's Wards with a Court of Wards, which undertook the administration of the land and sale of such lucrative wardships. Under Elizabeth I, the Court was supervised by Sir William

Cecil (Lord Burleigh), who was Master of the Court of Wards from 1561 till his death in 1598; after which the post passed to his son. He may not have purchased wardships, but probably shared in the revenue generated by those he sold to others.[1] The Court was abolished during the Long Parliament in 1646.

The pecuniary usefulness of wardships, particularly of women, lay in the revenue associated with marriage. Thomas More had two wards, one taken as an act of charity, the other as an investment. Margaret Giggs was the daughter of a neighbour who lived close to More in Cheapside. The neighbour's wife became wet-nurse to More's child, also called Margaret. After her mother died, and her father being often away, Margaret Giggs was raised as the Mores' adoptive child. She married Dr John Clement, previously tutor to More's own children. She was present at the execution of Thomas More, and her family lived as Catholic exiles in Louvain.

The second was Anne Cresacre, ward of the Crown when her father died one year after her birth. The wardship was bought by Thomas More about 1523. She married More's son John in 1529 when she was eighteen. The estate passed to More's family, Barnburgh Hall, which remained the home of their descendants until the early nineteenth century. John More died in 1547. His widow married George West thirteen years later; and shortly afterwards, her daughter Annie married George West's son: in an unusual family connection, mother and daughter married father and son.

Sir Matthew Hale

Most families of the gentry had the foresight to provide for their children in the event of bereavement. Matthew Hale was born in Gloucestershire in 1609, his father's family having made a fortune in the cloth industry in the preceding half century. His mother, Jayne Poynte came from an old Gloucestershire family of Norman descent.

Matthew Hale was orphaned at the age of five. His Puritan guardian and relative, Anthony Kingscott, ensured he was educated. First he was taught by a local Puritan vicar, and in 1626—at the age of seventeen—he went to Magdalen College, Oxford, to prepare for a career in the church. A guardian's primary responsibility was to manage the property of the orphan and deploy it for education or preparation for marriage. Hale's tutor was Obadiah Sedgwick, a Puritan preacher, and vehement opponent of episcopacy.

Matthew Hale exhibited conduct at Oxford which some ascribed to a lack of good parental example. He became 'frivolous and foppish', addicted to fencing, which predisposed him to a military rather than ecclesiastical career. He had no calling as a divine. In 1628, some former friends of his father in Lincoln's Inn kindled his interest in law. He enrolled in the same year. He studied English and Roman law, and became the protégé of William Noy in 1631, attorney general of Charles I. Hale was called to the bar in 1636. His clients were mainly Royalist. He represented Archbishop Laud at his impeachment trial in 1641. During the Protectorate, despite his Royalist sympathies, Cromwell made him a Justice in the Court of Common Pleas. Hale supported the Restoration, but retired to write and study. Made Chief Justice in 1671, he remained true to his heritage, a sober and abstemious personage, deploring the moral decay of Restoration England. He protected Protestant Nonconformists, maintaining that dissent was neither seditious nor criminal. On the other hand, at the trial of two old women, Rose Cullender and Amy Duny at Bury St Edmunds in 1664, he affirmed a belief in witchcraft, stating, 'that there were such creatures as witches he made no doubt at all; first, for the Scriptures has affirmed so much. Secondly, the wisdom of all nations had provided laws against such persons, which is an argument of their confidence of such crimes.' They were found guilty of bewitching seven persons and sentenced to death.

Matthew Hale married twice. With his first wife, Anne More, he had ten children, four of whom died in infancy. Of the other six, all but two predeceased him. His eldest son Robert had a wife who also died, leaving five orphaned children, whose care he undertook in old age, together with his second wife, Anne Bishop, formerly his servant. In his will, he described her as a most dutiful, faithful and loving wife, and therefore trusted the breeding of his grandchildren to her care.

He wrote a letter of advice to the grandchildren. In it, he said:

> I took you into my house when by the death of your father and mother you were left into the wide world wholly unprovided for; and the company of little children could not be very suitable to one of my condition, age and employment; yet I took you in, have borne with the infirmities and troubles of your childhood, have maintained you creditably, and have been studiously careful of your health, have provided convenient portions and subsistence for you all, have given you a becoming education and would be as glad to have you do well as your hearts would desire.

> If I should leave you all the wealth and honour of this world, yet without good advice to direct you, and the grace of God to go with you, these things would but make you more miserable, would fill you with pride, vanity, insolence, intemperance and luxury, and make you the mark of envy and hatred; they would shorten your life here, or make it a life displeasing to God, and to good men, and burthensome to yourselves; and when you die our happiness would be at an end whatever it were.

Of the five orphans, the three girls did not survive beyond their sixteenth, seventeenth and eighteenth years respectively.

Matthew Hale was a highly influential writer, and his History of Common Law, an account of the growth of English law, is his most celebrated work. Little record remains of the affective lives of orphans whose professional and financial status were overseen by their guardians. But the career and work of many suggest they were not socially or intellectually compromised by bereavement, whatever the emotional effect upon their lives. Matthew Hale's concern for his orphaned grandchildren must have been inspired by a memory of his own early privations; and this is reflected in his writings on the young of the poor, for whom he advocates constant and wholesome labour.[2]

Educational orphaning

It was the practice in the early modern era, of the upper and merchant classes to send their children to serve in other households. There, they would acquire accomplishments, both courtly and practical, under the superintendence of strangers; a training uninfluenced by family sentiment, which exposed them to more rigorous discipline than might have been expected at home. Although the word 'apprenticeship' was used, this was far from craft or parish apprenticeships. It implied a range of social skills, including manners, courtesy, and knowledge of the formalities of rank and precedence. Perhaps this tradition of sending the offspring of privilege from home at an early age was rekindled in the education of public schools. After all, it was a form of education attended by the asperities of subordination, flogging and finally, as they grew older, the consolation of disciplining younger boys in the same way.

This removal of children is also a form of orphaning from the affection of family, an influence considered too 'womanish' for young men in particular, whose destiny was, not only to superintend their estates, to hunt and shoot, but also to dispense justice to the poor at home and later, to the inhabitants of Empire. Girls, too, were ritually separated from birth parents. But their purpose in their households of exile was to become equipped for marriage, by following the example of their mistresses in the management of those who served them, and to acquire more than ornamental skills in the care of their own future household, including knowledge about food, medicine and the art of hospitality.[3]

Orphans of lesser degree

Children of freemen of London and other 'borough orphans' in England became the responsibility of the Court of Orphans. Formally established in London in 1492, this was of greater antiquity: borough oversight of orphan's inheritances goes back to the thirteenth century. Charles Carlton notes that in 1324, Agnes de Westhall forcibly abducted her nephew, John Chaucer—father of the poet—from London to Ipswich, where she married the twelve-year-old nephew to her daughter, in order to gain control of his inheritance.[4]

Investment of the inheritance of an orphan of a freeman could be profitable to her or his guardian. As boroughs freed themselves from seigniorial control, these wardships were often an article of the borough's charter. Guardians were appointed only with the consent of the governing body, to which account had to be made on the majority of the orphan. The next of kin, if enfranchised, had the first refusal of wardship. If there were none, the governing body could appoint anyone who accepted the charge.

Rules were drawn up as to the expenditure to be incurred on an orphan according to her or his station in life. The discharge of such duties was taken seriously. That disputes and dishonourable treatment of orphans was not uncommon appears in correspondence between central government and officials of the City of London relating to the rights, privileges, customs, trade and religious life of the City.[5]

15 March 1579

Letter from the Lords of the Council to the Lord Mayor, Aldermen re: order stating that, from information received by them, it appeared that Robert Huson, with the assistance of certain confederates, had stolen away Judeth Cox, an orphan, of the age of fourteen, and had conveyed her to Gravesend, where she was discovered by her friends and brought back, and directing steps at once be taken to arrest and commit to prison Huson and his confederates, in order that a stop might be put to this evil practice, which had of late greatly increased.[6]

13 Sept 1582

Letter from the Lord Mayor to the Lord Chancellor, informing him that Joan Martin, daughter of the late Sir Roger Morton, had come to full age, and desired to receive her portion. For as much as the City had the custody of, they were ready to pay, it appeared, by a decree made by his lordship to the Court of Chancery, that Alexander Denton, one of the executors of Sir Roger Morton, had, by colour of his office while he lived, got into his hands and converted to his own use some of the money. They therefore requested his lordship to take such steps as might appear to him desirable to recover out of the estates of the said Denton the remainder due to the said orphan.[7]

Charles Carlton notes that responsibility was solely for the orphans of freemen (of whom there were about 4,500 in London in 1501). It was the duty of the Mayor and Aldermen to see the child was fed, clothed, sheltered and educated, and to make sure the guardian looked after the inheritance until the child's majority (twenty-one for a boy or unmarried girl; eighteen for a woman married to a man over twenty-one).

Inheritances were increasingly deposited with the city Chamberlain, rather than invested by guardians. By the end of the sixteenth century, the amount deposited in the chamber exceeded that overseen by the orphans' guardians themselves. This was to have fateful consequences for the fortunes of London's orphans.

A 'freeman' was defined as one who had served an apprenticeship in the city and who could freely trade and manufacture within the city walls, so the number of children whose inheritance was safeguarded was limited. The Court of Aldermen was charged with overseeing the orphan's affairs. This included punishment of those who married heiresses without a licence and the return of defaulted securities. Strict rules governed the administration of the estate. One third was to go to the widow (excluding her 'widow's chamber', that is her personal linen and effects, including jewellery), one-third to be shared between legitimate children, while the final third was bequeathed according to the testator's wishes. A minor had no control over his inheritance. 'When Robert Harmer died just before his twenty-first birthday, he left his wife Anne half his £2000 inheritance. London's Court ruled that Anne had no claim on her husband's portion, 'which shall all pass to brothers and sisters.'

Records show the necessity for legal oversight. Widows were sometimes courted and married by friends of the deceased, or they sought to conceal some of his wealth; bad debts were exaggerated and sums owing to the deceased omitted. As the seventeenth century advanced, the Court, which by now held considerable sums, became also a kind of financial centre, providing loans to private and public entities. By 1680 it held over £500,000, and two years later, when London was overwhelmed by financial crisis, it was unable to pay the orphans' dues. It ceased to function; and with its abolition, the work of the Court of Orphans passed to the Court of Chancery (its labyrinthine workings satirised by Dickens in *Bleak House* in the 1850s). The number of orphans dispossessed by this loss is estimated at close to 2,500. Redress was slow, and in 1694 the Orphan's Act levied from the chamber a sum to defray all obligations. For the first few years, the chamber failed to reach its full contribution. New taxes—including a levy on each cauldron of coal brought into the port of London—eventually yielded a surplus and the Orphans' Fund was once more invested in such enterprises as Blackfriars Bridge and the Embankment. The debt was not cleared until 1832.[8]

The Court of Chancery

The Court of Chancery was originally a court of equity designed to mitigate the harshness and legal limitations of common law. Among its functions was to serve as *parens patriae*, that is, it fulfilled the duty of the Crown to protect all its subjects, including lunatics, idiots and infants (all wards below the age of majority); it took precedence over actual parents and guardians in the interest of such subjects, and settled the fate of orphans where guardians disagreed or failed to exercise proper supervision over their wards.

In 1727 the case of Mr Herbert recorded:

Mr Herbert was an infant of about eighteen years of age, and seized of an estate of 1200£ per annum; in a case depending in this Court, the guardianship of the infant was committed to the custody of Sir Thomas Changer. Mr Herbert, the infant, was sent to the University of Oxford, from whence, coming to town upon some occasion, he was drawn to marry a common servant maid, older than himself, of no fortune. One Philips, a parson, married them; and he had several blank licences under the seal of the proper officer which were used to be filled up by the said Philips; and one Williams, who pretended to be a counsellor at law, took him to be guardian to the infant and to consent to his marrying the servant maid. Wherefore being ordered to attend his Honour, the Master of the Rolls, it was insisted, by way of excuse, by the parson and Williams, that they did not know Mr Herbert was a ward of the Court, and not knowing it, could not be guilty of contempt of the Court. And with regard to filling up the blank licences, this was endeavoured to be justified by alleging it to be the common practice. The matter having been for some time debated, was adjourned over for further consideration. Afterwards on this day (July 21) the parties again attending, it was argued, that there had been several cases, where it did appear, that those who had drawn in infant wards of the Court to marry, and had been instrumental in bringing about such matters, although they did not know that the infants were in wardship to the Court, had yet been guilty of a contempt, as in the case of Mr Willis who had married the daughter and heir of Sir Edward Hanner, where the parson that married them, and other assistants in the marriage, were committed and lay long in custody...As to the blank licences, though this was admitted to be a usual practice, yet the same (it was said) ought highly to be discountenanced, as tending to promote unsuitable matches.

The Master of the Rolls: With regard to what is alleged by way of excuse, that the parson and the pretended guardian had no notice of the Infant's being a ward of the Court, it is to be observed, that the commitment of the wardship to Sir Thomas Changer was an act of the Court, and is a cause then depending; of which in the present case they unquestionably are, where one acts as the guardian of the infant who never appears to have known him before, and acts, too, not for the benefit but to the prejudice and probably to the ruin of the infant, in such cases, (I say) all the parties to the transaction ought to be severely censured for example sake, to deter others from like offices.

That the Court took seriously its responsibilities is not to be doubted; but the time and effort expended upon those of high degree offers an unhappy contrast with orphans who had none to protect them. Chancery was not solely concerned with the protection of wealthy 'infants' from fortune-hunters. It included such orphans of merchants as James Storke in 1730, whose right to be raised in the Presbyterian faith of their deceased father it defended, even against the Church of England.[9]

Edward Holden Cruttenden

For certain estates of wealthy orphans, private Acts of Parliament could be passed in order to contest or vindicate a will. This was the case with Edward Holden Cruttenden.

Cruttenden travelled to Calcutta in 1737 as a Writer for the East India Company. The Writers' function was to keep accounts of the Company's correspondence with London. Each letter was in triplicate, two being sent by different ships and one overland. (This is a possible source of later impenetrable Indian bureaucracy.) Cruttenden rose slowly through the hierarchy, with a modestly enhanced salary, which was not the source of his wealth. It was expected employees would grow rich in their private dealings, as long as they did not encroach on the Company's profits. Cruttenden became a Senior Merchant in 1744 and in 1752 was appointed Colonel of Militia. He married Elizabeth Jedderie in 1746 at St Anne's Church in Calcutta. Their three children, Elizabeth, Sarah and Edward were born in 1752, 1754 and 1756, respectively. He provoked the anger of the directors for advancing his own interests above those of the company, and was dismissed in 1755 for obtaining a contract fraudulently. He stayed in Bengal as an independent merchant, and was re-instated in the Company the following year.

He lived in Fort William, constructed at the end of the seventeenth century, and named after William III in 1700. Government House was finished in 1706, and was home to officials and Writers of the Company. In 1756 the Nawab of Bengal, Siraj ud Daulah, provoked by the Company's interference in the affairs of Bengal, laid siege to Fort William. This was the time of the incident of 'the black hole of Calcutta', a symbol of Indian atrocities against the innocent traders of the Company, and it entered British imperial folklore, together with the 'triumph' of the battle of Palashi in 1757. During the siege, women and children were evacuated from the Fort. Among them was Elizabeth Cruttenden and her three children. Supplies were scanty and conditions in the monsoon heat and rain unbearable. The ships reached the relative safety of Fulta, where Elizabeth died.

The three children returned to England in the charge of their ayah. A painting of them by Sir Joshua Reynolds, dating from 1759, is now in the Gallery of Sao Paolo in Brazil; the ayah's dark face wears an air of distant melancholy as she oversees three pale solemn children.

Edward Cruttenden returned to Calcutta as Lieutenant Governor of Fort William, re-built by Clive in 1758. In 1765 he became a Director of the East India Company and remained so until his death in 1771. He had brought home a fortune estimated at £50,000 in the late 1750s, and acquired property in Putney.

He had appointed three Guardians for his children, now orphaned. In his will he bequeathed 'considerable pecuniary legacies' for when they reached the age of majority, from which the cost of their maintenance and education would be deducted. In the interests of fairness, part of his estate was left equally to all three children, not just to his son, as would have been usual practice at the time. It turned out that the will had not been attested by any witnesses. Although it was authenticated and approved, the sale of the land could not proceed, because of failure to have the will witnessed, and would therefore pass only to Edward, the sole male heir.

A Parliamentary appeal was made by the guardians to sell land which was forbidden under common law. In other words, they requested an Act be passed to allow the desire of the deceased to take priority over enacted law. This actually broke existing law and created a new one solely to benefit the orphans. Parliament agreed, and the wishes of the testator were fulfilled.[10]

Orphans of a transgressive upper class

Percy Bysshe Shelley

It became common for the state to remove the children of the poor from parental care. In extreme cases it was prepared to make orphans of children of more elevated status.

Percy Bysshe Shelley, eldest son of Sir Timothy Shelley, was born in 1792. At the age of eight he went to school at Sion House in Brentford, where it was said of him that his 'delicate constitution and girlish disposition' earned him all the petty tyrannies and horrors of school. At the age of thirteen, Eton developed in him a hatred of flogging. He was sent down from Oxford at the age of sixteen for writing a pamphlet on atheism which he refused to disown. At the age of nineteen, he eloped with sixteen-year-old Harriet Westbrook to Scotland. He married her in a ceremony unrecognised in England, since parental consent was withheld. Their child, Elizabeth Ianthe, was born in 1813. They re-married in London to provide her with legal protection. Harriet became pregnant with their second child, Charles, born in 1814; but by that time Shelley had met Mary Godwin, sixteen-year old daughter of William Godwin and Mary Wollstonecraft. They eloped in July 1814. Harriet, deeply unhappy, became pregnant with a lover, and, after taking lodging in Hans Place, walked one day to Hyde Park and drowned her-self in the Serpentine. In a touching farewell letter she wrote:

> My dear Bysshe, let me conjure you by the remembrance of our days of happiness to grant my last wish—do not take your inno-cent child from Eliza [Harriet's older sister, who had lived with the pair soon after their marriage] who has been more than I have, who has watched over her with such unceasing care.

Shelley was in Bath with Mary Godwin, when he heard of his wife's suicide. He hurried to London to confront stories that he was the cause of her death, even that he had murdered her. Although all contact between them had ceased, he reproached himself for failing to exercise care over a woman so young and vulnerable. He said her death tore his being to pieces; that he almost lost his reason.

He was deprived of the care and education of his children, Elizabeth Ianthe and Charles, by an order of the Lord Chancellor. The Court of Chancery was prepared to interfere with parental authority.

A petition was presented in the name of the children to the Court of Chancery, (which administered the duty of the King as *pater patriae* to intervene in the lives of children injured by the father's misconduct or actions prejudicial to infants). This claimed Shelley had abandoned his wife, and had since unlaw-fully cohabited. Therefore the mother had returned to her father's house with the eldest infant, while the other was born soon after; since then they had been maintained by the mother and her father. Shelley, an avowed atheist, had demanded that the children be delivered up to him. He intended to get posses-sion of their persons and educate them as he saw fit. The Lord Chancellor (Lord Eldon) said:

> I consider that this is a case in which the father has demonstrated that he must, and does deem it to be a matter of duty which his principles impose upon him, to recommend to those whose opin-ions and habits he may take it upon himself to form, that conduct in some of the most important relations of life, is moral and virtu-

ous, which the law calls upon me to consider as immoral and vicious—conduct which the law animadverts upon as inconsistent with the duties of persons in such relations of life and which it considers injuriously affecting both the interests of such persons and those of the country.[11]

He and Mary Godwin went to Great Marlow in Buckinghamshire, where the radical poet was said to have been 'a great friend of the poor'. The breach with his relations was final. He suffered odium and abuse as a result of publicity from the Chancery Court application. Reviled and unpopular, they found it impossible to live in England and went to Italy in 1819. In Pisa, he was struck one day by an Englishman, who exclaimed 'What, are you that damned atheist Shelley?' His friend, Byron, declared he was the least selfish and mildest of men. The relationship with Mary Godwin was severely strained when they went to Lerici in 1822. She had already lost three of the four children she had borne, was pregnant again and suffered a miscarriage. Shelley was drowned in a boating accident off the coast of the Gulf of Spezia. He was twenty-nine.

Contemporary orphans of the middle class

Orphans today are rarely objects of such controversy. The parents of most orphans of the professional classes generally make provision for the (increasingly unlikely) occurrence that they will pre-decease their children.

Grace

Grace was a teenage orphan, whose parents died within a short time of one another. Her father was a cancer specialist, who monitored the abnormal clusters of cancers around the Windscale nuclear reactor. Her mother, daughter of a Methodist minister, trained at the Central School of Speech and Drama in the same year as Kenneth Williams. She never acted, but her histrionic ability served her well socially. During

the war she worked in London Transport, managing bus con-
ductresses whose husbands were away at the war.

Grace told me:

She and my father married in 1947. I was born two years later. My
mother had thrombosis and nearly died. They engaged a nurse to
look after me. There had been another nurse who raided the drinks
cupboard and was dismissed. My mother recovered, but was
advised to have no more children. When the NHS was founded,
new hospitals were built, especially in deprived places, and my
father became a consultant at Cumberland Infirmary. We lived in
a village with a green that sloped down to the river Eden. It was
very class ridden. I never socialised with village children, although
I was envious of them.

I went to boarding school at eleven in North Wales, where liberal
middle classes of the North West sent their girls. My mother was
attracted to its principles—dedicated originally to orphaned
daughters of the gentry who would otherwise have been poor gov-
ernesses or prostitutes. The head girl's parents had been killed in a
car crash.

The school had the same design as the local lunatic asylum. There
was a hall and ruined castle nearby, which were bought by the
school. We were vile to each other, but at the same time supportive
against authority. Girls are, I believe, generally more vicious than
boys. A lot of our time was spent doing nothing, around a one-bar
electric fire. We put our Harris tweed cloak over our beds because
it was so cold; ice formed on the inside windows.

They were very frightened of lesbianism. No one was allowed to
speak to anyone in the year below her. If two friends were in different years, they were not permitted any conversation. Of course
girls developed secret contact with each other. Life was full of
secrets—not sexual excitement so much as emotional security.
Waves of religious fervour occurred. We saw the film, *The Nun's
Story*. They discovered I had freckles in the form of a cross! We had
to wear our school uniform and plain veils to go to the parish
church. We wore hats in church, it was said, so that angels would
not look down and fall in love with us.

59

My last pash after my father died, was very kind and sat up all night with me when I cried. We were not well taught. The careers mistress was also the games teacher. She had no idea. I wanted to do Sociology at Nottingham or East Anglia. She looked at me and said 'Oh is there a university there?' Prefects were called wardens, because it was based on the Drapers' Guild system. Most girls became secretaries and nurses and left after O-levels.

My mother spoke to me about sex. She showed me her cap in the bedroom. At school I said the unsayable 'You'll never believe my parents have sex.' A friend said that was ridiculous, because hers didn't. My mother was ill and had a mastectomy. She wore what was called then a falsie. It seemed we could get on with life again.

Then my father fell ill. He had pneumonia, and slept on a camp-bed in the playroom downstairs. I wasn't frightened. I was protected from the early signs of his illness. He was referred to a hospital in Hammersmith, for which he had campaigned for a cobalt machine. He was provided with a portable cylinder of oxygen by his bed. He lived till the year of my O-levels. There had been panics during holidays, when he had been taken by ambulance to hospital. I said to my mother 'Is daddy going to die?' and 'Will I have to leave school?'

[She replied], 'No, let's see. School will be fine.' His dying took two years. At fourteen I heard that my friend's grandfather had died. I burst into tears, because I knew my father was ill. But nobody actually told me. We were all in denial at school: separated from our parents, it was like permanent bereavement.

Then one Speech Day they never came. I knew something was wrong. The father of a friend told me he had died. His funeral was in the church where they had married. The crematorium was packed. It seemed enormous to me. I went to Suffolk to my godparents. I loaded up the car, constantly unpacking and re-loading it. No one knew about the grieving process in those days.

At the same time, my mother's father died. I heard her crying. Is Mummy all right? She's just laughing. I knew that was deception, but I played along. I was not in a state about father's death. Other children saw my parents as glamorous 'like Princess Margaret.' There was a cocktail party for us from our old friends in Ipswich. I was in a pink Louis Feraud dress, pink—we all dressed like our mothers then, it was pre-Mary Quant, some of my outfits were my mother's cast-offs. I am looking competent in high heels trying to appear grown up. It looked as if everything was normal, yet we were in mourning.

I went back to school. I'd turned sixteen and got my O levels. Daddy would have been very pleased. We were in the Lower VI. The staff treated us like grown ups. My friend's father who was a teacher killed himself on the last day of term. A message came to ask me if I would tell her—they thought I would know what was needed to comfort her. It gave me responsibility. The Head took in three sisters who had been orphaned in some accident in South Africa. I was asked to look after the little one.

Then my mother became unwell. She turned yellow. Uncle Tony, my father's consultant and family friend, diagnosed jaundice and tuberculosis. I was tested and found to be clear. I went back to school. I don't remember anything of Lower VI. I did English, French and History. The staff were good apart from the French mistress. We were beyond her.

Deep down, I knew my mother was dying. Each house had a telephone to be used by the girls only in extraordinary circumstances. The Housemother allowed me to make calls to my mother. By the end of the Christmas holidays, she was really ill; the cancer was everywhere. Uncle Tony came to see her. I had gone to the village shop, and as Uncle Tony was leaving, he stopped the car and asked me to get in. He told me directly she was going to die. I was so grateful to him.

I was allowed to phone home. My mother's speech was slurred by medication. I asked the Housemistress for help. One of my father's old friends, a consultant in Birkenhead, scooped me up and drove to their home in Carlisle. Days passed. I was in the bathroom washing my hair when the telephone rang. They came up and said she had died. I was protected, by a fantastic social network of people all familiar to me. They knew what to do.

After the funeral I returned to school. Aunty Judy, my godmother and guardian, took me back after the funeral. I vaguely remember packing up my room. I had all my mother's and father's letters. Aunty Judy said 'Shall we light a bonfire?' We did. I regret that I cannot remember enough of my mother. I was concentrating on holding myself together. I can't recall leaving the house. Auntie Judy allowed me to take all the belongings I wanted, pots and pans as well as silver. They and my father's sister became my guardians. I was well protected. That summer I went back to Cumbria to spend the holiday with a friend's family. I didn't find it painful, I fell back into the old ways.

My guardian worked hard to include me, but it was different. I learned to play the part. Auntie Judy's father had built up a successful gentlemen's outfitter business for Suffolk county types. West Suffolk. They opened a wine bar and café on the outfitters' premises. Auntie Judy and Uncle Alec had a party there, launching me as a new member of the family. She carefully introduced me to people as 'my ward.' Judy had fostered children before. When I got married, the invitation said 'you are invited to the wedding of their ward.' It gave me a kind of legitimacy. I liked it.

After my mother's death, Aunty Judy would sit on my bed and stroke me. I pretended to be younger than I was and she talked about my mother and father. It was not pushed under the carpet. Judy and Alec evoked my parents' presence. I felt comforted.

I staggered through the rest of school. It was helpful being there— we relied on and looked after each other. Girls started going to university. We felt grown up, we could make tea, coffee and toast in our studies. We had poetry, music and singing societies. We even took driving lessons.

The female staff were a lost generation, bright women, all unmarried. They wanted us to flourish intellectually; perhaps they were also envious. The History and English teachers were inspiring. The Drapers' Company paid half my fees when father died and all my fees after mother's death.

I became a psychotherapist, helping people to manage their self-destructive impulses. I had not felt very clever at university. But afterwards I did psychoanalytic training. I had a partner, a home, a satisfying career. I worked at the Portman clinic for ten years, families with adolescents, then at the Tavistock in the adolescent development department. My whole career has been based on the psychology of loss.

Chloe

Not all guardians provided for orphans prove to be as reliable as far-sighted parents might have assumed.

Chloe is from a well-to-do family in Lincolnshire. Her father owned an extensive holding called at the time a 'market garden', growing flowers and vegetables. He was killed in Burma, and Chloe's mother died when she was two:

> I was told she died of grief. I tell myself I can remember her. I looked at the photographs so long, I think I conjured up her spirit. Her elder brother was my guardian. It was a terrible mistake. He was very rich. They had a flat in Knightsbridge. I went to a well-known private school on the south coast. I loved school. But I hated home.

> Uncle Frank's wife, Aunt Essie, was not interested in me at all. I think they led separate lives, and she always had some slightly androgynous young man in tow. That left the way free for Frank. I found him so repulsive, and I knew, from a child, that he showed an unhealthy interest in me. As I grew up, I dreaded going home. I managed to get invitations to stay with friends. It was horrible. When I went to bed at night he would say I will come and tuck you up, and even when I was only twelve or thirteen, he would linger, and be a bit too tactile. I couldn't bear his touch. I wanted to say to him 'For God's sake get your face away from mine and keep your hands off me.' He never actually went beyond the limit, so I couldn't point to some form of abuse or improper conduct.

> I tried to talk to Aunt Essie, but she gave vague reassurances about how much they loved us and their duty to my poor mother. I really think she knew, but pretended there was no problem. In the end, I confided in my friend's mother. She wanted to know if he had done anything he shouldn't. She understood when I said it wasn't that, it was just a feeling, an atmosphere he created around him. She let me stay at the house; and in fact she became more of a mother figure to me than Aunt Essie had ever been. As for Frank, whenever I saw him, he pretended to be hurt. He called me 'a deserter', and even threatened me with the terms of his guardianship. After I went to university, I never again went home to stay.

The brevity of orphanage; the length of its effects

Orphans are like child labourers, in that their condition does not last. Soon cast out of a role that inspires compassion into an abrasive 'real world', any forbearance they earned as minors is abruptly withdrawn. If the distress endured by loss of parents were as easily set aside as the charity extended to orphans, there would be no problem. But many suffer for the rest of their lives from lack of love, abuse in institutions, the unkindness of 'step-parents' (Old English *steop*, meaning 'orphan'); a deficit rarely made good. The disabilities of orphanhood are invisible, without mark or stigma.

Many children deprived of one or both parents are to be found as adults, both among those who have achieved positions of eminence, and also among the least favoured in society. It is not surprising that many living on the streets or begging had a childhood disrupted by death, absence or abandonment. They are pursued by loss which impairs their ability to participate in a social life which a majority take for granted.

On the other hand, early deprivation often serves as a spur to achievement. It may lead to compensatory efforts to earn the love of the phantoms their parents are, a desire to 'make something of themselves'. These selves have no reference to earlier generations—for their invention they find reservoirs of energy and determination not always available to those raised in stable and loving households. There is often an opportunity for self-creation, although this is scarcely a recommendation for orphanhood. Well-known public figures who were orphaned include US Presidents Andrew Jackson and Herbert Hoover, Eleanor Roosevelt, Nelson Mandela, Joseph Conrad, John Keats, Johann Sebastian Bach, Edgar Allan Poe, Leo Tolstoy, Ella Fitzgerald, William Wordsworth, Jean-Jacques Rousseau, Orson Welles, Marilyn Monroe and Steve Jobs.

The lives of such individuals appear to resemble orphan heroes of fiction and fairy-stories. Perhaps a distinction may be made between 'fictional' orphans and 'literary' orphans, although the categories overlap. In fiction, orphans often turn out to have been stolen or kidnapped, compelled to live out disreputable lives by those who have seized them from their rightful parents. In folk-tales and popular fiction, the fatherless often prove to be sons and daughters of kings or the nobility. They were stolen at birth and brought up by someone of lowly status; and restoration to their true estate is the culmination of the tale. Unbound by determinants of class or caste, they transcend social location, and their adventures take them, like Moll Flanders, into forbidden territory, moral as well as topographical.

Orphans of the rich rarely lose caste, particularly as wards of trusted friends and advisers of their parents, since their origins are no secret. But orphans of the poor are almost never reunited with the wealthy parents from whom they were not taken at birth by a wicked witch or dishonest scullery-maid. Many poor orphans work hard to gain recognition; often thanks to adoptive or foster-parents who have compensated for an absence of parental love; but many unloved orphans struggle to make satisfactory adult relationships. They distrust others, have a sense of unworthiness; characteristics exacerbated by orphanages, institutions, charitable endowments and official provisions for the child abandoned by death or design.

Rising above misfortune: the orphan as hero

Orphans who succeed are often promoted as models for emulation by the unfortunate, praised for having overcome the miserable conditions of their birth. Though for every exceptional individual able, by talent or will, to rise above circumstances, there are many more who fail in secrecy and silence, their struggles unacknowledged by sorrow or the indifference of adults charged with their care.

Although this book is concerned mainly with the lives of the poor and obscure, it should not be supposed that even those orphans whose lives are marked by often spectacular achievement are not also haunted by loss. It is worth dwelling on the experience of a few of these, since they sometimes articulate the feelings they doubtless have in common with those who left no record of their experience. Many suffer—or are driven to—early death; sometimes, it seems, in pursuit of those whose love they never received, or in collusion with their abandonment. Among these, Edgar Allan Poe was found unconscious on the streets of Baltimore at thirty-eight, Mikhail Lermontov was killed in a duel at twenty-seven and Marilyn Monroe took her own life at thirty-six. Philip Doddridge was exhausted in his forties, and although John Keats succumbed at twenty-five to the consumption that ran in his family, he had neglected his own health. John Lennon was killed by a gunman, but his own life had been profoundly marked by the death of his mother in a street accident twenty-three years earlier. Death—unsurprisingly—often haunts orphans; exercises a powerful hold over their imagination, and sometimes, influences their fate. When Samuel Taylor Coleridge, orphaned at eight, died in 1834, his close friend Charles Lamb observed 'It seemed to me that he long had been on the confines of the next world—I think he had a hunger for eternity.'[12]

Others have been borne up by strong family networks, or, like J S Bach, by kindred so penetrated by a sense of religion and music that this created a protective emotional sealant against desolation. Bach lost his mother and father in 1695 within a few months of each other. He was nine. His biographers have treated this almost as an incidental occurrence, recording that he soon settled down in the home of a married elder brother, where his love of music was further stimulated. There is nowhere a sense of the bereaved child; unless it appears in his work with an intensity that cannot be expressed in words. It is left to the linguistic power of a Tolstoy to articulate the sense of spirituality which remains after loss. Tolstoy cannot have known his mother, since he was only eighteen months old when she died, but he felt her presence. This is echoed by a very different orphan, Eleanor

Roosevelt, who wrote in her autobiography that although she did not attend her father's funeral, 'I knew in my mind that my father was dead, and yet I loved him more closely, probably, than when he was alive.'[13] Eleanor Roosevelt was well connected— her father's elder brother was Theodore Roosevelt, 26th US President. Her mother died of diphtheria in 1892, which also claimed her older brother the following year. Her father drank heavily after the loss of his wife, and was confined to a clinic, where he died in the summer of 1894. Eleanor was ten. She and her remaining brother went to live with their maternal grand-mother, where she was unhappy and insecure. Educated at home until she was fifteen, at her aunt's insistence, she was sent to a private finishing school on the outskirts of London. In 1902, she met Franklin Delano Roosevelt, her father's fifth cousin whom she would marry three years later. Of her father, she wrote, 'He dominated my life for as long as he lived, and was the love of my life for many years after he died.'[14]

Bertrand Russell was born in 1872, second son of Viscount Amberley and his mother Katharine was the daughter of Baron Stanley of Alderley. His mother died of diphtheria when he was two and his father died less than two years later. His sister died in 1876. Russell said he knew his mother from her diary and letters, which were 'vigorous, lively and witty, and original.' The family were exceptionally progressive, atheists who supported birth control and women's suffrage. When she died, his mother had no religious ceremony. His parents slept with their children's tutor, not for sexual enjoyment, but out of high-minded ideal-ism. He wrote that, 'My father decided that although the tutor should remain childless on account of his tuberculosis, it was unfair to expect him to be celibate.' After their death, Bertrand and his brother Frank lived with their grandfather, Lord John Russell, Lady Russell and her unmarried daughter in Pembroke Lodge in Richmond Park. Lord John Russell had twice been Prime Minister; and he died in 1878. Bertrand Russell was tutored at home until he went to Cambridge at eighteen; a soli-tary upbringing marked by continuous loss. Perhaps this gave him his lifelong sympathy for the poor and oppressed. The death which stalked his childhood may have contributed to his hatred of war, which only added to Nature's remorseless cull of humanity. His work as logician and one of the founders of modern analytic philosophy was attended by a restless sexual and emotional hunger which lasted until his fourth marriage with Edith Finch in the 1950s. He wrote in his autobiography, 'Three passions, simple but overwhelmingly strong, have governed my life: the longing for love, the search for knowledge and unbearable pity for the suffering of mankind.'[15]

The unhappiness of bereaved children often expresses itself as intense longing, or strong religious feeling; in purity of sound or poetry. It sometimes appears as a yearning for recognition, threnody for loss, or performance played out to the phantoms of their abandonment. For others, orphanhood means a life without limits: angry and anguished, they reproduce in their adult lives a disregard of boundaries and a pursuit of danger: a reflection, perhaps, of the want of loving care in childhood. Edgar Allan Poe, born in Boston in 1809, lost his mother to TB when he was three. His father had already disappeared. Raised by foster-parents in Virginia, he refused to enter the tobacco exporting business. He married a thirteen-year-old cousin in 1835, falsifying her age for the purpose of marriage. He drank and took opium, and much of his work shows his fascination with death: it has an incantatory quality, an orphan's summoning forth of the dead. He wrote 'The boundaries between Life and Death are at best shadowy and vague. Who shall say where the one ends and the other begins?'[16]

Many have sought to conceal their orphaned status—a reflection, perhaps, of social contempt for or indifference towards the orphans they were. Ella Fitzgerald, for instance, would never talk about the year she spent as a teenager in a reformatory in New York; perhaps it can only be heard in a voice that transforms pain and longing into anthems to life.

Henry Morton Stanley

Others did not simply remain silent over their early experience, but revised it, in order to draw to themselves affection or attention they lacked. The explorer Henry Morton Stanley remade himself. At the age of seventeen he went to the United States and became a journalist; later, as an accessory to the plunder of the Belgian King Leopold's Congo, he was resented by British colonialists, who saw him as an American interloper. He is unusual in having left, in his autobiography an account (perhaps also exaggerated) of his early life. Published posthumously in 1909, it is far from the way he wanted to be seen while he lived.

Stanley's father died within weeks of his birth. His mother left him with his grandfather, Moses Parry, a Wesleyan who lived within the precincts of Denbigh Castle. When the child was four, he broke a pitcher: his grandfather promised him a whipping when he returned from the field where he had work to attend to. There, he fell down and died. 'The visitation of God'. He was eighty-four.

The child was transferred to the care of an elderly couple at two shillings and sixpence a week paid for by his uncles. Dismayed by his appetite, they asked more for his keep. Both uncles had married, and declined any further charge:

> Consequently Dick Price, the son, took me by the hand one day and under the pretence that we were going to Aunt May, he induced me to accompany him on a long journey…[He] set me down from his shoulders before an immense stone building, and, passing through tall iron gates, he pulled at a bell, which I could hear clanging noisily in the distant interior. A sombre-faced stranger appeared at the door, who, despite my remonstrances, seized me by the hand, and drew me within…The door closed on him, and with the echoing sound, I experienced for the first time the awful feeling of utter desolateness.

> The great building with the iron gates and innumerable windows, into which I had been so treacherously taken, was the St Asaph Union Workhouse. It is an institution to which the aged poor and

superfluous children of that parish are taken, to relieve the respect-abilities of the obnoxious sight of extreme poverty, and because civilisation knows no better method of disposing of the infirm and helpless than by imprisoning them within its walls.

Once within, the aged are subjected to stern rules and useless tasks, while the children are disciplined and chastised in a manner that is contrary to justice and charity. To the aged it is a house of slow death, to the young it is a house of torture… It took me some time to learn the unimportance of tears in a workhouse. Hitherto tears had brought me relief in one shape or another, but from this time forth they availed nothing. James Francis, the one-handed school-master into whose stern grasp Dick Price had resigned me, was little disposed to soften the blow dealt my sensibilities by treachery. Though forty-five years have passed since that dreadful evening, my resentment has not a whit abated.

No Greek helot or dark slave ever underwent such discipline as the boys of St Asaph under the heavy masterful hand of James Francis. The ready backslap in the face, the stunning clout over the ear, the strong blow with the open palm on alternate cheeks, which knocked our senses into confusion, were so frequent that it is a marvel we ever recovered again. Whatever might be the nature of the offence, or merely because his irritable mood required vent, our poor heads were cuffed, and slapped and pounded, until we lay speechless and streaming with blood.

Francis had been a collier at Mold until an accident deprived him of his left hand. As he had some education he was appointed Master of St Asaph Union. He became more and more savage, until it appeared he had lost his reason. He died in a madhouse:

When I reached my eleventh year, the king of the school for beauty and amiability was a boy of about my own age, named Willie Roberts. Some of us believed that he belonged to a very superior class to our own. His coal-black hair curled in profusion over a delicately moulded face of milky whiteness. His eyes were soft and limpid, and he walked with a carriage that tempted imitation. Beyond these indications of him I remember but little, for just then I fell ill with some childish malady which necessitated my removal to the infirmary, where I lay for weeks. But as I was becoming convalescent I was startled by a rumour that he had suddenly died.

When I heard that his body was in the dead-house, I felt stricken with a sense of irreparable loss. As the infirmary opened upon the courtyard which contained our morgue, some of the boys suggested that it might be possible to view him, and, prompted by a fearful curiosity to know what death was like, we availed ourselves of a favourable opportunity, and entered the house with quaking hearts.

The boy lay on a black bier, and covered in a sheet, appeared uncommonly long for a boy. One of the boldest drew the cloth aside, and at the sight of his waxen face with its awful fixity, we all started back, gazing at it as if spellbound. There was something grand in its superb disregard of the chill and gloom of the building, in the holy calm of the features. It was the face of our dear Willie, with whom we had played, and yet not the same, for an inexplicable aloofness had come over it. We yearned to cry out to him to wake, but dared not, for the solemnity of his face was appalling.

Presently the sheet was drawn further away, and we saw what some of us insinuated might have been seen. The body was livid, and showed scores of dark weals. One glance was enough, and hastily covering it, we withdrew, with minds confirmed in the opinion that signs of violence would appear after death as testimonies against him who was guilty of it. After what we had seen, it would have been difficult for anyone to have removed from our minds the impression that Francis was accountable for Willie's death.[17]

Marilyn Monroe

Marilyn Monroe, born in 1926, was also re-created, not by fantasy but by her own charismatic reality; a dazzling presence who concealed the turmoil within. Her father was unknown, her mother, Gladys, a negative film-cutter at Consolidated Industries, emotionally and mentally unstable. Because of this, she placed Marilyn with Wayne and Ida Bolender, who fostered several other children. When she was seven, her mother retrieved her daughter and took her to live with her. Within months she had been admitted to a psychiatric institution, diagnosed with paranoid schizophrenia. She spent the rest of her life there and never saw her daughter again.

Marilyn passed into the care of her mother's best friend, Grace McKee. She was about to marry Erwin 'Doc' Goddard, who had bit parts in films. He abused Marilyn sexually; and she went through ten foster-homes between 1935 and 1942. At nine, she spent a year in the Los Angeles Orphans' Home. She was sexually abused again at eleven. Her mother would not permit adoption, because she hoped one day to recover and reclaim her daughter.

Marilyn returned to the Goddards, but in 1942, the family planned to move, and Marilyn, unwilling to go with them, married the twenty-one-year-old son of a neighbour. He went overseas with the army, while she worked in a munitions factory.

Her subsequent career is well known. Her vulnerable eroticism compelled and fascinated, but the image bore little relation to her inner insecurity. Her suicide at thirty-six supports the relatively lower life expectancy of orphans. Does death become the site where a relationship with absent parents is going to be resolved, or the 'truth' about parentage revealed; or is it simply that the burden of lovelessness becomes too hard to bear, broken relationships and an unfamiliarity with love which impedes the growth of enduring attachments?[18]

John Keats

Keats' father, Thomas, was an ostler in a livery stable in North London. He married the daughter of his employer, Frances, and was later left in charge of the business. John Keats was born in 1795, George in 1797, Edward in 1801 (died in infancy) and Frances Mary in 1803. John Keats attended a school in Enfield run by the Rev John Clarke. His father was killed in a fall from a horse in 1804. Within twelve months Frances had 'set aside her weeds' and made a disastrous remarriage with Charles Rawlings. The new husband now by law owned all her property, so that when they separated, and she returned to

Edmonton, to Mrs Jennings her mother, she had nothing. Fortunately Mrs Jennings had been left comfortably provided for by her husband. Keats' mother left the children in their grandmother's care and disappeared. John Keats left little testimony to his own early life. That he was sociable, passionate, combative, impulsive, yet also with an underlying melancholy comes from the memories of others. His mother returned after three years. Little is known of her intervening life—stories circulated that she led a life of dubious respectability. She had consumption, and died in 1810. Her return rekindled Keats' love for her, and, 'he sat up whole nights with her in a great chair, and would suffer nobody to give her medicine or even cook her food but himself, and read novels to her in her intervals of ease.'

Mrs Jennings drew up a deed of care for her grandchildren, and appointed two guardians. When she died, these failed to live up to the confidence placed in them. Some of the money was probably stolen, and in any case John was taken out of school and apprenticed to a surgeon. His indentures were cancelled four years later, and he became a student at the hospitals of St Thomas's and Guy's, passing his exams as licentiate at Apothecaries' Hall in 1816. He became a dresser at Guy's, but his heart was in the poetry which drew him from his medical work, and which produced, between 1816 and 1819, most of the poems for which he is known. His unconsummated relationship with Fanny Brawne was marred by illness: he returned from walking in the Lake District in 1818 to look after his brother Tom, who also died of the consumption that claimed him. He travelled with painter, Joseph Severn, to Italy in November 1819, where he soon died.[19]

Johann Sebastian Bach

J S Bach lost his mother when he was nine and his father a few months later. He was the eighth child in a family of musicians—

his father director of Eisenach's town musicians. His older siblings immersed him in music theory, while an uncle at Georgenkirche introduced him to the organ. His father taught him the violin and harpsichord. He also lost a brother and sister in childhood. He was supported by a wide network of kin for whom music and their Lutheran faith were effective psychological supports. He married twice—a cousin, Maria Barbara who died in 1720, and with whom he had seven children, of whom four survived. A year later, he married Anna Magdalena Wilcke, who bore thirteen children, of whom six survived to adulthood. There is great poignancy in such high child mortality among an orphan's prolific progeny. Whatever elements of loss and emotional privation he endured, Bach's profound faith penetrated all his work: 'Music's only purpose should be for the glory of God and the recreation of the human spirit.'[20]

Leo Tolstoy

Leo Tolstoy created a sense of having been loved by a parent he cannot recall:

> My mother I do not at all remember. I was a year and a half old when she died. Owing to some strange chance no portrait whatever of her has been preserved; so that, as a real physical being, I cannot represent her to myself. I am in a sense glad of this. For in my conception of her there is only her spiritual figure, and all that I know about her is beautiful, and I think this is so, not only because all who spoke to me of my mother tried to say only what was good, but because there was actually very much of this good in her.

Later, writing of his father in the present tense long after he died, he said, 'I am enchanted by my father's kindness, and taking leave of him with special tenderness, kiss his white muscular hand. I loved my father very much, but did not know how strong this love of mine for him was until he died.'

In 1837, when Tolstoy was nine, Tolstoy's father went to Tula on business. In the street on his way to the house of a friend, he staggered, fell to the ground and died of apoplexy.

This death made the deepest impression of Tolstoy's childhood. He said it called forth in him a feeling of religious awe and brought the question of life and death vividly before him for the first time. As he did not witness his father's death, he would not believe it. For a long time afterwards, if he looked at the faces of strangers in the streets of Moscow, he not only fancied, but was almost certain, that he might at any moment come upon his father alive. And this mixed attitude of hope and unbelief called forth in him a special feeling of tenderness.

Tolstoy's grandmother died nine months later of a broken heart. 'Pelageya Nicolayevna wept perpetually, and every evening ordered the door into the next room be opened, and said that she saw her son there and talked with him.' His father's sister became his guardian, and when she died in 1840, he went to Kazan, to another sister of his father's.[21]

Ella Fitzgerald

Born in 1917 in Virginia, Ella was the only child of the common-law marriage between William Fitzgerald and Temperance William Fitzgerald. Her parents separated soon after she was born. Her mother moved to New York with her boyfriend Joseph Da Silva. She died in 1932, and following abuse by Da Silva, Ella was taken in by an aunt. She worked as 'numbers runner' for gamblers, and as a lookout for a brothel. In 1933 she was sentenced to the New York State Training School for Girls in Hudson. This, opened in 1887, was the only state juvenile institution which accepted both black and white children. Girls were taken in for such reasons as being 'morally impaired', or because they were 'incorrigible' or 'wayward' or because they refused to comply with the 'lawful demands' of their parents. Black girls were segregated in two separate 'cottages' and were punished by beatings, shackles, a regime of bread and water and solitary confinement. Ella Fitzgerald was not allowed to participate in the choir, which was reserved for white girls.

Because all records were destroyed by order of the state, there is uncertainty as to when she left. She is said to have run away and lived as best she could, singing and living on the streets, until she won a talent competition at the Apollo Theatre in Harlem in 1934. The following year she joined bandleader and drummer Chick Webb's group… She would never speak of her time of confinement in the reformatory.[22]

Philip Doddridge

Philip Doddridge born in 1702, was the twentieth child of Monica Doddridge, wife of an oil merchant, eighteen of whose children had died in infancy. It appeared the baby was stillborn, thrust aside as a corpse, until the midwife noticed a flicker of life. She slapped the child. It cried and lived to become a luminary of the Dissenting church. His grandfathers had both been clerics: Monica's father had lost his living as a result of the Act of Uniformity in 1662, which had demanded that 'every Parson, Vicar or any other Minister whatsoever' be required to use the new Prayer Book and observe the procedures of the Church of England. He became pastor of a dissenting church in south-west London. His paternal grandfather was a Protestant minister who had fled Bohemia when Catholic forces removed the Protestant Elector.

His mother died when he was eight, and his spiritual care passed to another ejected Dissenting minister. His father died when he was thirteen. The boy said that although he had lost his earthly parents, 'God is an immortal Father; my soul rejoices in Him; He hath hitherto helped me and provided for me; may it be my study to approve myself a more affectionate, grateful and dutiful child.' A world where death was ubiquitous provided both consolation and meaning, in faith.

Philip Doddridge's guardian—a business associate of his father—became bankrupt, and the boy had to sell all that remained of the family goods, except the grandfather's Bible. A benefactor paid for his studies at a Dissenting establishment in Leicestershire. Doddridge set up an academy in Northampton in 1730, becoming pastor of the Church. In the same year he married Mercy Maris, with whom he had nine children, four of whom survived into adulthood. The academy was celebrated as a theological training school for independent churches; and even some Church of England ministers sent their sons there to avoid the 'corruption' of university life. He called himself a 'moderate' Calvinist, but attracted more liberal clergy by his belief that true Christians of all denominations should work together for religious revival. His health, always poor, was aggravated by the intensity of his devotions. Supporters of all denominations raised money to send him to Lisbon, where he died in 1751 at the age of forty-nine.[23]

John Lennon

John Lennon, shot dead outside a New York hotel when he was forty, was yet another orphan whose life was cut short, apparently at random. His mother Julia, was one of five sisters. She met a hotel bell-boy at the age of fourteen, Alfred Lennon, who later became a ship steward. They were married in 1938. The following day he went to sea, but returned on leave from time to time, and she became pregnant with John. After that, he was only an intermittent visitor in his life. Julia moved with the child to live with her father, but then, working as a waitress, met John 'Bobby' Dykins. They fell in love and set up home together. John went to his Aunt Mimi, while his mother and her new partner had two children, one of whom was Julia, John's half-sister, who says that Mimi waged war with her sister for possession of John. Mimi and her husband had no children; and it later appeared that Mimi, moralistic and disapproving, had for years been sleeping with the lodger in the family. John's mother maintained a loving relationship with him, until, when John was seventeen, she was knocked down and killed by a car. This had a profound influence on him. Julia, his half-sister says all his work was deeply coloured by his life and feelings.[24]

Walter Tull

Walter Tull's father, Daniel, the son of a slave, had come to Britain, embarking as joiner on a ship in 1876. He worked as a carpenter in Folkestone. He married a Kentish woman, daughter of a family of farm labourers, with whom he had six children. In 1895, when Tull was aged seven, his mother died of cancer. The following year, his father married his wife's niece, who had come to the home to help with the children. In 1897 a daughter was born. Three months afterwards, Daniel Tull died of heart disease.

His widow, Clara, could not manage so many children. The minister of their chapel recommended that the two boys at school should go to the Children's Home in Bethnal Green. The oldest boy was working, while the two girls could help with domestic duties. The boys were regarded as a burden on the family. The Poor Law guardians of the parish where they lived wrote to the orphanage saying, 'The father of these children was a negro and they are consequently coloured children. I do not know if you are aware of this or whether it will in any way affect the application.' It didn't, and the boys were there for two years. The parish paid four shillings a week for each of them.

The Home was a Wesleyan Institution. It arranged singing tours; and Edward was picked out at one performance by a dentist in Glasgow, who adopted him. Walter worked in the orphanage print shop, and when he was fourteen left school and started in the printing industry. A gifted footballer, he played for Clapton amateur club. Within a few months he had joined Tottenham Hotspur. He was only the second black man to play professional football in England. Two years later he played for Northampton Town.

He volunteered in the 1914 war, and, extraordinarily, was made an officer, promoted to sergeant, despite a rule excluding 'negroes' from the officer class. It was the view of the Army Council that white soldiers 'would not take orders from a black'. In 1916 he was invalided with trench fever. He returned with the army to the Italian front in 1917, and promoted to Second Lieutenant. Mentioned in despatches for 'gallantry and coolness', he was recommended for the Military Cross. He never received it. He was killed at the age of thirty in the Pas de Calais in 1918.[25]

To have been an orphan and a black man at the height of imperial fervour in England was an immense disadvantage. That Walter Tull persevered, made a career as a footballer and distinguished himself in World War One was a wonder; that his achievements went unremarked for so long is less so. Only in 1999, a memorial was erected at Northampton Town's football stadium. His martial valour was never commemorated.

PART TWO

ORPHANS IN BRITAIN

4

THE POOR LAW, 1601–1834

Children and the Poor Law

For the poore are by nature much inclined to ease and idleness; and therefore they are to be put forth very timely: for as a twigge will bend when it is greene, so children are fittest to be bound when they are young, otherwise by reason of their idle and base education, they will hardly hold service: but as they have wavering and straying minds, so they will have wandering and unstaied bodies, which will be sooner disposed to vagrancie than activitie, to idlenesse than to work.[1]

A tract of 1546 said:

…We are constrained to suffer our children to spend the flour of their youth in idleness, bryngying them up either to bear wallettes, other else, if thei be sturdy, to stuff prisons and garnish galow trees.[2]

The first mention of children in the Poor Laws stated in 1536 that children—distinguished from the 'able-bodied' poor and the 'impotent poor'—should be prevented from joining the growing numbers of adult criminals and vagrants. Wandering children should be set to work as apprentices. In the Act of 1547—the most punitive in our history—children between the ages of five and fifteen could be taken from their parents and set to work until the age of twenty-one for a male and twenty for a female. This was swiftly mitigated: in 1549 compulsory apprenticeships were introduced but only until the age of fifteen—or marriage—for girls and eighteen for boys. They were also permitted to change their employment if a master were cruel or oppressive.

A refinement of this, introduced in 1572, placed adolescents—those over the age of fourteen—at risk of gaol if they were caught begging, unless an honest employer came forward to take him (they were almost invariably boys) into service for a year. Younger children could face whipping or the stocks. Anxieties about the potential mischief of which young people (especially unattached or parentless boys) are capable long predates Elizabethan England; but in the late sixteenth century the tone was set for subsequent generations. Fear of idle youth has possessed the imagination of ruling castes ever since; in particular, the children of unbelonging, those of uncertain parentage. The 'changelings' of folklore, possessed of malevolent powers, were at best harbingers of mortality, at worst, offspring of witchcraft.

That the young were susceptible to disaffection, and might be enlisted in causes inimical to the Crown, certainly marked the period in which no standing army existed. But the fear persisted. Unattached young people, running wild, without parental control or guidance, were denounced by Puritans, disciplined by workhouses, reformatories and industrial schools and chastised and beaten by teachers. They were deplored by moralists, condemned by politicians convinced that paupers would beget more paupers, and that a lawless 'breed' of workless young men would create bastards to be supported by the parish. Nineteenth-century anxiety about pickpockets, thieves and 'savage street arabs' who terrorised the streets of London appears in the contemporary world as a fear of criminal gangs which recruit the suggestible, while the outcast and vagrant of an earlier age are thought susceptible to the appeal of political extremists, or the seduction of alien ideologies. (The word 'street-arab' has been in use since the middle of the nineteenth century. Combining the prejudices of both race and class, it assimilates the life of homeless children to that of nomadic Arab tribes.)

The remedy against disorder has always been the wholesome distraction of labour, to which children should be inured at the earliest age. Child labour was taken for granted by the existence of apprenticeships and in the Statute of Artificers in 1563. From 1576, Justices of the Peace were to 'appoint and order a competent stock of wool, hemp, flax, iron and other stuff' to employ the poor and needy of the parish.

And the countryside of Elizabethan England was peopled with youthful workers from infancy, cutting and carrying wood for fuel, fetching water, minding poultry, watching cattle. Perhaps—like children to be seen in rural India and Bangladesh today—they were also envying the cows their perpetual work of eating, since the children themselves often went hungry as they tended sheep, or frightened birds from the corn, often while caring for younger siblings. They were part of an economy of self-provisioning in cottage garden, picking vegetables, removing slugs from cabbages, pea-picking and shaking the branches of trees and scattering apples or damsons on the grass beneath; guarding the pig or cow on common land, boys with an ash or birch-twig in their hand; girls mending clothes or spinning wool, which they collected from the hedgerows where sheep had left tufts of fleece on thorn and briar.

That the 'parish' remained in Britain the principal source of succour to the poor right up to the nineteenth century lent poor-relief a borrowed religious lustre, even when provision had been largely detached from the church. The word 'parish' is significant. First found in English in the late thirteenth century (in the Old French it is *parroche*, from Latin *parochia*, which in turn comes from Greek *paroikia*), its meaning is 'sojourner', or 'stranger'. In the Christian sense, this meant exile from the life of eternity: a colony of residents for whom earth is a foreign strand; orphans indeed. It is a more than linguistic paradox that 'the parish' came to mean the homeplace, with its connotations of familiarity and limited vision. The Act of 1662, which sought to maintain people in their place of birth, had a double irony—'settlement' aimed to return individuals to their place of earthly exile.

However that may be, poor relief was more than a way of calming restive populations, however mean, dishonest and grudging it may have been; a sense of their *right* to relief remained among the poor. Poor people were often cowed and submissive, but were liable to protest and riot at times of dearth, hunger and failed harvests. Parochial duty was enshrined in the legislation of the Elizabethan Poor Law, a national system of relief overseen locally. Obligation to the poor has never died, despite the assault upon it by laissez-faire ideology and the neo-liberal revival. An aura of secular piety attended the establishment of the welfare state in the twentieth century: a renewal of commitment by the comfortable and well-to-do to the orphan and widow, 'the lame, the halt and the blind.'

Although a compulsory levy for the poor had been decreed in 1563, Sidney and Beatrice Webb estimated that, 'only in an infinitesimal proportion of the 15,000 parishes and townships and the couple of hundred cities and boroughs was any compulsory Poor Rate actually raised prior to 1598.'[3] After the consolidation of the Poor Laws in 1601, the practice of collection became more widespread, although far from universal.

We should be wary of reading into the history of legislation concerning the poor a reliable account of their actual fate, especially that of orphans and parish children. The Poor Laws, in both their most merciful and their most repressive aspect, were rarely applied with the rigour intended by those who framed them. The lived experience escaped many of the traps set for it; misfortunes were mitigated by the leniency of neighbours or aggravated by accident, pestilence or neglect.

Parish children were apprenticed younger than the children of independent labourers, boys to husbandry, girls to domestic service. The parents of pauper children had no control over the apprenticeship of their children, for if they refused, they risked losing their own relief. Orphans had even less agency, and prosperous householders were expected to take them without payment from the parish. Some were undoubtedly accepted as members of the household, treated with humanity and even affection. But it was not in the nature of hierarchical society to lavish much personal care upon paupers, in spite of abstract notions of Christian charity. Many led lives of semi-slavery. Margaret Pelling notes that in 1599, the mayor's court in Norwich declared eighteen-year-old Katherine Vardine should be dismissed from service, because both master and mistress had syphilis, 'whereby the said maid may in the like take hurt.'[4] This suggests official recognition that masters were likely to sleep with their young female servants. Many girls bore the children of their employers or of their adult sons. Such infants were often abandoned or done away with soon after birth (if they lived at all), or buried in woodland and meadow. There were always ways of killing unwanted children; just as there are today in poor communities. In parts of India, female children (whose presence is still often perceived as a burden) could be killed by the placing of a grain of uncooked rice on the tongue of a new born, which would choke her.

In spite of a determination to 'set children on work', throngs of beggars and vagrants crowded the highways of sixteenth century Britain, and were everywhere followed by 'flocks', 'swarms' or 'packs' of children: these collective nouns are scarcely accidental. The solution was to remove the children of 'harlots and beggars' from their parents; a practice which cast a long shadow, for it anticipated 'remedies' of later centuries that, in a form of wilful orphaning, separated children from incompetent or profligate adults in defiance of the sanctified bonds of kinship.

The Elizabethan Poor Law already empowered magistrates and parish officials to reconstitute households by binding out not only orphans but also pauper children as apprentices, thereby reducing relief expenditure by redistributing the burden

of children from the less well-off to the more prosperous households within and beyond the parish.[5] It should come as no sur-
prise that the well-to-do, who readily parted with their own
children by sending them to other substantial households, were
only too ready to subject poor children to a similar orphaning,
by assigning them to other families in order to spare the payers
of the poor-rate avoidable financial burdens.

Charity

Charitable establishments from the sixteenth century were
familiar in London, and reflect a compassion which Pinchbeck
and Hewitt claim was also exhibited by the Elizabethan Poor
Law, the most humane contribution to popular welfare in our
history until the welfare state.[6] Christ's Hospital was founded in
1552, when the youthful King, Edward Tudor, moved by 'a
fruitful and godly exhortation' by Bishop Ridley, set up an institution to receive 'fatherless and helpless children'. City notables,
alarmed perhaps at the mendicancy and vagrancy that affected
the City after the dissolution of the monasteries, readily sub-
scribed to the construction of the Hospital, constructed on the
site of the former Greyfriars monastery. It received 340 children
in November 1552, an event the King did not live to witness,
since the charter was established only a few days before his
death on 16 July of that year. Christ's Hospital, intended to
educate and nurture bereaved children as a means of helping
them to learn a trade and avoid poverty, continued to do so for
over a century. After 1674, following plague, fire and the Dutch
war, admission was restricted, although parents and guardians
were still expected 'on their child's behalf to petition the
Foundation's usual Pity and Charity to distressed Men, poor
Widows and fatherless children, to grant the Admission of said
child into Christ's Hospital...there to be Educated and brought
up among other poor children.' In 1809 it was laid down that,
'no child shall be admitted who is a foundling or maintained at

the parish charge'; also prohibited were any who were, 'lame, crooked or deformed, and none suffering leprosy, scald head, the itch or Scab.'[7]

Samuel Taylor Coleridge was admitted in 1782. His father, an erudite vicar in Devon died just before his ninth birthday. His mother—second wife—had borne ten children, nine of them boys, and Samuel was the youngest. Anne Bowden, his mother, was an untutored young woman from Exmoor, and their relationship was cool. He was the only child left at home when his father died, and with the help of a former student of his father's, he was accepted by Christ's Hospital, where he made a lifelong friendship with Charles Lamb. Coleridge said, 'I never thought as a child and never had the language of a child.' In *Table Talk* (1832) he remembered:

> The discipline at Christ's Hospital was ultra-Spartan; all domestic ties were to be put aside. 'Boy!' I remember Boyer (the headmaster) saying to me once when I was crying, the first day of my return after the holidays, 'boy! the school is your father; boy! the school is your mother boy! the school is your brother; the school is your sister, the school is your first cousin and your second cousin and all the rest of your relatives. Let's have no more crying!'[8]

Charitable and philanthropic endowments intended for the poor often mutate into institutions that lose their initial purpose in favour of the preservation of privilege. Indeed, the Poor Laws conceived by the Elizabethans to prevent poverty, had, by the late seventeenth century, become an ingenious game of avoiding expense for payers of the poor rate. Much subsequent policy upheld the elevated principle that public parsimony should take precedence over relief of the poor; a practice familiar to the present day.

Early emigrants

Other early strategies for ridding the country of poor and orphaned children included their removal to the English colo-

nies. Early in the seventeenth century the Privy Council prom-
ulgated an order:

> We are informed that the City of London, by Act of Common
> Council, have appointed one hundred children out of the multi-
> tudes that swarm in that place, to be sent to Virginia, there to be
> bound apprentices with very beneficial condition for them after-
> wards; and have yielded to a levy of £500 for the apparelling of
> these children and the charge of their transportation. Whereas the
> City deserves thanks and commendation for relieving so many
> poor souls from misery and ruin and putting them in a condition
> of use and service to the State...and that, among their number
> there are divers unwilling to be carried thither, and that the City
> wants authority to deliver, and the Virginia Company to receive
> and carry out, these persons against their will; We authorise and
> require the City to take charge of that service to transport to
> Virginia all and every the aforesaid children. And if any children
> disobey or are obstinate or oppose the requirement, punishment
> and disposal of them; and so to Shipp them out to Virginia with
> as much expedition as may stand with convenience.[9]

By the first quarter of the seventeenth century 1,500 boys
and girls had been sent to the American colonies, others to
plantations in Barbados. This forerunner of later schemes for
the emigration of children served a double purpose: while
populating the Empire, money was saved on their upkeep at
home. In the eighteenth century, when conveying indentured
servants to North America, unscrupulous private entities availed
themselves of the cash available for any they could persuade,
cajole, bully or 'spirit' (kidnap) to the colonies.

Peter Wilson Coldham cites an example from the Old Bailey
Sessions Papers for April 1776—right at the end of the period
of colonial deportations on the eve of American Independence.
A young woman aged seventeen was lured from her home by a
woman working for shipping agents (the 'human traffickers' of
a more humane age), and carried with a hundred other 'indentured servants' on the ship *Nancy* to America for a period of
twenty-one years. Her parents, outraged at this involuntary

orphaning, pursued the kidnappers, who had paid nine pounds seven shillings and sixpence to the agent of the *Nancy*. They received sentences of three months imprisonment, an eloquent comment on the value of lives diverted from their bleak course to the nobler purpose of colonial settlement.[10]

Orphanings, then and now

Lawrence Stone points to the brief span of the life of a family in the sixteenth century.[11] A bare majority of adolescent children had two living parents. 'In the early modern period this combination of delayed marriage, low life expectation and early fostering out of surviving children resulted in a conjugal family which was very short-lived and unstable in its composition.' Family life was, by force of circumstance, short and precarious, and marriages in consequence rarely lasted more than twenty-five years.

Despite far greater life expectancy, the average marriage contracted in England and Wales in 2016 will last a little over thirty years. This, of course, excludes all other relationships, some short-lived. The outcome is that time spent conjugally is little more in our age than it was in the sixteenth century. Then, it was abridged by death; divorce Stone describes as a 'functional substitute' for death in contemporary life; as is also avoidance of marriage altogether—what was called in a more moralistic era, 'cohabitation'.

A sixteenth-century orphan: an imaginative reconstruction

The infant was thrown at the bottom of the pallet of chaff on which the woman lay, not expected to outlive its mother by many hours. The father, a shiftless idler, had left a few days before the birth—perhaps for London or Norwich, where no one knew him. But the child was not ready to leave the world, for it continued to cry loudly. I thought it a sin to leave a poor scrap of life that had only a sister, a twelve-year-old girl, to care for it. Late in the night it continued to howl, which troubled me: I did not know if I was called to relieve its misery or warned to leave it to the devil. I could have left it to die of hunger and cold under the ignorant care of the sister; but the orphan's mother had been a good woman, who shared with us broken victuals and field gleanings.

I had three children of my own, a boy, a girl, and another sickly boy, from the frail tenement of whose body his spirit was eager to be free.

So I took the weazen creature and put it to the breast at which my own late stillborn had never suckled. I vowed not take it into my family. It would have to trust to the parish. There, it would not thrive and quickly go to lie with the unbaptised children outside the churchyard. My husband, home from the fields at dusk, asked if the baby had dropped from Heaven, or if I had picked it up in a ditch. He was angry at another mouth to feed, although the mouth would be fed by my body, and would not survive to eat bread. He didn't insist I throw out the orphan or refuse it shelter. The infant's sister was claimed by a kinswoman, covetous of sturdy limbs that could fetch a few pence for the family; but she wanted no charge of an infant which could not but be a burden on them in their poverty.

How the little thing clung to me! The vestry, persuaded of our charitable love for the orphan, provided six pence a week for her maintenance; which certainly disposed my husband's heart towards the poor child. My older son was already earning in the farmer's fields. I heard my own father say that we once had our own land, but it had been 'choked by the wool.' He said inclosures were the cause why rich men eat up the poor men as beasts do eat grass. My parents were reduced to vagabondage until they were able, by the grace of God, to find an empty cottage in Fawsley. We are thankful for whatever we receive, since it is sent for good or ill by the Most High. Our charity to this child will surely be rewarded. Indeed it should be, since in spite of our quarrels, when have we ever committed any unrighteous act against our neighbours? In the famine year, when the barley sprouted in the rain and the harvest was only a festival for the spirits, since nothing had been garnered from the sodden fields, we shared garden roots and pot-herbs with neighbours.

The little girl was baptised, and from that moment drew full breath and sucked at my breast till it was sore. We called her Margaret so she became our Peggy. I fed her with bread I chewed and placed into her mouth; and when the cow calved I gave her bisning-pudding, rich with cream streaked with cow's blood. When I knew she would live, I treated her as my own. She grew to be a proper little maid; always about my skirts wanting to be helpful.

She became a daughter to me. As she reached six or seven, my younger boy fell into a decline. I knew we would never keep him from the grave which is always hungry for young flesh. I blamed myself, for had the child I had killed not borne the same name? Neighbours said I should never have given to a newborn the name of one taken; for, they said, he would surely call his namesake away. Perhaps that is why he perished before our eyes. I harboured a suspicion he had been ill-wished by a woman who was barren and had no children; for she looked at mine with a jealous eye and a tight mouth. She may have worked some evil against them. I also delayed being churched after his birth, and some said a spirit might have entered him. I don't know. I only saw his life dwindle like a failing candle.

Peggy sat by him. She held his pale hand in hers, and told him tales of the village children and their games, and repeated what she had heard in church. She was forever bringing him something from the fields to tempt him—horse-mushrooms with the dew on them in August and cob-nuts; and to perfume the house she brought early violets and bluebells which to him, who had never seen the world beyond the yard, might have been treasures from heaven. She showed herself more able in housewifery than my own Mary, who dawdled over her work and put on a face to curdle cheese when disagreeable tasks awaited her.

I grieved for my boy who was a burden when he should have been minding the geese or picking stones from the field. Sometimes his father carried him outside so he could watch who went by— labourers going home in the twilight gave him a greeting that made him happy, since he said they were his friends. At home only the little wench had time for him. She made a daisy chain which he wore about his head so prettily, he looked already as if he was in a world beyond this one.

He died of the sweating sickness, closing his eyes without a murmur, passing out of life more easily than he came into it. We had already prepared his winding sheet, and as Peggy sat at work, he asked her what she was making, and she answered 'a shift for my marriage.' After he was laid in the ground, the poor little wench— who was now eight years old—wanted to watch for the corpse light over the grave, to satisfy herself that his soul had left the body for its true home. She took on daily work with her brother and sister in the fields to eke out a livelihood. As she was of an age to labour, the parish stopped payment. My husband was finding it hard to work, since he suffered a weakness in the bones, which sometimes broke as he was carrying away the animal dung to the fields or lifting bottles of hay; and then he had to lie while they knitted. We ate the sparse victuals of want.

After the boy died, Peggy became restless. She never feared work— carrying milk home in the frost, so that her hands stuck to the handle of the pail, fetching water from the well, from which I remember, as a girl, seeing the lifeless corpse of an infant lifted. She weeded the corn, pulled carrots and onions in the garden, planted peas on Good Friday. She removed hedgehogs from the byre, so they should not suck the milk of cows. She gathered Solomon's seal and comfrey leaves to heal the limbs of her father— as she called him—who had now taken the place of his son on the straw in the corner of the room. He coughed so from the cooking smoke that Peggy went to find fuel that would burn with a quick flame—she made clods of bracken and even broke hedges for twigs that burned bright, although I feared she would be caught and punished. But the omens of death were upon us—a bat flitted through the hole in the thatch at dusk, and the owl hooted at noon, while rooks cawed their hoarse song in the windy treetops.

Peggy longed to roam the countryside. I thought maybe she had got the itch for the bit of gristle that hangs between men's legs. She was only thirteen, but maids are early-ripe in these times. She watched the people who passed through the village as though she would have gone with them—beggars and vagabonds, a girl with a hare-lip who soured the milk with her gaze, and the dwarf who was said to be only six years old but already had a moustache and a member as frum as a grown man's. In her eyes I saw a strange light, perhaps the spirit of her mother. Some nights she wandered and did not come home at all. One Easter morning when she had stayed away she said she had seen the sun dance for joy at our Lord's rising as it came up over Cley Hill. She swore she saw it shimmer on the edge of the world; but the church had taught us such nonsense was Popish tricks to deceive honest people. I whipped her for it, and she wept and said she was sorry. I wondered once more what wrong we had done, that anyone should cast such spells upon us, when others we knew committed fornication to wither the crops and yet went unpunished. Sometimes she gathered fruits and nuts—chestnuts and blackberries, sloes and crab-apples, dandelion and dead-nettle, small wild strawberries that grew on the heath. But there was never enough to fill our bellies.

My man lying ill, and Peggy bringing nothing but odd pence from her work, she could no longer stay with us but would be put out as apprentice by the parish. She begged me and we wept together, but there was nothing else for it. With her gone, and my oldest boy already of an age to marry, we would not starve. It was with a heart like stone I put her away from me, for I still loved her; but how were we to make shift if she stayed? I had taught her what I knew, little enough, but of use in the service of some good people whose means would permit them bind her to huswifery.

The parish paid the indentures—three pounds I believe—so she should go to a middling farmer less than half day's walk from us. The parting was sorrowful. She promised she would come when she had a holiday. I walked with her to the farm where she should live. The farmer's wife seemed a kindly woman. I look my leave, certain she would receive godly and wholesome discipline, nourishment for both body and soul.

I did not know how harsh her master might be; and did not inquire what measures he might take to quiet her vagrant ways. When she came to what was no longer her home, she had become another person; hard as stone, and full of anger. No longer my Peggy, she was treated as a drudge, a scullion, a beast of draught. I did not know that the other farm servant was a boy of fifteen; and that in the garret where they slept, she had to share a bed with him. She was but thirteen, and I hold it a shame to this day that such a scandalous arrangement should have been made. I wish now I had kept her by me, in spite of hardship; but wishes turn back no time.

She saw us once more, the following year, after my husband was already put to bed with a shovel. I was as glad to see him go, since living in such pain is no fate for man or beast. We buried him one cold February day, when the snow-bones lay over the fields; and I returned to the cottage where the East wind tore the thatch and the fire would not draw; we ate a soup of bones from a cock that had died on a dunghill, with rye bread.

When Peggy returned she brought a few eggs from the farm, and stayed the whole day long—it being Rogationtide, a day of blessing the fields for a good harvest—but she told me little of her life, except that she was minded to run from her master. I begged her not to, since there was nowhere for her to go, and we had not room in our poverty to take her back.

She was fifteen, and I thought I recognised in her a swelling about the waist. She was sullen and angry and I did not pursue my inquiries. Only I had an inkling of something evil; and I fretted, wondering how it would finish.

It was not long before all was told. Dismissed, she would not return here, but was delivered of a child in an outhouse of a neighbouring farm. She went to join her mother in whatever cold place her bones were laid; and the child was taken by the parish. The serving-boy denied he was the father and swore she had lain with all the men of the parish, not all of them unmarried. I could not bring myself to give the child shelter. In any case, my breasts were withered, and we were surviving as we could, the parish collection, gatherings and roots and such kindnesses as the neighbours showed us. In a span of fifteen years one orphan died giving birth to another.

The imperative to labour

Well over half young people between the ages of fifteen and twenty-four (a majority young men) in the early seventeenth century were servants in husbandry. Annual contracts—often verbal—sent them from their birth families to live with the farmers they served. They left home with a bundle of scanty possessions, and probably walked the few miles to their place in a house of strangers. The tasks of younger children were simple—feeding and watering animals, fetching and carrying, domestic duties. Young people earned only as they approached adulthood; and women rarely received more than six-tenths of men's wages. They slept in garrets and outhouses, barns and kitchens on beds of straw, and washed in pails of icy water. They ate bread, root vegetables and drank small beer; attended church on Sunday, with moments of leisure in the ale-house, or at the sports of catching rats or stoning birds.

Rising before dawn for most of the year, only in high summer the early sunshine would illuminate their sleepy steps as they fetched fodder, groomed the horses and made good the instruments of their labour. Men were responsible for draught animals, cattle and sheep. They ploughed and carted. Women milked the cows, looked after poultry and geese, sowed seeds and weeded the crops.[12]

Breakfast would be at six o'clock, and by seven they would be at their tasks in the fields, ploughing, carting, picking stones, cutting wood, with longer hours in haytime in June and July and harvest between August and September, when day-labourers might also be hired. Dinner in the early afternoon gave a brief respite, before a return to cleaning stables, feeding livestock, preparing the fields or clearing them. Supper at around six o'clock was followed by a different kind of labour—there were clothes to be washed or mended, shoes repaired, corn to be threshed, malt to be ground, fruit or vegetables to be picked. An impermeable cycle of labour, advocated in the Elizabethan Poor Law, was calculated to keep them from mischief. The move, at puberty, to the homes and farms of others represented a mass fostering of the young: masters replaced parents to ensure industry, labour and obedience. It was a time of parental surrogacy, a pseudo-orphaning, since it was easier to keep other people's children in order than one's own—a significant contribution to the maintenance of social peace.

It did not, of course, prevent sexual relations, particularly where people lived and slept in such closeness, and where, in fields, woods and byres there was always occasion for dalliance. Relationships between servants were frequent, but so were those between masters and young women and the sons of the household with their fathers' servants. Pregnant girls and women often left the farm in disgrace to join wanderers on the highway. Marriage was generally delayed until the late twenties; but religious doctrines of continence were hard to enforce among young people engaged in manual labour in the natural environment.

The year was broken at Martinmas in the North (late October) and Michaelmas in the South (September), when many servants changed masters; then the roads were thronged with young people mingling with vagrants, the semi-permanent nomads whose numbers increased in the lean years and with the increase of population. Most servants were paid at regular intervals, but not frequently—four times a year, sometimes annually. The master of one young woman was ordered at Quarter Sessions to pay her for several years of service, which might have amounted to five or six pounds. Servants could be dismissed for drunkenness, quarrels and rivalries over young women, licentiousness; some ran away out of boredom or a desire to see a world beyond barnyard and cornfield. Some remained with the same master; saving their meagre wages, becoming unofficially betrothed, so that after ten years or so, they could marry and rent a small farm, becoming independent. Some masters retained beasts—a sheep or calf as part of withheld wages to help stock a holding of their own.

These were 'settled' people, despite frequent changes of master, and the customary 'orphanings' of leaving the parental home in the early teens. There was another less stable population. In the first half of the sixteenth century, prices rose, and the value of earnings fell; although for most servants, whose board was assured, there was little enough to spend money on, apart from ale or ribbons and lace from a passing pedlar. But population almost doubled in England between the mid-sixteenth and mid-seventeenth centuries: more young people had no place. The spectre of the unattached grew: gypsies, Irish migrants, but also families of houseless people, together with 'runagate'—or fugitive—servants. Women with bastard children, those with disabilities, amputees of kinship, especially orphans and parish children, were said to 'infest' the countryside, as well as the streets of growing towns, which also attracted the outcast and placeless. Disastrous harvests—1622 was one of the worst—and declining economic conditions in the 1620s and 30s, resulted in harsher treatment of vagrants, so that the dispossessed, scourged by the whips of propriety, moved faster and further than they had previously done. Between 1631 and 1639, 24, 867 persons were arrested for vagrancy.[13]

Many wanderers, vagabonds, beggars and petty criminals passed between village and fair, market and crossroads, town and city; but laws became harsher against those having 'no place to abide', 'no home but the highway', who formed a threatening class, to whom all kinds of evil were attributed: cutting purses, stealing from homesteads, disorderly behaviour, a menace to the respectable, practice of sorcery and witchcraft. Sturdy and robust idlers struck particular fear into settled people, because they represented permanent unbelonging—a class of orphaned persons who were believed to live by cheating and cozening, begging and thieving, feigning disease or impotence. They were also painted as violent, although this is far from borne out by the records of their arrest and dispatch to bridewell, gaol and house of correction. The absence of kindred or abode turned whole classes of people into suspects—jugglers, gamers, 'nightwalkers', discharged mariners or soldiers (particularly dangerous since they had experience of handling weapons), fortune-tellers, bear-wards, hawkers, minstrels and players.

These corrupted the young, exercised a fascination over people tied to the land, and were a lure to them to abandon their lawful occupations.

Most 'vagrants' experienced lives of itinerant misery; chased from one community to another, sleeping in out-houses and barns, under stalls and in porches, in stables and under hedges. Some lodged in town ale-houses, which were dirty, harboured smallpox, plagues and wasting fevers. Some were lifetime itinerants, covered many hundreds of miles, and often perished from malnutrition or exposure, and whose wasted bodies were interred in unmarked graves throughout the country.

Civil War and beyond

The Elizabethan Poor Law had been enforced by the Privy Council, which created a centrally organised hierarchy for the execution of the Poor Law in the parishes and municipalities of England and Wales. Admonitions to Justices, to Assize Judges, Lord Lieutenants and High Sheriffs, insisted that statutes relating to relief of the poor, to maimed soldiers, suppression of vagabondage, the binding of apprentices, the sale of ale and bread be properly observed; and although places remained where no poor rate had been levied up to the early eighteenth century, parishes varied in their practice. Although disruption occurred in some localities, parishes continued to function.

With the Civil War and the recruitment of soldiers—which diminished parish employment—provision for the able-bodied poor naturally fell away; but when the armies disbanded, towns and cities were besieged once more by migrants, tramps, the disemployed and men injured in conflict. If the stock of materials to set the poor on work dwindled, Houses of Correction expanded. These became part hospice for the needy and part penal institution for the incorrigible. During the Civil War, the overseers of the poor were diverted by orders to carry into effect the law for the demolition of monuments of idolatry, to attend to the observance of the Lord's Day and to draw up lists of all the men, arms and horses in their parish. Parochial and county officials were increasingly left to their own devices. The energy engendered by the vigour of the Elizabethan era was reinforced by the Caroline Book of Orders in 1631, during the economic crisis of 1629–31, which gave directives for 'laws and statutes tending to the relief of the poor, the well-ordering and training up of youth in trades and the reformation of disorder and disordered persons.' If compliance was grudging, this was scarcely improved by the proclamation in 1632 that the gentry should leave the cities of London and Westminster and resort to the several counties where they usually reside to carry out their local responsibilities.

During the Civil War the work of children, the binding of apprentices and the short lives of orphans went on as before in most parishes: cattle were tended, crops sown and harvested, domestic duties proceeded and the labour that rose and slept with the sun was not abated. But the war produced its own grim crop of orphans. Some children may also have fought in the conflict. In 2013, archaeologists discovered between seventeen and twenty-eight bodies buried in shallow pits close to Durham cathedral, soldiers defeated by Cromwell's army at the Battle of Dunbar: they were aged between thirteen and twenty-five, and the state of their teeth and bones suggest they were sickly and malnourished. Child soldiers are clearly no new thing.[14]

Making a profit out of the children of the poor

In the later seventeenth century, the desire to set the poor to work for their own sake was overtaken by the belief that it was possible to make their labour profitable. Puritan insistence on work, virtues of frugality and sound stewardship led to greater rigour against the poor, and also nourished the view that the poor were not so much the unfortunate of Providence as the disgraced of godlessness. Early in the seventeenth century, the stealing of victuals from orchards or gardens—prompted by hunger—was still dealt with more leniently than crimes committed for gain. Distinction was made between misdemeanours, punishable by mere whipping, and felonies, which incurred the death penalty. We can see continuing debasement of traditional Christian virtues (however imperfectly practised)—kindness to the poor, the just wage and a certain indulgence towards crimes of necessity— which had already begun the long, fateful journey, described by R. H. Tawney towards economic vices. Begging lost its association with Franciscan supplication and became an act of aggression against the ample purse of the well-to-do.[15] Those who gave were no longer venerated as caring for their immortal soul, but were despised as promoters of the idle and shiftless.

Under the evolving doctrine of moral culpability of the poor, it was natural that orphaned and abandoned children should also become responsible for their own maintenance as soon as they became capable of labour—an obsession which still holds in its spell the imagination of those in power. During the Commonwealth, in 1647, An Ordinance for the Relief and Employment of the Poor and the Punishment of Vagrants and Other Disorderly Persons (in which the word 'workhouse' was first used), the London Corporation for the Poor set up an Establishment on the site of two confiscated royal properties, intended to train up children 'in godly education.' Children were taught literacy and instruction in useful trades. This was promoted by Samuel Hartlib, a German émigré, who conceived of a wider system of welfare that would undertake a survey of the poor, provide free education and provide material for children to labour in the workhouse, and adults in their homes. This was halted with the Restoration when Charles II took possession of the royal properties once more. In 1662 A Middlesex Corporation of the Poor opened a workhouse, which was visited and admired by Samuel Pepys, who wrote of 'the many pretty works and the little children employed, every one to do something.'[16] In 1698, the London Corporation re-opened a residential institution, to educate children above the age of seven, employed spinning wool and flax, knitting, stocking-making, making and mending their own clothes and shoes. The anticipated self-financing of the scheme failed, and it closed in 1713.

Many efforts in the late seventeenth century were designed to wring profit from the labour of orphans and parish infants. Thomas Firmin, philanthropist and reformer, son of a Puritan Suffolk family, opened a linen manufactory in Aldersgate in 1677, from where he employed more than 1,700 poor spinners, flax-drawers and weavers, providing them with materials to work at home. He also sheltered the abandoned infant poor in what was called a 'working almshouse', where they could learn a trade and earn by their own labour (at six pence for a sixteen-hour day) enough for their sustenance.[17] This enterprise was also short-lived. The poor have never paid their way: that is why they are poor.

In Bristol in 1696, John Cary, merchant and social reformer, formed a Corporation of the Poor to establish a workhouse to serve a number of parishes. It opened in 1698 to provide for one hundred girls aged six to sixteen. A similar establishment for boys followed; then one for infants and another for the aged. The girls worked ten and a half hours a day in summer, less in winter, and four 'tutresses' taught them to spin. They were well-nourished—a diet including beef, pease, potatoes, broath, pease porridge, milk-porridge, bread and cheese, good beer, carrots and turnips. There was antagonism from some relatives of the poor girls: Cary wrote that when the girls were first taken in, 'we had a great deal of trouble with their Parents and those who formerly kept them, having lost the sweetness of their Pay, and they did all they could to set both their Children and others against us.'[18] Contests between charities, institutions and the families of poor children over their earning capacity would feature significantly in following centuries.

In any case, the yarn produced in Bristol was coarse and commanded a low price. Undeterred, the Corporation opened a similar workhouse for one hundred boys, employed 'spinning cotton wool and weaving Fustian'. The girls were taught only to read, but to this accomplishment boys were given the ability to write. Cary said, 'All do something, and though perhaps some of their labour comes to little, yet it keeps them from idleness.' The workhouse was unsustainable; the work degenerated into pin-making and picking oakum—traditional punishment for felons—and children were hired out as labour to local manufacturers. The building eventually became a refuge for 'the impotent poor.'[19]

The charity school movement

The Charity School movement was more successful in its purpose. It owed its existence to the Society for Promoting Christian Knowledge founded in 1699. Such schools were to be a means of 'taming' the children of the poor and training them—as was said at the time—'for that station in life wherein Providence hath placed them'. Learning was to be allied to labour; and charity children were publicly paraded as objects of condescending compassion. A child, selected to address Queen Anne at the Thanksgiving ceremony for the Treaty of Utrecht at St Paul's in 1713, spoke the words of his patrons:

> May it please your Most Excellent Majesty to Pardon the great Presumption in thy poor Children who throw themselves at your Royal feet, among the rest of your Glad Subjects, who here in crowds appear to behold your Sacred majesty. We, Madam, have no Father, no Mother, no Friend, or which, is next to me, and those who through extreme poverty cannot help us…All the Support we have is from the Unexhausted Charities of your loyal Citizens of London, and other Good Subjects, and the Pious Care of our Governors, who are teaching our little Hands to Work and our Fingers to Spin. These threads, madam (holding some yarn in his hand) are some of the early Fruits of our Industry. We are all daily employed on the Staple manufacture of England, learning betimes to be useful to the world.[20]

In 1713 Joseph Addison, having observed charity school children paraded in the Strand, referred to 'such a numerous and innocent multitude, clothed in the charity of their benefactors, was a spectacle pleasing to both God and man... Never did a more full and unspotted chorus of human creatures join together in a hymn of devotion.' He looked to charity schools as 'the most proper means that can be made use of to recover [the nation] out of its present degeneracy and depravation of manners. It seems to promise us an honest and virtuous posterity: there will be few in the next generation who will not at least be able to write and read, and have not had an early tincture of religion.' To show that he was not unaware of the wretched condition of the poor, he went on to advocate:

[A] provision for foundlings, and for those children who, for want of such a provision, are exposed to the barbarity of cruel and unnatural parents. One does not know how to speak on such a subject without horror: but what multitudes of infants have been made away with by those who brought them into the world, and were afterwards either ashamed or unable to provide for them. There is scarce an assizes where some unhappy wretch is not executed for the murder of a child. And how many more of these monsters of inhumanity may we suppose to be wholly undiscovered or cleared, for want of legal evidence?[21]

Monsters of inhumanity

The 'monsters of humanity' were exposed to pressures of destitution and despair that can scarcely have entered the mind, let alone the experience, of those who condemned them in such thunderous terms. In the sixteenth century, a woman had been punished for abandoning a child:

Wheare by the Lord Maior and his bretherne The aldermen it was adjudged that a woman named Norton dwellinge in Southwerke for leavynge and forsaking her chile in the streets should be whipped at Bruidewell and from thence sent unto the governors of Christe' hospital for a further reformacion, whiche thinge beinge done she was sent unto a pillorye in Chepe with a paper on his hed wherein was written in greate letters Whipped at Bridewell for leavyinge and forsakynge his childer in the streetes, and from thence caryed into Southwerk and banished for hir offence out of the citie.[22]

An insight into how the 'waste' people of history survived on the mercy of others is provided by the echo of pre-modern attitudes that survive in other parts of the world. In 2003 I met a woman whose home for herself and her baby was the verandah of the house of a pious man in Dhaka, Bangladesh. This woman had been taken from the village of her employers as a domestic servant when she was orphaned at twelve. She was a virtual captive in the house; even her free moments were bound by the metal grille of the place where she worked. When the (female) employer selected her, the husband was also consulted; since they were also seeking a suitable partner for the husband's bed. The wife did not want him to stray beyond the household. She became the regular partner of the husband, but when she became pregnant, accused of immoral behaviour, she was turned out to beg until rescued by her benefactor.

Many pregnant parish servants tried to conceal their condition, or used herbs—purgatives, pennyroyal, tansy or hyssop—and other traditional abortifacients, sometimes killing both the child and themselves in the process. Infants who survived were often boarded out to parish nurses, whose neglect ensured they never become adult encumbrances to the parish.

In August 1693, a midwife in Poplar who had received numerous parish children for nursing, 'bastards and by-blows', was arrested and charged with killing several of her charges. She had come from another place, remained aloof from her neighbours and did not attend church:

Then the Court spake to the Old woman thus: Mary Crompton, You are charged with the Murther of several Children, by starving them to death. You did take young Children from Parishes to breed them up, and you did not do it as you ought to have done; there were some found buried in a Cellar, others in a Hand-basket; and there was one in a Cradle, in such a condition, that the very Skin came off of its Head, the Ears rotted off; so that it did not die of any Sickness, but was really rotten, and that was from want of sustenance.[23]

She was sentenced to death.

The sea: refuge and oubliette

Early voyages to Virginia showed the sea as suitable receptacle for the burdensome poor, particularly the criminal, who were often bracketed with unwanted orphans. In 1703, a statute, invoking an Act of 1597, stated that:

[A]ll lewd and disorderly Man Servants and every such Person and Persons, both Men and Boys, that are deemed and adjudged Rogues, Vagabonds and Sturdy Beggars… shall be and are hereby directed to be taken up, sent, conducted and conveyed to Her Majesty's Service at Sea, or the Service of Her Majesty's Heirs or Successors, by such Ways, Methods, Means and in such a Manner and Forms as is directed for Vagrants by the said before mentioned Act of parliament…

This began a long association of derelict and orphan boys with naval service, since magistrates and overseers of the poor were empowered to apprentice to the marine service, 'any boy or boys who is, are or shall be of the age of ten and upwards, or is, are or shall be chargeable, or whose parents are or shall be chargeable to the parish, or who beg for alms.' The vast emptiness of the sea was a proper place for orphans to inscribe their anonymity or lapsed identity.

In the light of what we now know about the captives of an abusive care system in our time, we can imagine the numb terror in which children were consigned to the *Totenschiffe* that such vessels were, sometimes literally, bound for destinations many never reached. An idea of roaming the oceans, a life of adventure in exotic climes might well have dulled the spirit of those who condemned them to such suffering. But lack of nourishment, discipline, flogging, sequestration of offenders in cupboards and cabins without light or air, the predatory sexuality of adult men, physical brutality, arbitrary and repetitive labour, led to sicknesses of the heart and spirit. Apart from those who died, all traces of their existence effaced as they were consigned to the chill waters with minimal ceremony, what kind of life awaited any returnees among children sent to sea? How could they have 'settled', disturbed by this aimless marine servitude?

Many 'powder monkeys' were also orphans, some of whom had been kidnapped. They worked on naval warships to maintain a supply of gunpowder, which was kept deep in the magazine in a sealed compartment below the waterline. Their age and small stature enabled them to move nimbly with the powder required to keep the guns firing. Their skin was often stained by the blue residue of the powder, and they were always in danger from explosions, particularly when shots pierced the side of the ship.

Some were also exposed to the sexual attentions of officers. B R Burg's *Boys at Sea*, based on court martial records, allows the faint voice of the lowly and subordinate to reach posterity:

> …a large majority of the defendants were officers and in almost every case the officers were accused of forcing sodomy and indecent acts on unwilling boys…no officer was ever called to account for buggering another officer. Neither did men holding commissions or warrants select those immediately below them in rank as sexual partners. They chose only those in the lowest tiers of the naval hierarchy.[24]

The status of the children on the ships is rarely recorded, but many were orphans. Later, the book reveals:

> In a 1761 case, three youths charged Seaman Michael Berry of the Storeship *HMS Crown* with the non-capital crime of attempted sodomy. One of them, William Large, particularly attracted the scrutiny of the court. Questioning revealed that the fatherless waif from Petticoat Lane could neither read nor understand the mean-

ing of an oath, although he was fifteen years old. He was not allowed to give evidence.

Crewman on the 24-gun HMS Seashore found objectionable the conduct of sailor Richard Chilton, and the public display of affection he lavished on a fatherless boy named William Hoskins, who had been brought to the navy after his mother entered him into the Marine Society three years earlier. Clifton was seen with:

Hoskins between his legs...hugging the boy with his hand round his neck. Hoskins, a fifer, offered no objection to the attention according to the trial summary. But the sailor used force and the threat of flogging when the boy cried out at being buggered. There were enough witnesses to convict Chilton under the 29th Article of War; and the court sentenced him to be hanged.[25]

This anticipates cases of abuse in our time, in which the voiceless—or rather the unheard—of the care system have been victims. They have been sworn to silence and threatened if they make known assaults on them. Their powerlessness bestowed impunity upon those charged with their oversight and protection. In 1981, three members of staff at the Kincora Boys' Home, a spacious early twentieth-century mansion in East Belfast, were jailed for sexual offences against children in their care. The home had been opened in 1958 by the Health Authority. It closed in 1980. The principal accused was William McGrath, member of an extreme Loyalist group, whose conviction led to rumours of 'guilty men in high places' also involved. An inquiry of 1982 was never concluded, since three members of the committee resigned. The absence of any clear information only encouraged stories to persist, that the home had been a homosexual brothel used by the secret service to spy on influential political figures. An inquiry conducted by Sir Anthony Hart into abuse in children's homes in Northern Ireland from 1922–1995 was set up in 2013, and it reported in 2017 on a wide range of homes run by the state, local authorities, the Catholic Church, the Church of Ireland and voluntary agencies. It found physical, emotional and sexual abuse, not only in Kincora, but also in institutions run by the Sisters of Nazareth, the De La Salle Brothers and the Diocese of Down and Connor. Of the Kincora home, the report said there was 'no credible evidence' of any paedophile ring, nor that McGrath was a state agent; and that of the more than two hundred former inhabit- ants of the home, thirty-nine reported sexual abuse. It is aston- ishing how brutal repressions, consigned to the distant past by an ideology of progress, survive and present themselves once more in the altered landscapes of modernity

The sea as punishment

The sea had another part to play in the 'correction' of many criminal and wayward children until the nineteenth century, since the convict hulks, anchored in British ports, sequestered them effectively from the land, without even providing an opportunity to reach other, alien shores.

In any case, the shipping of young miscreants and orphans as indentured servants can scarcely have been more agreeable than the penal transportation of young men to the plantations of North America, as permitted by the Transportation Act of 1718. Transportation was an alternative to branding or whipping, and had the advantage of providing labour for the American colo- nies. Virginia had legislated for the indenture of children under the age of twelve in 1642. The labour of transported young men was certainly not skilled: of one shipload of convicts of ninety- eight felons, forty-eight had no recognisable trade at all, while sixteen were too young to have acquired one—which meant they were children. Between 1718 and 1776, about 50,000 people were transported to North America. Transportation was a primi- tive social cleansing: it emptied the gaols and lessened the disor- der of crowds at public punishments. Crimes for which individuals risked the relative leniency of being shipped to the colonies included: setting fire to underwood; stealing a shroud from a grave; receiving or buying stolen goods, jewels or plate; stealing fish from a pond; stealing children and their apparel (this was aimed at the apparel, not the children); bigamy; assaulting, stealing or cutting clothes; as well as manslaughter and assault with intent to rob. Returning aliens 'who had been sent out of the kingdom' could also be transported.

Coldham describes 'child-snatching for mercantile ends' in the eighteenth century, referring to Peter Williamson's *Life and Adventures*, published in Aberdeen in 1757: his mother died when he was eight and he was sent to Aberdeen to live with an aunt.[26] Playing by the quayside one day, he was approached by two men from a ship, who enticed him with promises of a new life of ease and plenty (a recurring pledge by 'friends of the poor'). These were recruiting agents for businessmen in Aberdeen, luring children to plantation service in alliance with the city's justices. Their efforts filled ships with seventy boys and girls at a time, who were presented to local justices in a parody of indenturing:

> In the troubled 1740s, a common sight in Aberdeen was a flock of local lads and lassies, mixed in with strapping youths from the Highlands being driven with staves and horsewhips along the main thoroughfares, under the superintendence of drovers', to an assembly point from where they would be shipped to America. Williamson averred that 'Almost all the inhabitants of Aberdeen knew the traffic…which was carried on in the market places, in the High Street and in the avenues to the town in the most public manner. The trade in carrying of boys to the plantations of America and selling them there as slaves was carried on with amazing effrontery…and by open violence. The whole neighbouring country were alarmed at it. They would not allow their children to go to Aberdeen for fear of being kidnapped.

With sixty-nine other young people Williamson was shipped to Virginia in 1743, where they were sold for £16 each. In Philadelphia he was later sold to another Scotsman, who treated him well, since he had also been kidnapped in Perth. He stayed with him until he was seventeen. He married in 1754, and returned to Britain, where he published his book;

and for his pains, he was fined ten shillings by the Aberdeen justices, who threw him in prison. He then prosecuted his detractors at the Court of Sessions in Edinburgh, where merchants and justices denied any collusion in the traffic of young persons to the colonies.

Jonas Hanway—perhaps recalling conditions in the Portsmouth dockyards of his youth, and the forcible kidnapping of young men for service—was a founder member of the Marine Society in 1756: this, at the beginning of the Seven Years War, also augmented the number of volunteers for naval service. Recruits were promised clothing, food and a measure of security. At the same time, poor parish boys were sent to the royal naval ships as servants; although priority was for the war effort rather than any redemptive intention for impoverished orphaned children. After the war, Hanway's recruitment of boys continued, and in 1772 an Act of Parliament legislated for the apprenticeship of poor boys to royal and merchant service. For subsequent generations 'the sea' became an ample vessel for holding the superfluous population of restless young men; while the no-man's-land of convict ships, moored between Britain and the ocean, were a receptacle for poor children, among whom it was difficult to disaggregate the orphaned from the delinquent. Indeed the categories frequently merged in the often clouded mind of Authority. Rowland Detroisier, a self-educated workman who founded the Manchester Mechanics' Institute, quoted a letter to Sir James Graham on *Impressment* from a naval captain in 1834:

> I go aboard the Euryalus convict-hulk in the Medway. There I find 225 little boys, whose only crime was not having been trained to virtue. These poor helpless victims of mismanagement and extravagance are kept in iron cages doing the work of women, making shirts. I ask if any of these children are likely to be reformed by this system? And I am told that none ever have been; I infer that none ever will be. I find the stench intolerable, the hatchways much smaller than they were originally, and no windsails down.[27]

The Euryalus had taken part in the Battle of Trafalgar. It was converted into a prison-hulk for boys in 1813. It is not difficult to imagine the atmosphere of fetid air, of violence and fear in the confinement of adolescents, many of them ignorant and ill-endowed, creatures of the streets, sentenced for trivial offences, pick-pocketing of handkerchiefs and pence, stealing a snuff-box or a thimble, theft of 'growing crops' or a fowl, perhaps injuring a rival in a knife-fight. They were bewildered children, permitted no outlet for feelings of abandonment. They were subjected to 'moderate whipping' if they misbehaved, to consist of 'no more than twenty-four stripes'; and none was allowed to go without an iron on one or both legs. Fettered in their dormitories, they were watched all night by an overseer. Classified according to behaviour they were allowed to mingle only with those in the same category. They rose early and washed in stone tubs under a low ceiling and the eyes of an overseer. Inadequately clothed in linen shirts and breeches, often without shoes or stockings, the silence was broken only by the rattle of chains, oaths and profanities, as they prepared for their nine-hour-day's labour. Labour included cleaning the vessel, mending clothing, working in the shipyards, carrying timber and repairing the frame of the ship, exhausting occupations designed to use up the repressed energy of boys, so all they would think about at night was sleep and not insolence. They were subjected to chapel-sermons on the Awful Judgments of the Most High on wickedness, on the wholesome doctrines of the established Church. Food was monotonous and not nourishing—ox-cheek soup, pease-pudding, biscuit that was often mildewed; while outbreaks of gaol fever or dysentery—water was drawn from the Thames and not properly filtered—ensured a death-rate, in some instances of 30 per cent. Funerals were perfunctory, in burial-grounds close to where the hulks were moored. Perhaps it was a measure of our loss of historical memory that prompted the use of prison-ships in 1997, when HMP Weare was moored at Portland in Dorset. It remained as a modern convict-hulk until 2006.

One late, sad example of the sea as destination for orphans in our own time is the story of a now-dead friend.

Alex was brought up in a Barnardo's home in Dumfries, having been evacuated from a Glasgow orphanage at the age of seven during the war. He has no memory of his parents. He was an effective—if not literal—orphan, because when he left in 1950, children were not encouraged to seek out their birth parents. A tradition that erased biological families, part of the practice of 'child rescue' from the industrial slums, continued well into the twentieth century. The upbringing in the Barnardo's community was adequate but chill and devoid of emotional care. Hygienic but loveless, it was 'a childhood of granite', marked by church attendance, order and discipline. It was always physically cold. The building itself was a former mansion; underheated, draughty, with shared dormitories and washrooms, without privacy or stimulus. Alex went to a local school, where the teachers showed more compassion than he received in 'the home'. He grew up concealing his feelings, since any display was considered unmanly, a sign of weakness. This, he said—in characteristic understatement—did not make it easy to establish relationships.

Many boys from such institutions went into the services. Alex was destined for the Navy. He went one Saturday to the recruitment centre. When he entered the building only one recruiting officer was present. He locked the door, pulled down the blind over the frosted glass, and sodomised the fifteen-year-old on the linoleum floor of the office. That, he said, was his introduction to human attachments. Later, he met an older man from South Africa, who befriended him and taught him what love meant; but he never fully overcame his distrust of people. Alex liked order and discipline. He had a natural intelligence, but was always quick to anger. He was unofficially 'adopted' by the South African, who, when he died, left him a stamp collection, the sale of which enabled Alex to buy a house. This man, personally honourable, was an ardent sympathiser with the apartheid regime.

After leaving the Navy, Alex worked in the Ministry of Labour. He lavished much care on his house. He loved crystal which he displayed on shelves illuminated from below, fine crockery, silver and glassware; a style of living remote from anything within his direct experience.

We once went with him for a holiday to the Southern Uplands; a warm wet summer, where honeysuckle perfumed the air and the pale saucers of dog-roses overflowed with soft rain. The hills were smudged by mist, beads of water trembled on grasses and red clover. We walked through shuttered Sunday streets in the somnolent grey town, holland blinds drawn and no sign of life in the Sabbath silence. It was hard to imagine the trauma he had suffered on that distant day, but which he felt as a continuation of a punitive childhood. He said he was judged guilty of losing his parents; a recurring theme in the experience of orphans and the darkness in which their origins remained until late in the twentieth century.

The abandoned child

Most foundlings in the seventeenth and eighteenth centuries were between two and six months old—old enough for mothers to have established strong maternal bonds, the more so since most women breast-fed their children. It was always driven by despair. More boys than girls were abandoned. More were forsaken in winter than in summer. When children were left in church porches or at the gates of hospitals, the intention was that they should live. Those discovered in streets or privies were either already dead or left to die. Valerie Fildes quotes from the Register of St Helens in Bishopsgate, 1612:

> Sept. 1. Job Rakt out of the Ashes being borne uppon Monday being the last of Augiust about viij of the clock in the morning was then presently lad upon a dunghill of seacole ashes in the lane going to Sr John Spencer's back gate ...wch child so layd and covered over with the same ashes was wthin an hower after

found out by Richard Atkinson, boxmaker, coming thither to shovel by the same dunghill into a wheele barrow, and by that tyme he had taken up twoo shovels of the same ashes he espied the child almost stifled therewith.[28]

The child died and was buried the following day.

Toni Bowers offers a corrective to any assumption that children left in church porches and convents or at the doors of the rich suggest the 'inhumanity' of mothers.[29] Minute Books of foundling hospitals show the grief and agony of mothers who found in them a haven for children from whom they had parted with bitter emotion, since poverty made it impossible to care for them. It is significant that abandonment rose in relation to the rise in bread prices in the late seventeenth and early eighteenth centuries. Parents were then described as 'wanton' or 'unnatural', people upon whom our knowing age has bestowed the slightly mitigating adjective, 'dysfunctional'. Children were relinquished with great pain, as explanatory notes, small sums of money, scraps of belongings and tokens whereby the child would be identified in a more favourable season, warm blankets in which she or he was wrapped, demonstrate. If the intention to reclaim the infant at some future time was seldom fulfilled, this was because the mother would never be free of the tangle of misfortune which had driven her. Coercive circumstances, not absence of feeling, prompted such sacrifices. We have an inkling of how it felt to these distressed women when we talk to mothers, within living memory forced to give up for adoption their illegitimate—but not unwanted—children. Grief and guilt shadowed their lives; as they no doubt did in a past that is less alien to us than we care to believe.

The Elizabethan system of boarding out orphaned and abandoned children broke down towards the end of the seventeenth century. Charity children who gladdened the hearts of observers after the Treaty of Utrecht were a symbolic minority, a comfort to the charitable perhaps, but of small help to most children of misfortune. Many parish infants died in the care of ignorant and indifferent nurses. In the eighteenth century mortality in some workhouses reached 90 per cent. Few children lived long enough to become orphans; rather, the Poor Law created generations of bereaved and grieving parents. No word exists for parents who lose their children: the word 'orphan' applies to children whose parents predecease them. Adults 'lose' their children, as they may lose their purses, and perhaps, their minds.

Guilt and shame—as well as more material pressures— haunted many who forsook their children. Tanya Evans in *Unfortunate Objects, Lone Mothers in Eighteenth Century London* says, 'The eighteenth century metropolis teemed with abandoned children.[30] Over a thousand a year were being let on rubbish heaps, in the streets and alleys and other public thoroughfares of the city...' But she confirms Valerie Fildes' view, 'Most parents left their children where others would be likely to find them.' A majority of those discarded were probably already dead; many of them the children of unmarried servants, who desperately tried to hide pregnancy and birth in order to keep their situation. Elizabeth Evans in 1740, in defence when she was tried for infanticide in 1740, said she 'found [the baby] dead, and therefore laid it away from her; and before she would have killed it, she would have gone a-begging with it.'[31]

In a house in Stonecutter Street in 1763, the purchaser of a derelict house 'found the bodies of three women, discovered almost naked, and in the garret, two women and a girl on the verge of starvation.' Two of the three dead women had been workers in Fleet market. Elizabeth Sturmer, the girl, was only sixteen. Her father had been a jeweller in the City. Elizabeth's parents died, leaving her apprenticed very young to the pauper trade of silk-winding in the insalubrious Spitalfields. She did not last long at this, and spent the next six years working for a washerwoman as a children's nurse. When she fell ill her mistress discharged her. With nowhere to go, she slept in the streets for weeks before finding a bit of shelter in the house. When she was strong enough she went out begging, coming back to Stonecutter Street at night. A couple of days before they were discovered, [one of the women] had pawned her apron for sixpence, which they spent on food.[32]

Court records

Aspects of orphaned lives appear in court records. If sufficiently notorious, they were commemorated in popular ballad and oral tradition. Such was 'Jenny Diver', who figured in John Gay's *Beggar's Opera* in 1731. Born Mary Young in about 1700 in the north of Ireland, she was the illegitimate child of a lady's maid. Her mother, discharged from her post, found shelter in a brothel, where Mary was born. She abandoned the child, who was unofficially fostered for several years, before being taken in by an elderly gentlewoman. She became literate and was proficient with her needle, which no doubt also made her fingers nimble for her subsequent career.

She travelled to England with an admirer, a servant who had stolen from his master to pay for the journey. He was arrested, returned to Ireland and transported. Mary went to London, where she fell in with a gang of pickpockets, and was so adept at the trade that she became leader of the gang, accomplished at 'cheving the froe'—or cutting open women's pockets. This earned her the nickname Jenny Diver, or 'Diving Jenny', from her ability to reach into pockets swiftly and without detection.

She had acquired an educated accent, and dressed respectably. Caught in 1733, she was confined in Newgate. Her death sentence was commuted to transportation to America. She remained there briefly, having bribed her way back to London, where she resumed her life. Caught a second time in 1738 under an alias which made it appear a first offence, she was again transported. Within a year she was back, but two years later taken and imprisoned once more. It was discovered she had returned from transportation, a capital offence. She was hanged in 1841 at Tyburn, before a great throng.

These wrongdoers were popular. Part-hero, part-villain, they represented vengeance of the poor against social injustice, and served as a warning and example to other would-be malefactors. Their daring aroused admiration; of their inner life virtually nothing remains—we can imagine hardening of their heart as they were passed from indifferent nurse to foster-mother, from one poor law authority to another, until finding a kind of comfort in the company of peers in street-gangs. This is familiar in our time, particularly in children raised chaotically, indifferently, with absent parents or in the care system. The streets—inhospitable, stony but full of niches, corners and other hiding-places—have always provided refuge for the outcast, where they developed their own versions of survival and solidarity. This life of picaresque and risky abandon must have required rigorous suppression of the feelings; a service (if that is what it was) assisted by nominal or heedless carers.

Past and present

The Newgate Calendar, a series of publications from the eighteenth and nineteenth centuries reminds us that horrors associated with contemporary society were familiar to the past.[33] In 1748, William York, aged ten, was convicted of the murder of Susan Mahew, who was five:

> This unhappy child was but ten years of age when he committed the dreadful crime of which he was convicted. A pauper in the poorhouse belonging to the parish of Eye in Suffolk, he was committed at the coroner's inquest to Ipswich jail for the murder of Susan Mahew, another child of five years, who had been his bedfellow.

The account gives gruesome detail of the injuries inflicted upon the little girl by a knife which 'cut her arm and elbow to the bone' and then did the same to her thigh.

> His next care was to conceal the murder, for which purpose he filled a pail with water at a ditch, and washing the blood off the child's body, buried it at the dunghill, together with the blood that was spilled on the child's clothes, and then went and got his breakfast.

When he was examined, he showed very little concern, appeared easy and cheerful. Also he alleged that the child fouled the bed in which they lay together, that she was sulky and that he did not like her. The boy was found guilty and sentenced to death; but he was respited from time to time on account of his tender years, and at length pardoned. He was sent to serve in the Seven Years' War, at a time when Britain established its naval supremacy; perhaps such a past was not considered a disadvantage in martial affairs.

This crime foreshadows national soul-searching following the murder of three-year-old James Bulger, abducted in 1993 from a shopping centre on Merseyside by two ten-year-olds, who killed him and threw his body into the canal. The murderers, for all their youth, became figures of hate. The sophisticated techniques of providing them with a new identity when they were released from detention were far less effective than the anonymity vouchsafed William York in war, since the popular press traced them and published stories of their subsequent lives. There was, of course, a significant difference. William York was described as a 'pauper'—to our sensibility a curious designation for a child, and without known parentage. That he shared a workhouse bed with a five-year-old girl also shocks us. It is impossible to know anything about his parents or those of the luckless victim; whereas we know a great deal about the families of Robert Thompson and Jon Venables. They were also, in their way, orphaned: their parents were separated, and the mothers of both lost, one to alcohol, the other to depression. This sense of *desertion* appeared in two waifs, occupying themselves with casual violence, fighting, bullying, shoplifting. Neighbours told stories of the heads of pigeons shot off with airguns and live rabbits tied to railway lines: 'a pair of empty, broken young lives', said *The Guardian* in November 2000, as they were released from detention. The trial judge had dwelt upon the responsibility of parents, or at least the mothers (there was a curious, and, alas, familiar, absence of blame attributed to the fathers); while the popular press insisted on the 'evil' of the ten-year-olds, which reflected popular response to the events. This extends, not entirely as metaphor, the idea of orphanhood. Rather than distancing us from a sombre past, it actually affirms continuity with it. For parents in the past were also often distracted from their children's needs: in the 1740s, the annual consumption of gin reached six gallons per person in England. This also must have contributed to the high mortality rate of the time.[34]

Philanthropy

Much has been made of the establishment for 'foundlings' created by the commitment of Thomas Coram. Little is known of his early life, apart from the brief reference in a letter to Benjamin Colman in 1824:

> …Through Mercy I discended from virtuous good Parentage on both sides as any Body. They were Families of strict hon'r and honesty and always of Good Reputation amongst the better sort of people, Yet I had no learning, my Mother dying when I was Young, my Father marryed again 4 or 5 years after at Hackney near the City. I went to sea, out of my Native place, the little Towne of Lyme in the West of England at eleven years and a half old, until five years later my Father sent for me hither and put me apprentice to a Shipwright.

His two brothers died in infancy, one also called Thomas. At eleven, he was 'sent to sea', scarcely a tender environment for an intelligent but uninstructed child. After his apprenticeship, he settled in Taunton, Massachusetts. Returning to Rotherhithe in 1719, he was shocked by the number of infants deserted on the public streets. A deep personal and religious commitment inspired his radical concern for the waste children of Britain. He sought patrons and government approval for the shelter and nurture of foundlings. It was nineteen years before a charter, granted by George II, led to the Foundling Hospital in 1739: delay came from the fear of its potential patrons that, 'it might seem to encourage vice by making too easy a provision for illegitimate children.' Coram was a churchman, traditional in allegiances, radical in his recognition of deserted children, in whom he may have seen something of his own experience.[35]

The Foundling Hospital became a fashionable charity, Hogarth and Handel among its supporters. At first no questions were asked of mothers who left their children to its care. The only conditions were that no child should be more than two months old and should be free of the, 'French pox, leprosy, Evil or diseases of that Nature.' The demand was so great that many had to be turned away. In 1756, the governors turned to Parliament, which agreed to finance the Hospital, provided that no child was refused admission. The intention of Parliament was, 'to render the hospital of general utility to all the children which should be offered under a certain age'….and 'that proper places be opened up in all the counties of the kingdom for the reception of exposed and deserted young children.' The age limit was raised to six months, then to twelve months. This 'General Reception' lasted about four years; during which time 14,934 children were admitted. The institution became so well known that people brought their babies from all over the country. No equivalent opened up elsewhere. But so great was the throng that subsidiary branches of the hospital had to be set up outside of London, with wet-nurses to suckle the babies.

An echo of this occurred in China in 2014, where, in order to discourage people from leaving unwanted children on the roadside, twenty-five so-called 'baby-hatches' were set up, attached to orphanages in ten provinces. Children could be safely left in such refuges, from where they could be received into State homes. In Guangzhou in south China, the scheme had to be closed, after 262 children were left at the 1,000-bed depository next to the orphanage. Most of the abandoned children had some illness or disability—cerebral palsy, Down's syndrome or heart disease.[36]

In 1760, Parliament insisted the Coram foundation be self-reliant and depend upon its own funds. Between 1760 and 1800 only 2,301 children were accepted, and the condition was that they had been orphaned by their parents being 'lost in Battle' or by 'sickness'. After 1762 they were admitted only from London and on the presentation of a petition. In 1801 the Hospital was restricted to illegitimate children, and this remained its function till 1950.[37]

This institution was important, even though foundling hospitals already existed all over Europe. It answered only a fraction of need, and its function was soon limited; but acknowledgement of the right of the most wretched children to protection struck contemporaries as humane and necessary. Britain is good at symbolic gestures that demonstrate our humanitarian temper, even if a majority of the needy remain untouched. Other examples include the Kindertransport before the outbreak of War in 1938/9, which took in children from Nazi Germany. There was also the ostentatious (and soon abandoned) acceptance of children from the Calais refugee camp in 2016: refuge had been promised to 3,000; numbers were limited to a few hundred. Thomas Coram is represented in a stained glass window in the church at Lyme Regis where he was born: a panel in the medieval embrasure of the porch shows him, benign and expansive, sheltering children who have grown to a prosperous and useful adolescence.

Jonas Hanway

Jonas Hanway was known in Britain for publication of an account of his travels in Persia and Russia in 1755. In 1756, when fear the French would 'descend on the kingdom from Brest', he published his *Thoughts on Invasion*. This prepared the ground for his establishment of the Marine Society, 'to collect such vagabond boys as either were brought before the magistrate charged with petty offences or were found wandering and begging in the street.' It had been enacted under Queen Anne that every master of a vessel above 30 tons should take a parish apprentice; but this had been neglected. Hanway, aware that the war required more seamen than existed, believed boys should be trained before they reached manhood. The society, formed with merchants and ship-owners, would fit out volunteers and boys to serve on the king's ships. Hanway declared:

> We found a great number of young fellows in danger of becoming a prey to vice through idleness who, as soon as the garb of seamen was offered to them gratis, gladly entered into the service; and a number of boys loitering in filth and rags, and as the forlorn hope of human nature, ready for any enterprise; and we considered that the preserving of such persons and rendering them useful, promoted the great end of government, and true policy in a double view.'[38]

Hanway lost his own father in early childhood. Moved by the condition of parish orphans, he paid £50 in 1858 to qualify him as a governor of the Foundling Hospital for life. With the ending of the general reception, Hanway turned his energies to other ways of preserving the lives of such children. He discovered the low life expectancy of children raised in the London 'bills of mortality', the 147 central parishes of the city: 80 per cent of children born in London workhouses died in the first year of their life. He campaigned for the introduction of a comprehensive Register of Poor Children—already part of the (lapsed) duties of each parish. No reliable record existed of children who perished by neglect or of those simply left to die in the hedgerows or on the streets soon after birth. An Act was passed in 1762 requiring an annual register of all parish poor infants.

In 1760 Hanway induced Parliament to set up a committee to inquire into the facts. The Committee found that:

> ...taking the children born in the workhouse or parish houses or received under twelve months old in 1763, and following the same in 1764 and 1765, only seven in a hundred survived the short period'.... (and whilst 1,419 children were apprenticed between 1754 and 1762) 'only 19 of those born in workhouses or

received into them under twelve months old comprise any part of the 1,419, and even of those received as far as three years old, only thirty-six appear to have survived in the hands of the said parishes to be placed out as apprentices.

Six years later he published *An Earnest Appeal for Mercy to the Children of the Poor* which showed that in some parishes of London all babies received into the workhouse in the preceding year had died before their first birthday.[39] In 1767 an Act of Parliament decreed that, 'all infants below the age of four belonging to parishes within the Bills of Mortality shall not be nursed in workhouse, but shall be sent to nurse between three and five miles from the cities of London and Westminster.' The same Bill also reduced the maximum period of parish apprenticeships to seven years; and the payment to masters was to take place in two instalments—first at the beginning of the apprentice's time and second after a lapse of three years.

This legislation suppressed abuses at the point where they were most critical. The country nursing of infants decreased the death-rate within the bills of mortality, but led to the practice which in the nineteenth century became notorious as baby-farming—the nursing of babies by women who, sometimes in collusion with the mother, showed no great zeal for their survival. As for London parish apprenticeships, some involved removing youngsters from London workhouses to serve the new manufactories in the north of England.

Orphan chimney sweeps

An emblem of derelict children in popular folklore is the climbing-boy; apprenticed to chimney sweeps, often stunted and misshapen by years of scraping their bones against chimney-bricks and inhaling the sooty deposits they have removed. In 1785 Jonas Hanway took up their cause. In his *Sentimental History of Chimney Sweepers in London and Westminster*, he wrote, 'Orphans who are in a vagabond state, or the illegitimate children of the poorest kind of people, are said to be sold; that is, their service for seven years is disposed of for twenty or thirty shillings, being a smaller price than the value of a terrier.'[40]

Hanway describes a child:

> ...blasted with chilling cold, wet to the skin, without shoes or with only the fragments of them, without stockings, his coat and breeches in tatters, and his shirt in smutty rags; sometimes with sores bleeding, or with limbs twisted or contracted whilst his misery is rendered more pungent by his task-master, who has no feeling for his sorrows! ...It is moreover well known, that there are some disorders peculiar to persons so employed, against which they ought to be guarded by a climbing dress, and due caution suited to such circumstances. If I am rightly informed, the climbing frequently occasions great heat in the scrotum, which if irritated by friction, brings on cancerous disorders. I have heard of four such, who were attended in one workhouse at one time.

He singles out one:

> ...particular object of misery...The object in question, to judge from his discourse, has the full exercise of his reason, and all its glorious faculties, and affections not inferior to the common run of men. He is now twelve years of age, a cripple on crutches, hardly three feet seven inches in stature. He began to climb chimneys before he was five years of age, his bones not having acquired a fit degree of strength... Being out of his time of servitude, as a REWARD for his labours and sufferings, he has become an object of parochial charity... Being asked if he ever went to church, his answer was 'I have no hat for my head no buckles for my shoes.' This boy, from a certain active spirit and goodness of heart, still performs his duty to his master, although he cannot move on the surface of the earth without the assistance of crutches and has aid from the parish, he climbs and sweeps a chimney.

Hanway's observations foreshadow a very 'modern' appreciation of the rights of poor children and parish orphans. Just as we in this age have no monopoly on humanitarian sentiment (as the British government's response to refugee children from Syria and elsewhere attests), so our ancestors had their visionaries who were outraged by abuses then taken for granted or accepted as part of the 'natural' landscape. John Scott, Quaker poet, landscape gardener, author of *Observations on the Present State of the Parochial and Vagrant Poor*, 1773, expressed a resonant anger:

> Neither is the cruelty of him who expatiates on the follies, when he ought to supply the necessities of the necessitous, greatly inferior to him, who, instead of extending an arm to save a drowning wretch from immediate destruction, should stand calmly to censure his temerity in venturing on the water.[41]

If the Enlightenment led to more humane attitudes towards oppressed humanity, it also nourished scientific and technological practices in industry. These, allied to the ideology of laissez-faire, engendered new hostility towards victims of industrialism including children. Resentment of the poor was renewed; their propensity to increase in number (despite levels of infant mortality) disquieted ruling castes and rising entrepreneurial classes alike. The children of the poor would overwhelm order and propriety: what alienated, menacing humanity might not spring from the stunted loins and distorted bodies of those who laboured in mine, mill and manufactory?

The workhouse as deterrent

Knatchbull's Act of 1723 had permitted parishes to send to the workhouse all who required relief. They were expected to contribute towards their own maintenance by working for the parish. This introduced, for the first time, the idea of workhouse as a place of deterrence. It foreshadowed the Poor Law Amendment Act of 1834, with its 'law of less eligibility', which insisted that the poorest labourer outside the workhouse should be better off than the best provided pauper within. An alternative to the workhouse was for parishes to farm out the poor to contractors, who, for a given sum, would house, feed and employ them.

In such conditions many infants saw barely a gleam of light of the world before they passed from it. Workhouses—which, in small parishes, were often simply ordinary dwelling-places— were frequently ill-ventilated, dirty, their floors covered with rushes in summer and straw in winter, and people slept promiscuously, two or three to a bed. By the 1770s there were over 2000 workhouses in England and Wales.

Despite the London legislation, children in the rest of the Britain continued to die in their thousands. R. Potter, in his *Observations on the Poor Laws, or the Present State of the Poor and on Houses of Industry*, 1775, describes the poorhouses of East Anglia as:

> ...those wretched receptacles of suffering indigence. These miserable tenantries are, many of them, open to the roof like barns, with ten thousand fluttering cobwebs pendant from the thatch; if they have chambers they are in this condition; few of them have any floor besides the naked earth; their site and precinct is generally damp and unwholesome; the door seems to let in the light and let out the smoke; for the windows are generally so small and so patch'd, that they serve but little purpose but to admit the bleak and howling winds and driving snows; their beds are filthy masses of unsheltering rags that beggar description; and many of them elevated from the bare earth only by a little rotten straw; in one room you shall find an aged couple, whose shivering limbs ache for want of better covering; contiguous to them a younger pair, with three of their children in the same bed, and in a corner of the same room a son and a daughter, each arrived at the age of puberty and couching together. In the same room lodges a decent man of eighty, hoarsely insulted by two wanton wenches, each holding to her breast the fruits of unlawfull love. One room contains three, sometimes four beds with persons of different ages and sexes. One bed contains the husband, wife and four children, two more lodged on straw. One bed contains the father and mother and two daughters, one of fifteen, the other of twenty years. These are not cases of particular necessity or particular neglect, but the common and general abuse of the Clause of the Statute of 43 Elizabeth, which empowers the Overseers to place inmates or more families than one in one cottage or house.[42]

A changing sensibility

The spirit of the Enlightenment crept through chinks in the closed minds of poor law officials. Gilbert's Act of 1782 empowered parishes, or groups of parishes, to provide workhouses especially for children, the aged, infirm and impotent, and those unable to support themselves by their labour. For such people William Gilbert who, before he entered Parliament had been a land agent to Lord Gower, was determined to bring reform to parish workhouses which he called 'dens of horror'. He saw the workhouse as a shelter, no longer a repellent to all but the most desperate. Orphans and poor children were to be housed until they were, 'of sufficient Age to be put into Service, or bound Apprentice to Husbandry or some Trade or Occupation.' The number of parishes that took advantage of the Act was limited. History of the poor must be read between the lines of official policy, while the story of orphans was barely legible at all. In parishes which took advantage of Gilbert's Act, children knitted stockings, made mops, picked oakum, and made bags and sacks.

Children who survived long enough to be bound apprentice were put to ill-paid and dangerous labour. Many became agrarian or domestic drudges. Although legislation existed for redress of cruelty to apprentices, few were in a position to make use of it. It is easy to imagine the circumstances in which a ten-year-old girl was put to service. Her day began before dawn, feeding fowls or other domestic livestock, preparing breakfast, washing clothes, swilling floors, tending children, fetching water, serving dinner, with only an interval for family prayers before supper, clearing away the remains of the meal before retiring to a straw mattress under the eaves, stifling in summer, numbingly chill in winter.

The London orphan asylum

The stratification of orphans was severe. Philanthropic institutions devoted to the illegitimate and outcast existed; but most orphanages were designed for the meritorious classes—orphans of those who had served in the military, trade and the professions. In 1681, there were so many abandoned babies at St Bartholomew's Hospital that the Governors issued instructions that, 'the beadles are to walk the cloisters all day to prevent children being left there'.

The unfortunates of premature mortality among the middling ranks should not be contaminated by the progeny of indigence. As Mrs Trimmer observed in her 1801 *The Oeconomy of Charity:*

> It would be thought cruel to send the child, or orphan, of a pious clergyman, or a respectable but reduced tradesman to be brought up among the offspring of thieves and vagabonds, in the schools so happily and judiciously founded for those most wretched of poor children, by the Philanthropic Society.[43]

> The education of the children of the poor therefore should not be left to their ignorant and corrupted parents; it is a public concern, and should be regarded as a public business, so far as is consistent with that freedom which it would be an injury to the community to infringe.

This desire to separate a new generation from irretrievably vicious parents strikes against the idea of the sanctity of family, which even the most charitable would prefer to observe:

> The poor might probably resist in these times of licentious freedom, that authority which would force them to give up their children entirely to the state; but they are, in general, glad to accept of eleemosynary education for them; and the bounty of the rich cannot be better employed than in providing it.

During the Napoleonic Wars, the London Orphan Asylum was founded by Andrew Reed, a Congregational minister whose influence on later London orphans stretches even to living memory. Patrons included royalty and members of the nobility. Its prospectus stated it was 'for the reception of destitute orphans, particularly those descending from respectable parents.'[44] It went on:

This class of charitable objects is probably more extensive than any other. Our manufactories, our merchandise and above all the long-continued wars in which we have been engaged have stripped innumerable families of their head, and reduced them to a condition the most destitute and deplorable.

The first claimants on this charity were children, 'whose parents had been in respectable circumstances, and children whose parents have lost their lives in the ARMY, NAVY, MARINE and MANUFACTURING services in general.'

Children were admitted between the ages of seven and ten. The aim was to train the 'ductile' mind of the unformed character, rather than leave it to the time when the deepest features of the personality are fixed, to prevent the necessity for later forms of charity. Before admission, it was required that the marriage-lines of the orphan's parents be shown to those in authority.

There were other limits—no diseased, deformed or infirm child was eligible. No child was to be dismissed before its fourteenth year, nor continue beyond its fifteenth. No dog, bird or rabbit was allowed on the premises, and no person visiting was permitted to give the children drink, sweetmeats or rewards of any kind. The rule was that:

...the friends of the children be allowed to see them in the presence of the Master or the Matron in the Easter, Whitsun and Christmas week (Sundays always excepted) between the hours of nine and twelve and two and five only; that they are not to remain more than two hours on any account...A possessive quality is detectable in the oversight of orphans, a vigilance to ensure that nothing from her or his past interferes with inculcation of principles of probity and diligence.

A list of the first 109 children admitted ('elected', as it is described) to the orphanage survives, with a brief biography of each, adverting to the devastating circumstances which have brought them there:

Mary Ann Richards: neither father nor mother; seven children left with an Aunt, who is unable to support them; were respectable.

Mary Appleby: neither father nor mother; six children dependant upon the industry and exertions of the elder sister, who is in service.

Clarissa Walker: no father, who was a Mariner; mother in a decline, with 4 children dependant upon her exertions.

Eliza Jane Evans: no father; was a boat builder; mother dying; 5 children destitute; were in respectable circumstances.

Amelia Evans: father, who was a tax officer, died suddenly of an apoplexy; while the mother was confined of her sixth child; were respectable, very destitute.

Josephine Bowcock Wilson: no father; was a mercer and draper; under severe losses he put an end to his life; mother is in ill health with five children wholly dependant; the eldest afflicted with spinal hurt; were very respectable, now very distressed.

Among the boys were:

Thomas Richards: neither father nor mother; father under pressure of serious losses, terminated his existence; the mother shortly after died of Grief; leaving seven children unprovided for.

Samuel Oram: father distressed by embarrassed circumstances, put an end to his existence; the mother and four children are reduced from comfort to want.

Walter Partridge: father Captain Partridge murdered off Dieppe; mother has ten children, eight wholly dependant [sic]; very distressed.

Peter Swan: father Captain in West India Trade, perished with the crew off Scotland; three children dependant on the mother; were respectable; very distressed.

Mark Perry: no father, who died in St Luke's Hospital; mother has eight children, one deaf and dumb and one an idiot, dependant; very distressed.

Frank Hammer Wigmore Hawkins: father a Master Shipwright; losses in trade brought on insanity, of which he died; mother in ill health, with five children, four wholly dependant; were respectable; very distressed.

The orphanage provided for them far more effectively than the wintry mercy of the parish. Despite limited details of their circumstances, there are patterns: economic losses and suicide of the father are recorded without comment, as though this were an honourable course of action for those ruined in trade. Suicide, a sin and a crime, was evidently a less grave offence than illegitimacy. There is often sudden death and the only remaining relative an aged grandparent. The use of the past tense—'were respectable'—suggests the abyss that awaited families wholly reliant on the profession of the father.

The fate of the orphanage reflects subsequent social history. An imposing classical structure dating from 1820 in semi-rural Clapton was, by the 1860s, engulfed by urban expansion. A site was acquired in Watford, and a substantial Gothic construction opened in 1871. It was re-named 'The London Orphan School' in 1921, and in 1939 became 'Reed's School' in honour of the founder. During the war, the girls were evacuated to Devon and the boys to Northamptonshire. After 1945, the girls were moved to a country estate in Hampshire and the boys to Cobham in Surrey. In 1955, boys and girls were re-united on the Cobham site. It is now a private school.

Dr Reed's Asylum for Fatherless Children, founded in 1844, was to be, 'free of any denominational catechism.' These— also from the respectable classes—were provided with a new building in Coulsden, Surrey. This has also now been demo- lished, replaced by 'luxury flats'—that defining institution of our time.

Dr Reed adopted a child orphaned when a labourer, engaged on a building in East London, fell from the scaffolding and was killed on the spot. After the sad event his pregnant wife gave birth, but she, too, died and was carried to the grave of her husband. Dr Reed heard this melancholy story, and on making inquiry, found that the posthumous infant was one of eight left friendless. He chose instead to take her under his own care and she was placed to nurse in the village of Hendon. He supported her until he died, without the circumstances ever becoming known beyond his own family.

Hetty Day

Hetty Day spent ten years of her childhood in Reedham Asylum for Fatherless Children. She relates:

> My father died when I was eighteen months. He was repairing the engine of an old car and cut his finger. He wrapped the wound in an oily rag, and got blood-poisoning. Within a week he was dead. The story is that he and my mother were to go out that evening. His arm was swollen and throbbing, and he felt ill. But my mother wanted to dance, and so they went. My father fainted, was taken to hospital and died a few days later. My sister was six, and my mother three months pregnant with my brother, James.

> It was 1929. My sister went to Reedham Orphanage. I stayed with my mother for a while, when she got a job as housekeeper. When my brother was born, I joined my sister in Reedham.

> Although non-sectarian, it was certainly not secular. We had religion crammed down our throats. Religion and charity were our staple diet. The food was inadequate and it stayed that way. We were fed on bread and butter, potatoes and gravy. I remember a boiled egg once.

> I remember my first day clearly. I'd been encouraged to see it as a great adventure. I was told it was a school, and I was very proud. We went into the nursery, and my mother said 'Oh, look at the lovely rocking-horse.' I wasn't particularly interested, but I went over to it, to please her. And when I looked round, she'd gone. I still feel the sense of loss I had then.

> I went into the Babies' Department: children from eighteen months to five. We were severely treated. If we talked when we shouldn't, we had to sit and hold our tongues between our fingers. If we talked after we'd been put to bed, they pulled the sheets over our heads, and I was always afraid of the dark. By four, I was no longer considered a child—I had to help look after the younger ones, make the cots, prove myself useful. The food was inadequate

and it stayed that way. My time in the Babies' Department is a blur of unhappiness.

From five till seven you went into the Infants and started school. I was happy only in the classroom. One of the biggest wrongs was that we were not allowed to continue our education. We were clever. My brother won a scholarship to the county school but couldn't go.

Mothers signed a contract to say the Orphanage should take care of you till you were fifteen. The only release would be if the mother married again. My mother had a man friend, and I wished they would marry, because I would get out of Reedham. I worshipped my mother, this idol, this beautiful woman. I invested her with the opposite of the bad things in the Orphanage. She came one day, Festival Day, and left one of her blue lace gloves behind. I treasured that glove, it smelt of my mother's perfume. I caressed it and kept it beside me. Whenever I wanted my mother, I'd take it out and the smell of it evoked her. I was lovesick for my mother all those years.

We had orphan clothes, rough, durable. We were inadequately clad, always cold and hungry. It was all punishing, to remind you of your dependent state.

We had cotton vests, navy blue knickers like workmen's dungarees cut off, with bibs and straps, a navy blue jumper, very thin. Nothing was ever ours: it was put on the pile. You never owned any clothing—it was passed on to you. You wore a liberty bodice, itchy black woollen stockings with garters to keep them up; all in navy blue: the only splash of colour at the collar, where you wore the red and yellow colours of the school. Even the shoes were never our own. You were not known by name, only a number. I was G80, my sister G90, my brother B52—Girl and Boy.

The school was kept clean by the inmates. A boy was picked each term to blow the bugle, a dubious privilege because he had to get up at six. This woke the whole school. We dressed and washed, stripped the bed, folded the blankets exactly right, turned the mattress: everything just so. Then we had our duties—cleaning the stairs and washrooms. When you'd finished your task, the mistress inspected it. Any mistake, however minute, you had to do it all over again.

Cleaning the stairs was unpleasant, because you would drive splinters into your hands. Each stair had to be dusted and polished.

The boys were allowed a newspaper to get some idea of what was going on in the world. The girls didn't. I expect they thought it was none of our business. We were so institutionalised that when I left I was afraid to cross the road and terrified of going into a shop. Your life was so structured that anything out of that routine was a frightening adventure.

Prayers were at nine; church every morning to thank God for blessings which were not often evident. The sexes were severely divided in everything: the girls did domestic science, the boys woodwork and chemistry. There was more than a hint of service in the training we received.

I knew why we were sent away, but I didn't understand. I felt sympathy for my mother. The shock of losing my father suddenly must have been dreadful. She did various jobs—receptionist at a hotel, matron of a boarding school at one time. I thought it odd she was matron of a boarding school while her own children were at Reedham. She rarely visited us. It was a red-letter day if she came. If she was expected I would go crazy.

I protected my brother, who never really knew our mother at all. I grew up fast: I realised how James depended on me when he came to Reedham at two. For the first year he was fussed over; they were quite good with the tiny ones. I was constantly hungry. Food played a big part in our games. He used to say 'Tell me a story.' I made up stories about ourselves: two children lost in a wood; an old woman found us, took us to her cottage and gave us rabbit stew.

If you found a chocolate wrapper, you would pick it up and smell it, and as you smelled the chocolate, you imagined you could taste it too. If anybody got an apple, we would gather round and beg for the core. Even orange peel, you chewed it to get the taste.

Apparently, when I went to Reedham I had rickets. I remember pains in my legs and being unable to walk. At six, I was being pushed round in a pram because my legs were so weak. I was sickly; mostly from lack of love.

At meal times, at the first whistle, we had to wash our hands, file past the mistress to have them inspected, make sure our nails were white, our hair perfect. At the second whistle, get in line and march into the meal. We stood at the table and said Grace. I never did learn the words till after I left. You could la-la-la them.

'Be present at our table, Lord,
Be here and everywhere adored;
….His mercies blest, and grant that we
May feast in Paradise with thee.'

We ate in silence. If we talked, we had to stand on the bench and remain there for the rest of the meal, with nothing more to eat. Then we sang again 'We thank you, Lord, for this our food, And every other needful good…' At tea-time, we were allowed five minutes' talk before dispersing. The mistress patrolled the room throughout the meal. At the end of each day, we filed into the classroom for the evening service. We sang, 'The day thou gavest, Lord, is ended'—a hymn usually reserved for funerals. The Infants knelt at the foot of the bed to say prayers. Infants went to bed at six. The mistress walked round the beds. If anybody's hands were anywhere near their private parts, she removed them and placed them outside the bedcovers.

Betty's sister left school to help her mother who was managing a wool shop. Then she joined the Auxiliary Territorial Service, and her mother wanted companionship. She asked if I could leave Reedham. I was making good educational progress, well ahead for my age. The Headmaster did me this wrong—he gave me the choice. He asked me if I wanted to leave. Of course, it was the one thing I'd dreamed of for ten years. And as I was 14, they said I could leave. My teacher shed tears and said it was wrong to break off my education. But you can imagine my excitement at being reunited with the woman I'd worshipped from afar all those years. I went home. And then for a year I cried to go back.

I was broken-hearted. It was the most unhappy year of my life. I don't know why I didn't leave and run away back to Reedham. My fantasy of my mother crumbled. She had never read a book in her life, and she nagged me every time she saw me do so.

Hetty was damaged by her experience. She had a close relationship with a woman who sensed the intensity of her feeling, and arranged for her to meet—and marry—a man who had been one of the guinea-pigs, that is, had had reconstructive surgery on his face. He had been badly burned when his Coastal Command plane came down. Hetty says they were both wounded—he physically, she psychologically; and although they had four children, it was a difficult and controlling relationship; and she only really began to live when she was widowed in her fifties.[45]

Continuities

Hetty's story shows how a tradition of abuse of the orphaned and disinherited continued. Contemporary prejudice against the poor is no recent development; and no fable in today's popular press surpasses the lurid evocations of eighteenth-century 'observers' of the roguery of the poor. The writer of the anonymous *Trip from St James' to the Royal Exchange, with Remarks, Serious and Diverting on the Manners, Customs and Amusements of the Inhabitants of London and Westminster* in 1744, begs leave:

> …to give an Account of a Ramble I took one day into the Heart of the good Parish of St Giles in the Fields, where I stood staring and gaping about, like the Mayor of a Country Corporation in the Court of Requests, being surrounded on all sides by Thieves, Knaves and Beggars. At length I came to a place called the Infant Office, where young children stand at livery, and are let out by the day to town mendicants. The first scene that presented was a little Vilain of about seven years old, who, upon my asking him some questions, told me that his father had been a house carpenter in Dublin where he broke his neck by a fall from a scaffold in repairing a cellar window, and died about seven years before he was born. A woman of about fifty would needs have a baby that was sucking at the Breast; and another who had a Complexion as sallow as a Portuguese Sailor, must be accommodated with a Child as fair as a smock-faced Parson. One woman had no less than four for the Day, two packed up behind her like a Scotch Pedlar's Budget, the third was to run by her side bawling out for Victuals, and the fourth she held in her Arms, like a tuneable Instrument to be set to Musick when she came in the view of any seemingly well-disposed People. An ancient Matron, who had the superin-

tendency of the Office held forth in her Arms a pretty Poppet of about a Year old, telling them there was a sweet innocent Picture, a moving Countenance that would not fail making a Serjeant at Law feel for his Halfpence, and might extort Charity even from a Divine. A Beggar Woman, who was vastly in Arrear for the Let of Children, being refused any longer Credit till she had paid off the old Score, made no more to do but throw and old ragged Riding Hood over her Shoulders, cursing 'em all for a Parcel of unchristian old B*tches, in forcing her to tell the Town ten thousand lies by saying she had three poor Infants sick at home.

Everyone being suited according to their Circumstances and Consciences, it was not altogether an unpleasant Sight, to behold this little Auxiliary Army march off to lay a great Protestant City and its Suburbs under Contributions.

Orphans and convicts

It is a small step from moral condemnation to criminalisation. Lists of transported felons, political dissidents and others in the late eighteenth century often include 'convicts and orphans': convicts are not easily distinguished from those without parents; and in records of their trials at the Old Bailey categories readily overlap.

A report from 1783 tells that:

John Hudson, (a child of nine years old) was indicted for burglariously and feloniously breaking and entering the dwelling house of William Holdsworth at the hour of one in the night, on the 19th October last, and feloniously stealing therein one linen shirt, value 10s. five silk stockings, value 5s. one pistol, value 5s. and two aprons, value 2s. the property of the said William.

Court to Prisoner: How old are you?—Going on nine.
What business was you bred up in?—None, sometimes a
    chimney sweeper.
Have you any father or mother?—Dead.
How long ago?—I do not know.
Court—I wanted to see whether he had any understanding
    or no, we shall hear more of him by and by.

The Court was told how William Holdsworth, a 'chymist' in East Smithfield, was informed by a maid that the house had been robbed. The glass of the skylight had been broken and some 'small sooty toeprints' were discovered. A woman lodging at a nearby shoe warehouse found John Hudson in a water-tub, washing the soot from his body. She was angry because this was water intended for drinking. She found a damask cloth a parcel of silk stockings and a pistol concealed in a thread stocking. A pawnbroker testified that the shirt had been brought in by the boy that same morning. The boy was made to confess by the threats of the lodging-house keeper, but insisted he had been assisted by an older boy. The Court was disinclined to accept such a confession, and said it should not be allowed because it was made 'under fear.' The Court stated, 'I think it would be too hard to find a boy of his tender age guilty of the burglary' (which would have required sentence of death); 'one would wish to snatch such a boy, if one possibly could, from destruction, for he will only return to the same kind of life which he has led before, and will be an instrument in the hands of very bad people, who make use of boys of that sort to rob houses.' He was found guilty of the felony, but not of the burglary, and sentenced to transportation for seven years.[46]

A notorious convict transported at that time was Mary Wade, who, at the age of eleven, was indicted with another girl, Jane Whiting, aged fourteen:

> ...for feloniously assaulting Mary Phillips on the King's Highway in 1777, and putting her in fear, and feloniously taking from her person, and against her will, one cotton frock, value 3s one linen tippet value 2d one linen cap value 2d, the property of John Forward' [the girl's father].

> This drama occurred in New Pye Street, near Perkins' Rents, where the frock was pawned for eighteen pence. Wade said, 'I wish I had not done it' to the big one, and the big one said, 'It was your own fault.' Then the little one said 'I was in a good mind to have chucked the child down the necessary and I wish I had done it.'

The child whose frock was stolen, knew 'the little one', whom she had seen 'sweeping the streets.' Inattentive or absent parents—whether kept from minding their children by poverty, drink or indifference—created a moral orphaning of their children. Mary Wade's parents were not in court. The child said 'They live at Wandsworth, they was here today, only they could not come to me.' Her father was a drover. Mary made a living as best she could, as street-sweeper. She had not learned her catechism, although she claimed to know the difference between truth and falsehood. When she came to be sentenced, the Judge said to the mother:

> I hardly can ask you how your child has behaved; for I am afraid you are as much in fault as she is; by not taking proper care of her, keeping her at home and making her industrious; letting her run about the streets, was the sure way to lead her to the place where she is now; therefore I ought rather to ask you, what you can say for yourself then for her?

[The mother replied]; 'It is the other girls that induce her to go a begging with them; I never brought her up to go a begging.'

The Judge summed up the evidence to the jury, saying:

> For the sake of example, I cannot recommend to you, if you should be of the opinion that the crime is sufficiently fixed upon them, I cannot recommend you to say it is of a less degree of atrociousness than robbery; the tender years of these persons may be a circumstance to be attended to in other views; but as to the demonstration of the crime, I think it would be a dangerous thing for society, if you were to be induced, by any humanity, to lessen the offence at all below the rank of actual robbery. So that if you say that they are both or either of them guilty, I think you must say they are guilty of the crime for which they stand indicted, robbery, not larceny.' They were sentenced to death.[47]

In April 1789, George III, declared cured of porphyria, by way of thanksgiving, commuted all death sentences to transportation. Mary Wade had spent ninety-three days as an eleven-year-old awaiting execution before the reprieve was announced. She sailed on the *Lady Juliana* in 1789, the first convict ship to consist solely of transported women and girls. The voyage took eleven months. She was taken to Norfolk Island, where she gave birth to two children. Her companion disappeared on a whaling trip and she lived with another man and bore twenty-one children. When she died she had three hundred relatives; former Australian Prime Minister Kevin Rudd is among her thousands of descendants.

The severity with which the children of want were treated was official policy: the lowest age of criminal responsibility was seven (raised to eight in 1933 and to ten in 1963). That the reformative power of this criminalisation of childhood was negligible was widely acknowledged, but a punitive inertia inhibited change. A report from 1814 records a death sentence passed on five children:

> It has been said, and said truly, that while we employ a terrific apparatus to punish crime, we are shamefully remiss in taking measures to prevent it. If anyone doubts of the truth of this assertion, let him read over the Calendar of the criminals tried at the Old Bailey: he will then find that no longer ago than the 16th February 1814, five children, the youngest eight and the oldest twelve years of age, were condemned to death: Fowler and Wolfe 12 years, for burglary in a dwelling house; Morris 8, Solomons, 9 and Barnall, 11, for burglary and stealing a pair of shoes. On the next day, 17th February, Cook, aged 15, Young, 13, Sandiford, 12, J Thompson, 12, and B Thompson 15, were condemned to transportation for stealing cheese from a shop.[48]

Glimpses of the Bridewell

William Pennant, eighteenth century traveller and naturalist, produced in 1790 *Some Account of London*, where he records his visit to the female section of the Bridewell prison:

> The first time I ever visited the place, there was not a single male prisoner and about thirty female. They were confined on a ground

floor and employed in beating hemp. When the door was opened by the keeper, they ran towards it like so many hounds in kennel, and presented a most moving sight: about twenty young creatures, the eldest not exceeding sixteen, many of them with angelic faces, divested of every angelic expression; featured with impudence, impenitency and profligacy and clothed in the silken tatters of squalid finery. A magisterial! A national opprobrium!! What a disadvantageous contrast to the Spinhuis in Amsterdam, where the confined sit under the eye of a matron, spinning or sewing, in plain, neat dresses, provided by the public. No trace of their former lives appears in their countenances; a thorough reformation seems to have been effected, equally to the emolument and honour of the republic.[49]

Popular opinion

Certain cases of mistreatment of orphans were perpetuated in ballads circulating at executions; others were lost in the anonymity of the lives of the poor. The execution of Elizabeth Brownrigg at Tyburn for torturing to death her female apprentices was an example: that spectacular acts of wickedness and cruelty can always be turned into compelling popular entertainment lives on today in TV dramas of sensational court cases.

Brownrigg was the mother of sixteen children (of whom only three survived into adult life).[50] Having practised midwifery, she was appointed by the overseers of the poor to look after poor women in the workhouse of St Dunstan's Parish. In 1765, Mary Mitchell was apprenticed to Mrs Brownrigg, and the same year, Mary Jones, a child of the Foundling Hospital was also placed with her, alongside a number of other young girls. The word 'apprentice' was an exaggeration, for the girls were cheap servants who helped Mrs Brownrigg in her private business with the lying-in of pregnant women. The orphans were treated with great savagery. Mary Jones was whipped and beaten. She escaped one night and managed to reach the Foundling Hospital, where she was examined and found to be covered with bruises and sores. The governors of the Hospital wrote to James Brownrigg, threatening prosecution if he failed to account for the injuries to the child. There was no response. The Hospital thought it unwise to indict at common law. Mary Jones did not return to her place of employment.

Others were subject to merciless ill-treatment. Mary Clifford was chained and forced to sleep in the coal-hole, persistently whipped until she bled. Eventually freed, her whole body was found to be ulcerated. She died in St Bartholomew's Hospital a few days later. Elizabeth Brownrigg was indicted and executed at Newgate, her body then placed in a hackney-coach, conveyed to Surgeon's Hall, dissected and anatomised. Her skeleton was hung up in Surgeon's Hall.

Orphans of early industrialism

Early industrialism increased concentrations of the outcast and the deprived. In manufacturing areas, the 'labouring poor' were transformed from the ragged clodhoppers of the rural landscape into regimented workers pressed into service of mill and factory.

This also reversed the dawning sense of humanity towards the poor of the late eighteenth century. Industry conjured forth a wild, intractable population who might combine to commit all kinds of mischief. On his travels through the English Midlands between 1781 and 1794, the Honourable John Byng (later Viscount Torrington, writing in 1790 of the Derwent Valley) observed 'The simple peasant is changed into the impudent mechanic'; capturing in a phrase the epic upheaval which would re-shape, not only the people themselves, but also the social attitudes of their superiors. [51]

That poor children could be civilised by exposure to the behaviour and manners of their betters became less plausible as industrial society developed, since the number of the poor multiplied, even as the wealth of the nation increased. This paradox hastened a further moralising (or immoralising) of the poor: in the presence of such riches, what could be the cause of their failure to avail themselves of opportunities provided, if not innate laziness or perversity? The very opulence of power, conspicuous display of liveried servants, glittering ballrooms and gilded equipages suggested effortless accumulation, open to all but those who wilfully spurned the wealth which they were invited to share. The migrations of the era appear small to the eye of a posterity which takes easy mobility for granted; but at the time, the shift from rural homestead to city tenement represented a profound uprooting, which broke familiar networks and left its scattered orphans and abandoned to survive or perish at random. Sylvia Lynd, writing in 1942, said, 'The story of the Industrial Age throughout Europe is the story of the martyrdom of childhood.'[52] The abhorrence of 'idleness' became almost pathological as a result of intensifying faith in salvation through labour.

Parish children were taken from London to water-powered mills in the late eighteenth century. Fragments of subjective experience—literary as well as biographical—remain; among them, the well-known testimony of Robert Blincoe, who gave his story to John Brown in Manchester in 1832, a few years before his suicide.[53]

Blincoe was sent at the age of seven from St Pancras Workhouse to a cotton mill in Derbyshire, in a consignment of parish orphans in a mutation of 'apprenticeship' to the North, which would turn them into productive members of society, and rid metropolitan rate-payers of the burden of their subsistence. This practice, in theory halted by Peel's Bill of 1802, continued long afterwards.

There was no record of Blincoe's parents on his entry into the workhouse. In the workhouse, during recitation of the catechism, when it came to the Fifth Commandment, he would burst into tears, 'I cry because I cannot obey one of God's commandments. I know not either my father or mother.'

Blincoe recalled St Pancras as, 'a gloomy though liberal sort of prison house.' When boys were selected as apprentice climbing boys for chimney sweeps, he was passed over to his bitter disappointment. In August 1799, he was excited to learn he was to go to a cotton mill near Nottingham. Only 'volunteers' were accepted, but since the children were told they would be turned into 'ladies and gentlemen', would remain until they were twenty one, be fed on roast-beef and plum-pudding, ride their masters' horses, have silver watches and plenty of cash in their pockets, the 'voluntary' nature of their enrolment was scarcely surprising.

They set off with new clothes, one shilling, a pocket handkerchief and some gingerbread.

After a four-day journey in wagons, they arrived at the mill ten miles from Nottingham: a large building with a cupola, which the child mistook for a church. The apprentice-house was half a mile from the mill. The master had a horse-whip. The first meal was of thin porridge and rye-bread that stuck to the teeth 'like bird-lime'.

Blincoe found no soap, no plates, knives or forks. A multitude of ill-clad and dirty apprentices slept in two-tiered cribs around the chamber, two boys to a bed on flock mattresses. Work started at five o'clock after a breakfast of black bread and blue-milk porridge. They worked fourteen hours a day, except Sunday, and received an extra halfpenny if they worked the dinner hour.

Blincoe ran away from the mill, but was caught by a tailor who specialised in runaways for the five-shilling reward. He recalled accidents, including one that passed into industrial folk-lore: a girl caught in the machinery by her apron and whirled around the whole shaft so that almost every bone was broken. This story became a symbol of capitalist production: worker and machine indivisible, so it was impossible to tell where machine stopped and humanity started. In this instance, the girl, miraculously, survived, but was permanently crippled.

The mill failed and Blincoe was transferred to Lowdham, a two-day journey. It was gloomy, the apprentices filthy and ragged. The diet was water-porridge and oaten cakes. Lodging and bedding were filthy and foul. They rose at four o'clock in the morning, and washed once a week. Their verminous bodies were covered with weals. They slept fifty to a room and worked a sixteen-hour day. They were so tired boys would give an older boy a halfpenny or part of their dinner to be allowed to lean on him on the way back to the prentice-house. There were contagious fevers. Dead apprentices were replaced by parish children. Pitch and tobacco were burned in the chamber and vinegar sprinkled on beds and floor to dampen infection. The sick were worked to exhaustion and then wheeled in a barrow back to the prentice-house.

There was wanton cruelty: the children working as piecers, scavengers and minders were forced to eat dirty candle pieces or to lick up tobacco spittle. They were sometimes compelled to open their mouths for the wretches to spit into: a suggestion of brutal eroticism.

After finishing his time, Blincoe stayed another year for four shillings and sixpence a week, and then got a job in a neighbouring mill at eleven shillings. He eventually went to Manchester, worked as a stoker, and became a dealer in waste cotton on his own behalf. He married 'for a bet'. He saved and invested in cotton machinery as part owner of a mill which burned down. He died by his own hand in 1830.[54]

Katrina Honeyman, claims the life chances of parish children sent as apprentices were better than if they had remained in the workhouse.[55] She disputed the assertion of the Webbs, that agents 'carted off the children literally in cartloads'; and she traces the fate of parish children in their removal, not only from the London workhouses, but also in the more frequent shorter distances from country towns to local employers. She stresses the relative meticulousness with which parish officials and employers 'distributed' parish children, and maintained contact with them. Very few were below the age of seven, although almost half were under ten. There were virtually no 'infants'; and in any case ten-year-olds were expected to earn their living as 'free labourers.' Complaints of the apprentices, which were filtered through the officials who received them, included principally 'bad diet', 'homesickness' and 'exploitation.' She writes:

> Parish orphans are frequently portrayed as orphans. The apprenticeship registers indicate that only a minority has in fact lost both parents. A much larger number had at least one living parent with perhaps a second of unknown whereabouts. It was uncommon for parish factory apprentices to be in possession of two cohabiting parents, but not as rare as is often assumed.

The point is, surely, that they became orphans by their removal from the home village or parish, banished from the touch of affection or even friendship. It is perverse to admire the efficient administration of the factory apprentice system in the early industrial period. The British were also quite efficient in administering Bengal at the same time, and oversaw the first great de-industrialisation of the modern world, as weavers were dispossessed, and the great city of Dhaka fell into ruin, abandoned habitations of the weavers overrun by wild flowers, and animals. That this was intimately connected with the industrialisation of Britain and its child labour tarnishes the glory of the sometime 'workshop of the world.' I met a garment-factory owner in Bangladesh in the early years of this century, who waved a gracious arm over the bent heads of 400 girls—some of them extremely young—at their Juki sewing machines. He said, 'See how happy the children are, employed on useful labour in our spacious factory, rather than idly watching cattle or picking grass.' Some of them, too, were orphans, brought to Dhaka by agents or bogus 'aunties', who placed them with employers to contribute to the industrial success of Bangladesh. Honeyman claims:

> The fact of factory parish apprenticeship was large in scale, extended over a wide geographical area and liberated the industrial labour market. The increasingly flexible, unconstrained labour

market that emerged later in the eighteenth century, facilitated the establishment and growth of nascent textile manufacturing enterprises, a number of which would not have existed without parish apprentices.

The view that the liberation of markets might take precedence over the enslavement of children is a judgment no doubt rendered more fashionable by our renewed subservience to laissez-faire ideology.

When mills ceased to depend upon water-power in remote hillsides, pauper apprentices were no longer required; a resident urban population and their children provided the labour. Occasionally, later in the nineteenth century, labour shortages prompted employers to contract with parish officials and workhouse masters for young workers. From 1879 children were brought from Liverpool workhouses to the textile factory of Calvert in the upper Calder Valley in Yorkshire.[56] Principally orphans, they worked without wages for food, clothing and shelter in cottage-style homes. In the graveyard of Luddenden Dean Wesleyan church, a gravestone bears the following inscription:

In Memory of Orphans employed by I and I C Calvert,
Wainstalls:
Mary Ellen Clark, aged 14 years
Alice Devitt, aged 12 years
Elizabeth Edwards aged 17 years
John Johnson aged 12 years
Sarah Shaw, died May 17 1892 aged 15 years
Anne Larrings, died March 7 1895, aged 16 years
Mary Emery, died January 27 1895, aged 15 years.

They were buried in a common grave. That a Christian burial was given and memorial erected is supposed to show the humanity of the employers.

Apprentices

Ill-treatment of parish apprentices erupted in scandals that threw doubt upon the belief that Britain was the cradle of social, as well as industrial, progress. In 1801, a Mr Jouveaux, employed seventeen parish apprentice girls as tambour workers. (This is embroidery, stitched onto fabric held taut over a tambourine-shaped frame.) He so cruelly ill-treated and starved them that five died 'in a decline'. The girls embroidered on muslin from four or five in the morning till eleven or twelve at night, sometimes till two in the morning, occasionally all night. Their food was bread and water, a few potatoes or rice boiled in water without salt. They ate at their embroidery frames. The seventeen slept in a garret in three shared beds. When there was no work they had Sundays to themselves. Jouveaux moved his establishment from Hackney to Stepney Green at four o'clock one morning, because the neighbours had called out, 'Shame'. The girls' shrieks had been heard and they had been seeking in the hog-trough for food.[57]

I found an echo of these 'tambour workers' in Delhi at the millennium. I met Harish, pastorally called 'field worker' with a non-government organisation. It was the work of this NGO to comb the dark places of Delhi in search of small captives bringing profit to their employers and unfair competition to the honest toilers of the blameless—and rich—world. One day, it was a small metal-making unit, then a zari-shop, or a place where trace metals were recovered from discarded computers.

I accompanied Harish to East Delhi, a maze of unpaved streets between concrete buildings. Narrow workshops spilled onto the public spaces. Young men and boys were welding: some wore eye-shields of scratched plastic, but most were exposed to the hazardous fireworks from their torches. They brushed off lingering sparks that stung their flesh. A boy looked at us through a shower of stars: an oily wraith glittering in the stony waste.

We turned into a *gali*, structures of corrugated metal on either side and stopped at a building. The door was closed but not padlocked. Harish pulled the clasp from the lock and stepped inside.

The first sensation was of heat. On an earth floor, about twenty boys sat in front of wooden frames, over which was pinned taut fabric. Under instruction from older boys they were embroidering the cloth with coloured thread—gold, silver, peacock blue, crimson and lime-green—sequins and small confetti-like discs. The motifs were birds of paradise with long, shimmering tails, abstract filigrees of gold, garlands of rosebuds and lilies. It was shocking, that from this inferno of heat and dirt objects of such splendour should appear.

As soon as the door opened the children ceased work. Some held their needle poised in mid air; others stared, open-mouthed. A few began to cry: on their nose mucus formed a yellow crust. Flies circled everywhere. Beside each child—the youngest about seven, the oldest barely adolescent—stood a bottle of cloudy water. The only light came from yellow bulbs that oscillated on their flex like pallid eggs—inadequate for the work they illuminated. The boys blinked in the wedge of orange sunlight that came through the door. A slight breeze moved the stagnant air. Harish was calling the police on his phone. In a couple of minutes, two corpulent officers appeared, their belts tight over bellies grown fat on rice, beer and bribery. They asked 'Malik kahan?' If the children knew where the boss was, they were not going to say. They sat, skinny, cross-legged, passive. Harish, meanwhile was summoning a journalist, who also appeared out of nowhere to complete the scene of triumph over the forces of evil. The flash of a camera disconcerted the children. Some rose to their feet, unsteady on their thin legs.

By this time, a crowd had gathered outside—workers from industrial units and garment factories—and infants darting between the legs of adults. The children looked hungry and sleepless. The journalist asked them questions in the hectoring tone usually reserved for politicians. Where is your home? Who brought you here? Who owns the factory? Where are your mother and father? The boys remained mute, a tableau of puzzled servitude.

No one spoke. Some of the rescued children, bored, resumed work. The policemen sat on metal barrels outside, smoking, perhaps thwarted of their expected pay-off from the proprietor. A boy of about eleven approached us. He asked Harish what he proposed to do with the children. 'You will go to a government school.'

The boy asked 'Who will pay our wages?'

'You are too young to be working. You should be in school.'

The crowd was hostile: they regarded the rescuers as villains, ruining the livelihood of families whose only support was these ragged urchins.

'Come.' A wiry young man of about nineteen with intense eyes and a halo of dark curly hair, seized Harish by the wrist. 'This'—indicating a younger boy—'is my brother. He is learning *zari* work. He is an apprentice.'

We followed paths between workshops and makeshift dwellings of rough brick with tin roofs. The area was strewn with garbage—orange peel, banana skins, vegetable refuse, plastic bags, shit, discarded rags, rusty cans. The stench of a polluted canal was overwhelming. Bubbles on the surface burst in evil-smelling crepitations. I almost trod on a dead rat, the innards of which had been crushed like the inside of a pomegranate.

Outside some dwellings women were lighting small stoves, fuelled with waste straw and plastic, which warmed pots where rice simmered in pearly water. We stopped at a particularly wretched hut. The young man opened a plywood door. We stooped to enter. Adjusting our eyes to the darkness, we saw a bundle of rags in the corner, on which lay the emaciated body of a woman. Her eyes shone through the gloom.

She was at an advanced stage of consumption. A dark blot on the dirty cushion at her head might have been blood. In a hoarse whisper she said she was the grandmother of the two boys. Their father was dead, and the mother, her daughter, had thrown herself in front of a train. She had been a maidservant until, too weak to work, her employers sent her away. Iqbal, the *zari*-worker and his brother who worked in shoe-factory, were the sole support of two younger sisters and the grandmother who would not live to see them grow up. She wept at the thought of leaving them; and spoke of her gratitude to Allah, who had surely sent us to her.

In the presence of such dereliction, Harish fell silent. I took out my wallet and gave the young man two five-hundred rupee notes. He took them without a word. We went outside. Iqbal followed us along the glassy canal. He took my hand and would not relinquish it. Harish told him he wouldn't get anything else and should go and look after his grandmother.

Parish orphan labour

Sir Robert Peel's Bill of 1802, *The Health and Morals of Apprentices*, was rarely enforced, since there were not enough investigators for the purpose. 'Morals' as well as the health of apprentices were included, for moral laxity was considered as injurious to trade as weakened bodies. According to the Act, all rooms were to be ventilated and lime-washed twice a year. Each apprentice should have two sets of clothing. Work was not to exceed twelve hours a day, should not start before five or continue after nine at night. During the first four years of apprenticeship, each child should receive four hours instruction a day in writing, reading and arithmetic. Boys and girls should sleep separately, with no more than two in each bed. On Sundays they were to be instructed in the principles of the Christian religion.

Most parish children did not even enjoy the melancholy benefits of 'apprenticeship'. They remained in the poorhouse or workhouse, where, if they survived, they were to, 'be bred up to labour, principles of virtue being implanted in them at an early age and laziness discouraged.' Prevention of adults becoming paupers had priority over concern for the children they were. Among the work of parish children cited by Sidney and Beatrice Webb were:

Weaving and knitting wool and hemp into sacking, making plough-
lines and other kinds of twine and cordage (Norfolk); Teasing wool
by hand and braiding twine for fishing nets (Kendal, 1800)

Beating carpets for the nobility and gentry of the West End (St
Paul's Covent Garden).

Other employments included polishing horn, making paper
bags, heading pins; in Hackney, boys span 'shule' for floorcloth
manufacturers, while girls span flax, and picked feathers. The
Webbs concluded:

The docility and complete dependence of these little workers [the
tens of thousands of orphan and neglected children] and their
inability to abscond, the facility with which they could be punished—seemed to make their compulsory labour almost as profitable as if it had been freely tendered for wages to an employer,
while the superior authority exercised by he workhouse master
appeared to give him, in this exceptional case, a positive advantage
over private enterprise. At a certain stage in the industrial processes, when machinery has superseded physical strength and has
not yet itself become rapid or complicated—a stage which various
textile industries passed at different times during the eighteent century—the labour of little children was particularly applicable.'[58]

The training of apprenticed children bore no relation to
demand: they were prepared for overstocked trades, acquired
archaic skills for which there was no call; in certain places—the
Webbs mention glove-making in Worcester, nail-making in
Bromsgrove and stocking-weaving in Tewkesbury—the labour
market was already saturated with such employments as children were fitted for.

Contemporary descendants of parish orphans

Two hundred years after these parish orphans, the last vestiges
of such a population—young people leaving care—are still pursued by disadvantages accumulated over centuries of neglect.
How long it takes for evils believed to have been abolished to

play themselves out. And with what punitive relish politicians, police and other public functionaries turn upon injured children who, overnight at the age of sixteen, eighteen or even twenty one, cease to be vulnerable objects of 'care', and became idle, disorderly and workless, to be scorned and castigated as they join the enduring ranks of the undeserving.

Nurjehan

Nur has three documents—passport, driving licence and birth certificate: all symbols of uncertain identity, since all bear a different version of her name:

> I was born in Paddington and lived with my mother till I was four. She was an Irish nurse from Cork or Limerick, I'm not sure. I have no memory of being with her. I never knew my father, but he was Indian or Pakistani. This was the 1960s, when mixed-race children were being removed from their parents; an old fear of 'miscegenation'. Nobody would adopt them—'half-caste' was the word used. The then wisdom—ignorance—was that neither black nor white communities would want them.

> My first memories are of a care home in Oxford. Actually, there are two lies in that phrase—it wasn't a home and it had nothing to do with care. I never met my real father, but my sister Yasmin did.

> The court placed me with the local authority, which had complete responsibility for me. My mother didn't give me up. I was forcibly removed. Many years later she showed me the papers, so I knew she never gave consent. I would have been better off with her, even if she was an alcoholic. The experience I had could not have been worse.

> I was fostered for three years by a family on a farm; this gave me a love of animals. At that time, you could only be fostered only for three years if your birth parents were alive. My mother was not allowed near me. I was fostered again at five, but when I was seven, my foster-mother died of cancer. Her husband had three sons and a daughter, so he sent me back to the local authority.

I was sent to Borehamwood in Hertfordshire, an out-of-town home for Camden and Westminster, between fourteen and sixteen children. The woman ran it like an army camp. She wouldn't allow us to make a sound. Already in her sixties, she retired a few years later. She hated Irish, Jews, blacks and Indians. She took an instant dislike to me. We were the dregs. My foreign name was a give-away. I changed it to Jean. The woman was full of hatred. Her husband was a fireman, but we never saw or spoke to him. He was known as Pop. He had nothing to do with us.

It was about three in the afternoon on the day I arrived. She sat in the front room, knitting. She had piercing blue eyes, silver hair. She gave me paper and pencil and told me to draw a flower. I drew one without petals. 'You stupid girl'; she grabbed me by the arm with a pressure that told me she was boss. I knew then this was not a good place. She told me to change my clothes. I never saw them again. I kept one toy, a stuffed monkey.

I went downstairs, and tried to stroke the cat. It clawed me. I thought this was an evil place. The children were seated round the table by four o'clock. Without warning, she seized me by the scruff of the neck, pinched me in the back and sat me down. The others looked at me. We all knew we were there for a reason, but we did not know what reason.

That was my introduction. My farewell, eight years later, was similar. Nobody said goodbye, not even the new housemother. I was in care until I was fifteen. I was fostered to a Christian family at eleven, who picked me out of a Christian newspaper. By that time, I was already into drugs and cider. They had an eighteen-month old baby. I was their worst nightmare. All the blue-eyed, blond-haired kids got fostered first. You would come home from school: kids had gone and there would be somebody new.

The house-mother had favourites. I was brought up under her regime as second-best. Every day fifteen pints of milk, twelve loaves were delivered to the doorstep. There was a gardener, an ironing lady, a cleaner. We never went to shops, except Millett's, to get a set of clothes for summer and another for winter. They were signed for. We never saw money.

I didn't know my mother lived fifteen minutes away. Not only did they not give me my name, they never let me see her. I hid my name and lost my identity, because I was of mixed race. The Mayor came once a year. He went to all the children's homes in his Bentley, with his chain. One day when he came, I had had a beating. She never hit our face or anywhere where it would show. We had to stand in line, smiling.

We all had jobs. Mine was cleaning the toilet. Others had easier work—folding serviettes, putting away cutlery. You were never an individual. She would say 'Sit up. You don't want people to think you're Orphan Annie.' I had no idea who Orphan Annie was. There were years of beating. Two of the children had a brother in the army. Sometimes he stayed over at night; both me and Jackie were sexually abused by him from age seven till I was eleven. He would draw a plane and a vapour trail coming from it: 'Look, a plane', then his hand would be down my pants. Every time I see a plane on a clear day leaving a trail, it comes back to me.

I had an adult relationship when I was seven. I don't know if I am gay because of that, but I know it damaged me for life. I have always found intimacy difficult. I have had fabulous girlfriends, but it never lasted. I reported him about ten years ago. I went to the police. They said they couldn't do anything because of the passage of time.

In any institution you get abuse. When you look at the late 1960s and 1970s, it was drink, dope and sex. Children's homes were riddled with drugs. I smoked my first joint at twelve, and started drinking at eleven. I was alcohol-dependent by the time I left care.

The house-mother hated kids. She should never have been there. One day she rubbed all the skin off my neck with a scrubbing brush. I should have run away. A lot of the staff were students of nineteen or twenty. The youngest children were babies, so they got all the attention and we left to our own devices. One member of staff we called Alcoholic Anna. It was the culture of the kids to get the better of the staff. At least they got a wage for it. We were there because we had to be. It was like Lord of the Flies. I started at the bottom of the hierarchy. Even when I had been on the farm I nicked the egg money because somebody had called me a 'wog.' I had such a complex about my colour.

At fifteen, you left and were on your own. I slept with the house-father at fifteen, because I had nowhere to go. In winter, I went back to the home. I had nowhere to live. The housefather gave me sherry, put a Marvin Gaye record on. Later he went to Thailand and I believe he committed suicide. He was wanted by the police, because one girl had been interfered with there. She got £40,000 hush money.

Where there are no parents, you'll get paedophilia. We were sup-posed to have social workers. You'd see them once a year. When they were due to come we were ordered to keep quiet. School was horrendous. I was illiterate. I am self-taught.

My childhood was constant stress and anxiety. I was diagnosed with depression at fourteen and given sleeping pills. I feel I'm a refugee in my own country. If I've managed to survive, it's by God's will, not my own.

Dealing with illiteracy, sex and alcohol as a child, it makes you unsta-ble, let alone the emotional neglect and lack of identity. We had an annual holiday with the home. On one occasion I had a relationship with a waitress. Once that door was opened, I fell in love with a woman. When I came out of care, I found the Gateway Club.

When the house-mother left, the regime went too. She had done everything like clockwork. She had migraines. We had to be quiet. Even today, I still hide all my possessions, and always close doors quietly. There were layers of abuse. I carried on drinking. At twenty-nine I went into rehab. Reality hit me. I lived with a stock-broker, musicians, scientists, I had great lovers, all blonde and blue-eyed. I found women liked me—I'm dark and have jet-black hair. I was also assertive. I can be quite aggressive. The boys were always trying to get into your knickers in care, especially when you went to the bathroom.

I remember the names of those in care. Staff came and went. There were no attachments, no cuddles, no birthdays. There was no stimu-lation, no play, no mental welfare, no education, no nursery rhymes, no *Blue Peter*... Just the house and silence. I was only happy when I was not in the same room as her. She beat me so badly I wet myself; and that earned another beating.

When she left—her husband had a heart attack and they retired—another woman came. One day we smashed up the house, trashed everything—every window, door, table, chair, plate and cup. We wrecked the house. Only then did we realise we had freedom—it was fight or flight. We had been so suppressed.

Even today I have to do things in a routine. After she left, it went to the other extreme. There was no structure, so we drank: bottles of sweet Martini—I told the staff it was Lucozade. I drank daily from the age of twelve. One day, I attacked a teacher at school and was expelled. I was taken to a psychiatric hospital in St Alban's and injected with Largactil. When you wake up, it is as if your brain has been erased. I didn't know where or who I was. Mood-altering substances were officially given.

Why did they allow me to drink? I was in pain and denial. You don't know who you are, or even who you are supposed to be. I was brought up in shame. Only the strong survived. Of the kids I was with, one committed suicide, one is in a psychiatric hospital, others in prison.

The second house-mother left. Next was a woman from South Africa who had her own son. A social worker told her she could never do anything with me because I was 'too damaged.' I had never known anyone like this South African. My own sexuality was awakening. She was beautiful and intelligent. And she talked to me. I had a crush on her, but it was a life-changing experience. On my fourteenth birthday she gave me three Rod Stewart records, a record-player and a birthday cake. The only birthday I ever had. Most birthdays and Christmas, children went to some relative or other. Only one or two of us were left. We had nothing.

I would wander off when I could. We were taken on holidays on orange-coloured buses, Borough of Camden on them. The children took their clothes in black bin-liners. Imagine, arriving at a holiday camp. I was on cider, watching James Cagney movies till midnight.

If I had known… We had nothing to compare it with. We were enclosed, separated. The younger children's basic needs were met, but the older ones were on our own. No books, no toys. I was an adult before I was a child. In rehab, they asked me what I would like to become. I have always been artistic—I would like to have been a writer or painter. Art therapy saved my life. At fourteen I had suicidal thoughts. I put it off, thinking I'll do it at eighteen, or twenty-two or whatever—the thought has always been there.

I'm not a victim, in spite of the sexual abuse and lack of care. When I think of this lack of care—it cost £600–£800 in the 1960s and 1970s: what a waste. And then to come out homeless.

One day, cleaning the office, I opened a drawer and stole my file. I couldn't read it, but I recognised the word Holloway. I wanted to be a Jones or a Smith, not a Malik or a Murphy. I got a girl to read it to me. I burnt it then. Reality was too painful. You had to be someone. All my Indianness had gone. What I wanted was to go to Harrods for tea with an English girl.

My mother lived in the Harrow Road, ironically near to the Social Services office. I went into all the pubs, asking if anybody knew my mother. It was a common name—Margaret Murphy. Eventually I met a friend of hers.

I went to see her. I had never seen such poverty. In the home, we had been kept clean and had good meals. This was a broken-down house, damp and dirty. She came to the door, her hair in a towel. [I said], 'Mrs Malik? Sit down'.

She looked at me. 'Who are you?'

'I'm your first-born.'

She fell to pieces. She showed me the court order that she had refused to sign. But she chose alcoholism over her children. I was horrified by where she lived—one room, a bed, a gasfire. It was 1973. She gave me a drink. I wanted a mother/daughter relationship. She couldn't do it. I started taking stuff to her from the home—plates, cups, food. I got caught. I tried to help her but couldn't.

After I was homeless I went to a bed and breakfast in Praed Street. All the dysfunction came back again. I lived in a hotel for £6 a day. I got a job working in the kitchen at Harrods. I would make a pot of tea and pour red wine into it, so I was drinking all day.

But I survived. Between the ages of twenty and thirty I lived with girlfriends. I was great at cooking, cleaning and keeping house, and that was it. I lived with one of the first women stockbrokers. We went to the Seychelles, Caribbean. But my drinking increased, depression got the better of me. In my late twenties, I could not be like these white people. I had no friends from school. I was with her for four years. I got a mortgage in 1989–90. At the time of the poll tax, she palmed off one of her properties on me. If I had stayed with her, I would never have been sober. I was always there, loyal, obedient. I didn't have anything. Girls felt sorry for me, but it wasn't enough. I was good-looking, hot in the bedroom, a good housekeeper. No wonder they didn't want me to leave. I couldn't be emotionally intimate.

Dogs have been my saving grace. I loved them ever since the farm. I left the stockbroker, and I worked for a cleaning company. I got my own business. I made money, but it all went on drugs and alcohol. I'm generous, but lousy with money. My women friends have all been white, middle class, educated. No ragamuffins or ethnic minorities. I was brought up racist. My mother and I are the only whites in the family, all the rest are black.

At thirty-two I fell in love with Clara, a singer, member of a Greek duo. I'd been in rehab, stopped drinking. It opened the flood-gates. Tears, all that had happened. I loved her, but I did what I always do—push people away before they rejected me. Nothing made me happy—not the job, the mortgage. Only dogs.

I was angry while I was in care. Which is worse—rigid structure or being left wild as the wind? At thirty-four I finished with Clara. I was housed by Camden in my flat. I went to do some GCSEs, did an Access course, and went to Middlesex University, Theatre and Drama. I was useless. I didn't fit in. But I blagged my way through. I got my degree, even though I was drinking again. I was thirty-eight, but then I lost eight years as a full-time drunk.

I did stand-up comedy. I was a hit. I had developed a great sense of humour. But at forty-six, I went into rehab for the third time. Six months. And this time it worked. I knew the only other choice was suicide or alcohol.

I've been sober ten years. I've got my home, jobs, dog-walking. I'm independent. I live on my own, I paint and read. I do three hours dog-walking. I've had no relationship for seventeen years. My mother died of alcoholism at forty-five.

I started painting at fifty. It was a compulsion. I just sat and painted and painted. I don't like the outside world. Maybe I am ready for a more mature relationship now, but I'm fifty-eight. It was either university or prison. I have survived, but at what cost!

The slow pace of reform

Reform has always been slothful, resisted by the force of habit or tradition. Following a House of Commons inquiry in 1816, it was found that the Apprentice Act was widely evaded, and many children in cotton-mills were still working from five in the morning till eight in the evening with one hour for meal-breaks.

In the debate preceding legislation in 1819, which would extend protection to all children in factories, Francis Horner said:

That these children were often sent one, two or three hundred miles from their places of birth and separated for life from all their relations, and deprived of the aid which, even in their destitute situation they might derive from their friends—a practice repugnant to humanity, which had been suffered to exist by the negligence of the legislatures. It had been known, that, with a bankrupt's effects, a gang, if he sought to use the term, of these children had been put up for sale, and were advertised publicly, as a part of the property. A most atrocious instance had come before the King's Bench, two years ago, in which a number of these boys, apprenticed by a parish in London to one manufacturer, had been transferred to another, and had been found by some benevolent persons in a state of absolute famine. Another case, more horrible, had come to his knowledge…that, not many years ago, an agreement had been made between a London parish and a Lancashire manufacturer, by which it was stipulated that with every twenty sound children, one idiot should be taken.[59]

The 1819 Cotton Mills and Factories Act prohibited employment of any child under nine in spinning, and limited labour of those under sixteen to twelve hours a day. This, incidentally, reflected a concern common in the nineteenth century—fear that parish children, the illegitimate and outcast, might receive more favourable treatment than the children of honest labourers. No preference must be shown to those who flouted social norms; and if such lessons were lost on reprobate adults, they would devolve upon their children. We still live with the consequences of this. Reformulated in the 1834 Poor Law Amendment Act, as the law of less eligibility, it was reasserted in 2010 in the Coalition's welfare 'reforms'—that no one on benefits should be better off than those in work.

This morbid fear lest any pauper should enjoy a better life than the lowest labourer has long possessed the mind of officialdom. Objecting to the boarding out of pauper children in 1869, Henry Fawcett was concerned that this would:

> ...exercise a demoralising influence which will most powerfully promote the future increase in pauperism. Children sent to healthy country homes; care in selecting foster-parents who will receive 4s. a week, excluding school fees and medical attendance which are also provided by the Guardians as well as 10s. a quarter for clothes. To children who are ill is given an extra allowance in order that they may have nourishing food. None must live in a house where there is an adult lodger. Above the age of seven they must not sleep in a room with a married couple. Children between two and ten must be given to foster-parents of the same religious faith. They must also be supervised. They will be brought up under conditions more conducive to health than a majority of the children of the working class.[60]

Slavery

Slavery, too, was a major generator of orphans; not only the collusion in taking captives between traders and their collaborators in sending countries, but the forcible separation of children from their families. As the end of the slave trade neared in 1807, numbers of children despatched to the plantations of the Caribbean increased to prolong the institution of slavery beyond the cessation of the trade. James Walvin in *Black Ivory*, records:

> Throughout the era of the slave trade, children made up about 34 per cent of the African population. But before 1800 fewer than 20 per cent of slaves carried across the Atlantic were children... But as the slave trade developed, the overall percentage of children found on the slave ships rose quite markedly.[61]

The advantages of shipping children were obvious: more likely to survive the journey, a greater number of their slender bodies could be crammed into smaller space and they would also serve as a source of future slaves. 'Between 1811 and 1867 more than 41 per cent of all slaves shipped across the Atlantic were children.'

Olaudah Equiano, born in 1745, kidnapped by African slave-traders at the age of eleven; sold and resold several times, was taken to Barbados where he was sold again. He later worked on a slave-ship and was sold on to a merchant in Philadelphia. An enterprising individual, he traded on his own account and raised the £40 to buy his freedom in 1766. He then worked on merchant ships, settled in England in 1777 and supported the abolitionist cause.[62]

This is one of the few stories of survivors, since Hugh Thomas observes, 'Any historian of the slave trade is conscious of a large gap in his picture. The slave himself is a silent participant in the account.'[63]

Harriet Beecher Stowe's novel of slavery, *Uncle Tom's Cabin*, not only anticipated the war to come between abolitionists and a slave-owning culture, but also lived up to its subtitle, sympathetically portraying 'life among the lowly'. Its tone of pious sentimentality strikes the contemporary sensibility awkwardly, and makes it harder to appreciate its range and depth. That the term 'Uncle Tom' has become a contemptuous description of black 'collaborators' with their white masters should not hinder appreciation of her portrait of a culture which tore children from their parents, making orphans of them by selling them as separate 'items of property', separations that lasted a lifetime. In any case, Uncle Tom is the very reverse of collaborator: in the face of extreme cruelty and violence, he will not yield his soul to any earthly master, preferring death. His earthly quietism has nothing to do with acceptance of slavery.

It is significant that in Russia *Uncle Tom's Cabin*, constantly reprinted up to the time of the Revolution, appeared in fresh editions in the 1920s and 1930s: the book spoke to people in the Soviet Union of violent disruption of family life in purges, deportations, summary executions and arbitrary campaigns against 'enemies of the state'.

Slavery's mirror-image

A bitter coda to this trade is the mirror-image of these voyages of despair: the present-day movement in the opposite direction—people seeking release from servitude, debt and hunger *at home*, in former colonial possessions, by migration to rich Western countries. These, too, involve poignant separations, as well as elective orphanings, which often bring, not prosperity and contentment, but cruelty and early death, as has been frequently seen on the beaches of southern Europe.

There is another cruel historical echo in such journeys.

Just as it was widely argued that slavery released people from the darkest savagery and brought them into the clear light of Christian truth, so the rhetoric of a 'better life' promised to children of dereliction in Britain by their transfer to the colonies, promised a fresh start in 'new' countries, with unpolluted air, soaring mountains and rolling prairies. Such children were promised, not the 'plum cake' which beguiled Robert Blincoe, but unlimited opportunities to 'get on in the world.' That many were exploited and abused in desolate farmlands where they were without friends was not part of the prospectus of what came to be called 'philanthropic abduction'; a term that might have appealed to the defenders of slavery.

The forced orphaning of children severed from families who loved them has resonance in our time. The better life which beckons people from the war-scarred landscapes of the Middle East, parts of Africa and South Asia, is now an iconography of luxury, ease and prosperity which the 'developed' West has tirelessly projected to an admiring world which it has sought to re-make in its own shining image. But even when they have followed the disinterested advice of their mentors, these countries are still ravaged by insufficiency, violence and disease; and have, in consequence, sent many of their children—not their unwanted, but their most cherished—to seek an elusive better world.

Strife in the countries they leave creates new orphanings. Parents, killed by sectarians, civil war or criminal gangs, leave their children to fend for themselves in informal camps and enclosures of unbelonging, from Calais to Lesbos, Lampedusa to Zaatari in Jordan (the country's fourth biggest city), and to swell the population of Turkey's cities. Poor families in Africa have also smuggled their children through gaps in the fortifications of Europe—to relatives, neighbours or acquaintances—where some have also experienced bizarre new forms of orphanage.

This reversal of the slave trade is worse than the accidental loss of parents, since it is inflicted by the parents themselves, who voluntarily send away their children, poor human sacrifices, to ambition and hope.

Orphans of hope

A woman living in France, a French citizen, visits her relatives in Ivory Coast. She offers to take one of their children to France, to give her an education and a fuller life. The parents are happy: who doesn't dream of their child going to the West, and returning, doctor or teacher, happy and rich, to share her good fortune with kin and community?

One such child was Victoria Climbie. Her great-aunt, Marie-Therese Kouao, took her to Paris in 1998. Kouao was divorced, living on social security benefits in France with her three sons. In Paris, Victoria failed to attend school, and became the subject of a Child at Risk Emergency Notification. A social worker observed 'a difficult mother and child relationship', for such Kouao claimed it was. When she left France, she owed money fraudulently claimed from the social security system.

They travelled to England. Kouao told social services she wanted to improve her English, to upgrade her work with an airline in Paris. She was elegant, well-dressed and forceful. The contrast with the waif she brought in her wake, ill-clad, wearing a wig and malnourished, seemed to astonish no one.

Within eleven months of arriving in England, Victoria Climbie was dead. Admitted to hospital in February 2000, her temperature was too low to be recorded by a hospital thermometer. She had 128 injuries. Transferred to intensive care, she did not survive the day.

Kouao boarded a bus one day, and talked to the driver, Carl Manning. Within days she had moved into his one-room flat. Victoria was an embarrassment, no longer necessary for claims upon the welfare system. Ill-treated and incontinent, she was banished from her sofa bed to sleep in the bath. Later, placed in a plastic bag, her hands and legs tied, she was fed like an animal. Twice she was hospitalised on suspicion of non-accidental injury. The contact between Kouao (ostensibly the child's mother) and four social service departments, the police child protection service, two hospitals, and various evangelical churches, one of which tried to exorcise the evil spirits believed to be possessing Victoria, failed to rescue her from the real demonic possession—that of her great-aunt and Manning.

The welfare system failed to identify Victoria's suffering. Rarely spoken to by social workers, these saw the 'mother' as their client, who was plausible and controlling. She claimed that Victoria's injuries were self-inflicted, and her apparent middle-class status forestalled closer questioning, which a less articulate migrant might attract. Discrepancies in her stories were not checked: she said she was recently widowed, and Manning was a friend; he and his fiancée were accommodating her and Victoria temporarily. The photograph in Victoria's passport was not hers. It was of a child called Anna, whom Kouao originally wanted to take to Paris, but whose parents had second thoughts. She nevertheless called Victoria Anna: in an eerie echo of the fate of Victorian orphans, even her name was not her own.

Victoria was virtually invisible: rare interactions with social workers were limited to a greeting. All that remains is her dazzling smile and her appalling injuries. When Victoria was seen with her 'mother', the fact that she sprang to attention, the absence of an affective bond, the fear and incontinence the child showed in Kouao's presence, were ascribed to culturally determined characteristics—'respect and obedience towards elders'.

The inquiry, like those that preceded it into the deaths of other children—Kimberly Clark, Jasmine Beckford, Maria Colwell—was a penitential document, committed to the never-again principle, so that the violent death of a child may light the way to a more humane future. It was, however, more searching than previous inquiries. The picture that emerged was of numerous functionaries—social services, the NHS, police, housing department officials, who came, often briefly, into contact with the case, and of an uncoordinated, chaotic system, in which no one's judgment took precedence over procedures, which were, for the most part, followed perfunctorily. Inadequate resources, constant restructuring of children's services, ill-trained personnel, high turnover of demoralised staff, excessive dependency upon short-term agency employees, overwork, and consequently, poor communications and record-keeping, created a system which determined the fate of the child.

The trajectory of urban nomads like Kouao is a tragic example of a globalisation which kindles a desperate desire in the poor of the earth to reach the shores of Atlantis. Victoria's parents were eager to sacrifice their beautiful daughter, who became a for-profit orphan of a false foster-mother. In a touching effort to make something meaningful of her death, they started a fund to establish a school close to their home, so parents will not send their children to distant countries for the sake of an education: for the 305 days that she lived in London, Victoria was never enrolled in any school.

The outcry after the event had a profoundly unnerving effect upon social services departments in Britain. The numbers of children taken into care rose, as social services departments 'erred on the side of caution' in the official phraseology of what happens after any public scandal over the death of a child known to social services. In a paradox created by the mysterious liaison between capitalism and welfare, yet more pseudo-orphans were generated by this tragedy.

5

AFTER 1834

Professional orphan-makers

Historically, the condition of orphan was created by low life expectancy, famine and disease; although the state has also been complicit—in war, in penal laws, transportation and capital punishment, which robbed children of parents. But systematic and wilful orphanage had to await the deepening of industrial society in Britain.

If the report of the Poor Law Commission of 1832, which investigated existing provision for the poor, exposed many examples of cruelty and mistreatment of poor orphans in institutions, the Amendment Act, which followed two years later, would furnish even more material for the zeal of reformers.

The Commissioners, for example, found the workhouse in Grimsby 'in a filthy condition', and described the condition of one inmate in particular:

> ...an unfortunate lad of eighteen or twenty. I was shown the sleeping place of this poor wretch in an outhouse in the yard, with a very damp brick floor, half of which he had pulled up; his bed a heap of filthy litter, with a miserable rug full of holes for covering; his clothing, though in the middle of winter, consisted of nothing

but a long shirt of sacking; and a leather strap with a chain fastened to the wall was in a corner, to make him fast when he was unruly. The whole presented a spectacle alike disgraceful to a civilized country and to the parish where it exists.[1]

Orphans of other ideologies

Reports of such conditions did not end with the nineteenth century. Cathy Feierson, and Semen Samuilovich Vilenski recorded conditions in Soviet orphanages that strike the British reader with a shock of recognition.[2] Revolution and war left some 300,000 orphans by 1917. Ten years after the Bolshevik seizure of power, there were an estimated six million children without parents—survivors of the 1921–22 famine, of the purge of Social Revolutionaries, of the families of Orthodox priests, later of 'saboteurs' and Trotskyists, the displacement of recalcitrant nationalities, war on Kulaks and other 'enemies of the State.' Conditions in orphanages are reminiscent of Poor Law establishments of the eighteenth and nineteenth centuries, but without the discipline. A report in 1925 stated:

> Conditions in the home in Tula for morally defective children are truly scandalous. There are not enough beds; consequently children sleep two to a bed; for ten beds there are no wooden planks. So that these children have to sleep on metal slats; the mattresses are filthy, the blankets are junk, there are no bed-linens whatsoever... there is a complete absence of any school materials; and there is not enough food.

A note on an orphanage in Omsk surpassed even the horrors of Mr Drouet at Tooting in 1847. 'The children fell victim to smallpox, typhus, cholera. Dead bodies were stored on the verandah of the orphanage until there were so many they had to be taken away and cremated.' In the purges of 1937 and 1938, 1.4 million children lost at least one parent to execution. In labour camps for political dissidents and 'state enemies', there also existed a population of orphans, street-urchins and homeless children. They lived under the bunks on which prisoners slept, unfed, naked... These were the forgotten street-children, often convicted of vagrancy or petty theft, children who had lost their parents—killed, starved to death or driven abroad with the White Army. By 1925, there were an estimated 80,000 children on the streets of Moscow, more than the most pessimistic assessment of observers in Victorian London.

Echoes of the capitalist Poor Law in the Socialist utopia do not end there. Many children whose parents had been arrested as 'enemies of the people' had no relatives willing to take them in, since they were afraid of the social stigma. In an even more brutal analogy with the administrators of the Poor Law in England, Soviet authorities feared the 'taint' of parents executed or removed to camps and prisons might also be heritable. Just as the 'taint' of pauperism pursued children in Britain, the stigma of political 'deviancy' hung over the youth of Soviet Russia. Many orphans were gathered into institutions, often structures requisitioned from 'bourgeois' occupation—semi-derelict mansions, shells of habitations of the old regime. In the Soviet republics of Russia, Ukraine and Byelorussia in 1921, there were 1,701 orphanages. By 1933 there were 2,588. These housed 147,289 and 345,836 children respectively.[3]

Consequences of the Poor Law Amendment Act

Within five years of the 1834 Act almost 100,000 people were in the workhouse, 47,767 of them children. Some had entered the house with their parents, from whom they were separated on admission, although children under seven were allowed to remain with the mother. Adults were segregated by sex. Mothers were expected to have reasonable access to their older children, including 'a daily interview'.[4] Other orders stated that, 'workhouses in or near populous towns commonly contain boys and girls between the ages of twelve and fifteen, whom it is more expedient to class with the adult men and women than with the other boys and girls.'

About half the children were orphans or had no known close relative. They undertook supervised labour in the workhouse, including help with nursing the sick or impotent, but were permitted no position of responsibility which might threaten the good order and discipline of the house.

Whatever the abuses of the Old Poor Law, it had provided a certain security for the people; a condition that jarred against the new faith in an abrasive laissez-faire. Indeed, the 8,000 pages of the Report of the Poor Law of 1834 provided evidence for views already conceived by those who produced it: a denunciation of the mendacity and mendicity of paupers and the labouring poor, as well as of the venality of the more lowly administrators of the Poor Law. Indeed, the same themes also furnished the Coalition Government in 2010 and its Conservative successor with rhetoric, no doubt modernised for our enlightened age, but unmistakeable in its source. It echoed the conviction that those 'on benefit' were idlers, cunning and workshy, ready to live at public expense for doing nothing; that the true victims of social injustice were taxpayers, at whose expense the poor were enjoying a high life of daytime television, sleep, drugs and drink.

Punitive propaganda

In the nineteenth century, the persuasive powers of politicians, churchmen, writers and bureaucrats were deployed to demonstrate the beneficent effects of laissez-faire. The free market, left to its own workings, would create harmony between supply and demand, and ultimately, eliminate poverty. An influential proponent of this view was Harriet Martineau, Whig translator of Auguste Comte, early enthusiast of weaning people from dependency and restoring them to that sturdy independence once apparently characteristic of the British. In her publications, she extolled the harsh law of 1834; in her stories, she was at pains to show the favourable outcome of a regime of severity in the workhouse.[5]

One story, set in a small seaside town, has, as protagonists, two orphans, Harriet and Ben, whose mother is dead and whose father was drowned at sea. The children are taken from the parish by an idle fisherman and his wife for one shilling and sixpence each a week. "'Tis little enough, but you must get work out of them to make it answer…They ought to be able to do a deal at their age.' The children are aged ten and nine. Mr Barry, a newcomer to the community, 'a man of small fortune', finds 'only drunkenness in the streets, idleness on the downs, discontent in the farm-house and pining-away in the hovel, but fraud, spreading from the transactions of the overseer's office till it tainted all the deals of the place.' The high poor-rate is driving people of substance away from the town. Mr Barry takes over as overseer of the poor. He withholds rent from cottagers and the customary supplement to their wages. Some accept the alternative of the workhouse; but there they find no pay for the labour of stone-cutting or breaking bones with a hammer. There is only bread and water, no beer, tobacco or tea. The paupers complain it is worse than prison. They are told they are free to leave. Next morning, they quit the workhouse, and miraculously, find work felling trees, selling limpets, collecting and selling wild birds' eggs, picking pebbles for the road or sand for domestic use.

The orphans, meanwhile, set to work with relish, gathering grass for plaiting and rushes to make lights. They try to do good and please their foster-parents. Harriet prays 'to her parent, the parent of the orphan.'

The workhouse master is instructed, 'You will always bear in mind the rule that they (the paupers) are to have whatever comes below the limit of what is enjoyed by the independent labourers who help to support them.' The story expresses nostalgia for a time when, 'private charity visited the fatherless and the widow in their affliction, and relieved them of worldly cares till the mind had become fit once more for exertion'; but that happy era was 'before parish interference had stepped in to close the hearts and hold back the hands of neighbours for each other.' A fisherman is drowned, but the widow and her five children do not have to enter the workhouse, because neighbours take in the children and provide food and she is exempt from 'being exposed to the blight of a corrupted legal charity.'

The foster-mother is confined and Harriet looks after the baby. 'The three weeks during which Harriet held the office of manager at home did more to make a woman of her than all the tasks, troubles and pleasures of the preceding years.' The orphans prove their worth; and when the foster-mother dies, they bear up the desolate father and maintain the household. Offered assistance from the parish the children proudly refuse it. 'I do not see why there should not be plenty such as Ben and me, if orphans were timely taught and tended in some place out of the workhouse. In the workhouse they do not know whom to look up to, to thank and repay for the care of them, and so, too often, grow up thankless.'

The children look after the home, help bring up the children, pay the rent and actually contribute five pence to the poor-rate. The parish prospers. People of quality move back, private charity ensures bequests to care for genuine paupers, the old, impotent and lame. The neighbours do the rest, and in the end, the workhouse is empty. The combined forces of morality and market have led to universal self-reliance; the fiction of the propagandist is at one with the ideological fiction.

Orphan stories

The reality of orphan lives had little to do with the idealised creatures of Martineau. Orphans abandoned in public places were occasionally rescued by strangers. Ellen Barlee tells of two foundlings.[6] One was discovered by a soldier in the water at Southsea. Revived, she was taken in by some charitable ladies, who baptised her Minnie Bath. From there she went to the workhouse, and later, to Brockham, a home founded by the

Honourable Mrs Albert Way, near Dorking. There she was renamed Marina. A second girl was renamed by the same institution as Terrena. She was found by a labourer on his way to work at five o'clock one morning. He heard a cry, looked round and saw nothing. Hearing another cry, he noticed a loose turf, which he pulled aside. It revealed a female infant buried alive. She was taken immediately to the workhouse, where she was called Eliza Towpath, after her place of interment, before being received at Brockham, where she acquired her new classical name.

Fragments reach us about the condition of orphans of the past. Margaret Pelling records that the census of Norwich in 1570 described poor children as young as six as 'idle', implying a more desirable alternative, and noted the occupations of working children of both sexes around that age.[7] Alexandra Shepard notes that Fraunces Goosey (aged ten) and Amy Goosey (aged four), daughters of the lately deceased Thomas Goosey, 'having no means or friends' to maintain them, were bound apprentices in Southampton to a victualler and a serge weaver respectively.[8] It was reported from the Royal Foundation School of Queen Anne that the—evidently luxuriant—hair of a little girl was cut and sold for £4, to be kept for her at 5 per cent interest 'until such time as she should go out into the world.' A child from Victorian London, taken on a holiday to the countryside, gazed with awe upon some swans swimming in the river and asked if 'these were angels.' Florence Davenport-Hill tells of a girl who went to service being called stupid, because she did not know the names or uses of kitchen articles: she could not understand grate- or candle-stick cleaning, because the workhouse had been artificially lighted and heated by gas.[9] Some children born in the workhouse died in their youth without ever seeing the world outside. Davenport-Hill tells of, 'a girl sent to her first place and supplied with a candle on going to bed. She came down again with a request that her mistress would be so kind as to show her the tap to turn out the light, as she could not find it.' She had been brought up solely with gaslight.

Vivid images stand out in accounts of the orphan experience. Thomas Pennant, writing of boys who 'beat hemp under the eye and lash of a taskmaster, from eight till four in winter and from six to six in summer';[10] or Crabbe, describing the infant abandoned to the parish 'a slave of slaves, the lowest of the low' (that he subsequently made good was certainly an exception);[11] the teeth of the poor drawn to furnish the mouths of the rich; children of the workhouse with sacks tied to their feet against the cold for labour on farms; the excitement of apprentices in November when the pig was killed and salted down for winter meat.

Two orphan girls broke the windows of the workhouse, so that they might be sent to gaol, since the food allotted to felons was reputed better than that offered to paupers. The theft of a child did not become illegal until 1814. Hugh Cunningham quotes the case of a woman indicted for feloniously receiving a child's cap and gown.[12] She had arranged for the abduction of the child and then passed it off as her own. The Chair of the Bench told the jury that they should take no cognisance of the theft of the child, but only of the clothes it was wearing. In 1761, a woman who put out the eyes of two children with whom she went begging was sentenced to two years in prison.

Orphan institutions

In what Charles Dickens called 'The Paradise at Tooting', the Infant Poor Establishment run by Mr Drouet on behalf of the Guardians of thirteen London unions, an outbreak of cholera in 1848 killed 180 children out of a total of 1,372, twice the number the institution was supposed to accommodate.[13] A verdict of 'manslaughter' was returned against Drouet, of 'negligence' against the Guardians of the Holborn Union and of inadequate supervision by the central Poor Law authorities. The children testified they had not enough to eat and could not get as much water as they wanted. They 'had no one to complain to' and were frightened, since children who objected were beaten or flogged. They slept in close, unhealthy dormitories. Children examined by surgeons of the Royal Free Hospital showed a complexion 'pale and sallow', the protuberant belly 'characteristic of scrofulous children'. There were cases of scabies or itch, and 'those cutaneous affections which arise from a low state of the system.'

When cholera broke out, the children were placed four to a bed to contain the infection. Dickens reported, 'The dietary of the children is so unwholesome and insufficient, that they climb secretly over the palings, and pick out scraps of sustenance from the tubs of hog-wash. Their clothing by day and their covering by night are shamefully defective. Their rooms are cold, damp, dirty and rotten.'

The scandal was heightened by favourable reports of Mr Drouet's 'farm' by the Guardians of the Holborn Union and of the twelve other unions whose pauper infants dwelt there. Indeed, a hundred and fifty investigations had taken place in the course of a year, by some three or four hundred gentlemen, 'selected', as *The Tablet* reported, 'for parish functions on account of their supposed aptitude; by men of business, men of science, men of religion; and yet they and all of them are unable to see anything but matter of praise and eulogy.' Their enthusiasm had been on public display for the 'healthy and satisfactory state' of the children, 'their comforts attended to', the 'generally healthy and cleanly appearance of the children', 'food of a wholesome and nutritious quality.'

The invisibility of the suffering of children to those charged with their oversight has a long history. They were a different order of humanity from that among which these functionaries moved; and, convinced that pauperism was contagious (in this it resembled cholera), they were easily satisfied that the meagre commons and density of occupation at Norwood were suited to the modest needs of infants in their station of life.

In a parliamentary debate that followed in 1849, it appeared that all but one of the unions had withdrawn their children from the home. The Union of Chelsea reported to the Poor Law Board that, notwithstanding every endeavour on their part, they had been unable to find a suitable place:

> The workhouse was already full, and the owners of private property were naturally unwilling to receive into that property persons coming from an establishment where the cholera had existed. The number of children now at Mr Drouet's was 223, consisting of those belonging to the Chelsea union, and other parishes, who had laboured under cholera, but were now convalescent, although they had not yet been certified as in a fit state to be removed.

In April 1849, Drouet was tried at the Old Bailey for manslaughter. The report from the trial stated it was:

> ...clear that the death (of James Andrews, one of the children who perished) [was] consequent of the visitation of the cholera, and not caused by any neglect of duty on the part of Mr Drouet. No evidence has been adduced to show that the child might not have died of the cholera if that treatment had not been exhibited, and in the absence of any such evidence, in his opinion, in point of law, the prisoner ought to be acquitted.[14]

Drouet retired to Margate, where he died three months later of 'disease of the heart and dropsy'.

Such events presage similar enquiries in our time; not in relation to pestilence, but rather to human visitations—the 'epidemics' and 'outbreaks', the 'contagion', 'the rash of cases' of child abuse. The language of sickness persists: although such things are a result of human agency, they remain as mysterious and unaccountable as circumstances attending cholera in the early Victorian period.

Child abuse: a contemporary epidemic

Following disclosures that Jimmy Savile, famous for his charitable work, and much lauded by politicians, luminaries and royalty, had systematically abused hundreds of children during his time at the BBC and in work for the National Health Service, further inquiries revealed the involvement, not only of other celebrities, but also of the staff of children's homes, religious institutions and local authority institutions. Most victims, powerless, over-awed or disbelieved by authority, had maintained their secret, often with disastrous consequences to their own psychological and sexual wellbeing, well into adult life. Many were wards of the state or under the protection of organisations that not only failed to shelter them, but actually exploited them with, until recently, apparent impunity: the heirs of those who had been for centuries treated with punitive disregard by the state.

An Independent Inquiry into Child Sexual Abuse was set up by the British government in 2014, as the catalogue of 'historic abuse' expanded. In the first two years of the inquiry, there were four heads. Two of them resigned because of alleged 'closeness to the Establishment'—in other words members of government who held positions of responsibility for depart-ments concerned with child welfare—and the fourth because, as a New Zealander, she felt insufficiently familiar with British law. The present Head, Professor Alexis Jay, is looking into thir-teen organisations in which abuse is alleged to have occurred. The relative zeal with which this is being pursued is advertised as a measure of the 'progress' we have made in response to generations of the undefended and unprotected; but it also shows how traditional attitudes live on, even in an ostentatiously child-centred culture.

And even this change of heart is regarded with suspicion by some victims of abuse who have no faith in the investigation. Among them is the Shirley Oaks Survivors Association, whose members have refused to give evidence. They take exception to the present Chair who, after a lifetime in social work, they feel, will be unable to present an impartial account of organisations in which social workers failed to keep watch on places to which they sent children.[15] Shirley Oaks was an eighty-acre site of cottage-style homes, opened in 1904 by the Bermondsey Board of Guardians for four hundred children, many orphaned, abandoned or neglected. The movement for redress against systematic abuse was started by Raymond Stevenson, who was in the home from the age of two until he was eighteen. Since he set up the survivors' movement, almost 700 former inhabitants of the homes have made themselves known. Lambeth Council superintended the institution, which closed in 1983. A network of abusers found their way into employment, overseeing the welfare of some of the most vulnerable—and abused—children in society. A senior housefather was jailed for twelve years in 2016 for the abuse of boys over a twenty-three year period, some of the time at Shirley Oaks. He is the fourth former member of staff to have been convicted. The site, which was sold off and 'developed' is now known as Shirley Oaks Village, a complex of new houses, flats and parkland; 'landscaped' like many other monuments to cruelty and exploitation.

The humanitarian monopoly of the present

We are mistaken if we believe that our 'concern' for the ill-treatment of poor children is a reflection of progress and that such behaviour went unchallenged in the past.

The author of *Old Bailey Experience, Criminal Jurisprudence & The Actual Working of Our Penal Code Laws* describes the perfunctory and contradictory machinery of the legal system.[16] On the effect of an Act that punished with death 'stealing in a shop or lifting anything of a counter with intent to steal', he cites the case of:

> …one Mary Jones [who was] executed whose case I shall just mention: it was at the time when press-warrants [legitimising the enforced induction of men into the military] were issued, on the clamour about the Falkland Islands. The woman's husband was pressed, and their goods seized for some debt of his, and she, with two small children, turned into the streets a-begging. 'Tis a circumstance not to be forgotten, that she was very young (under nineteen), and most remarkably handsome. She went to a linen-draper's shop, took some coarse linen off the counter, and slipped it under her cloak; the shopman saw her, and she laid it down: for

this she was hanged. Her defence was (I have the trial in my pocket) 'that she had lived in credit, and wanted for nothing, till a press-gang came and stole her husband from her; but since then she had no bed to lie on; nothing to give her children to eat, and they were almost naked; perhaps she might have done something wrong, for she hardly knew what she did.' The parish officers testified the truth of this story, but there had been a good deal of shop-lifting about Ludgate—an example was thought necessary— and this woman was hanged for the comfort and satisfaction of shopkeepers about Ludgate-street. When brought to receive sentence, she behaved in such a frantic manner, as proved her mind to be in a distracted and desponding state; and the child was sucking at her breast when she went to Tyburn… It was for no injury but for a mere attempt to clothe two naked children by unlawful means. Compare this with what the state did, and what the law did. The state bereaved the woman of her husband and the children of their father; who was all their support; the law deprived the woman of her life and the children of their remaining parent, exposing them to every danger, insult and merciless treatment, that destitute and helpless orphans suffer.

This was yet another way in which the state created orphans. Such children were rarely at the centre of the literature, but existed as an afterthought, as in 'widows and orphans', or 'the children of the poor and orphans', a pathetic coda of humanity trailing behind the principal players, insubstantial wraiths into whose parenthetical status small enquiry was ever made.

The Book of the Bastiles

From its introduction the Act of 1834 prompted opposition. In his *Book of the Bastiles*, which he called—perhaps prematurely— a history of the working of the New Poor Law, G R W Baxter published in 1841 a compendium of newspaper reports, extracts from speeches and parliamentary debates.[17] Much is angry polemic, but it shows how the policy was viewed, both by opponents and supporters. It contains considerable detail on the treatment of children. James Bronterre O' Brien—fiery and uncompromising member of the Chartist 'physical force' faction—wrote in the movement's newspaper, *Northern Star* on 1 August 1838:

> I see in *The Times* this day a statement to the effect, that, in the Hartismere Union, a pauper boy named Quentin, between eleven and twelve years of age, having watched the mouse-trap set in the men's attic, secured a mouse from it, and skinned, roasted and ate it in the men's sitting-room in their presence. Mott, the Assistant-Commissioner says that the Governor of the Hartismere Union Workhouse considers this to have been a mere 'lark'; but a Mr Rodgers asserts that it can be distinctly proved and by a person (not a pauper) who interrogated the boy on the subject within twenty four hours after the roasting that hunger was his inducement for having eaten the mouse, etc.

Most inquests on deaths in the workhouse state 'Died by the visitation of God'. So numerous and frequent were these occurrences that it can only be concluded that God, although omnipresent, showed a particular delectation for these grim institutions, many of which he perhaps, in view of their architecture, mistook for tabernacles.

The reports have a Dickensian irony. One declares:

> A lad of not more than ten years of age was charged by policeman Downey of the B Division, with an offence which has been frequently considered at this office as of a most dreadful nature, that of being found sleeping in the open air. The policeman stated, that he had crouched himself under the portico of St George's Hospital, but that situation afforded him little protection against the rain, which at this time was falling in torrents; and upon the prisoner not being able to give an account of himself, he took him down to the station-house. The boy, who shivered with cold when placed before the Magistrate, said that his name was George Fisher. He did not recollect his mother, but he knew very well that his father had been transported. Mr Gregoire: 'For what offence was he transported?' The boy burst into tears and said for breaking machinery in Buckinghamshire. Since his father had been transported he had not

a friend in the world. He was willing to do all he could for himself and had come up to London to seek work. Mr Gregoire: 'Before you left Bedfordshire how did you live?' The lad replied 'As well as I could. I did jobs; sometimes slept in the manger, sometimes in the yard.' Nobody cared about me.' Mr Gregoire: 'Did you apply to the overseers of the Union workhouse?' 'I did, but I could get no relief.' Mr Gregoire: 'To whom did you apply?' 'I went to Hobbs, a publican at Woburn; he is one of the overseers; but before I went there they told me if I hadn't friends it was of no use; and I found it was true, for they would not give me a halfpenny, and so I came by Mr Jolly's waggon to London.' Mr Gregoire: 'Did you apply to the Guardians of the Poor?' 'I did not, for I was left without friends, nobody helped me.' The policeman Downey, said that he was himself born in Bedfordshire, and only lately having joined the 'Force', he knew and could swear, that the overseer in that part of the country wouldn't allow a destitute man or woman to be introduced to the Guardians, no matter as to the business they might have with them. Mr Gregoire ordered the poor lad to receive immediate relief, and that a few shillings should be given to him from the poor-box. He would himself take care that he should be sent back to the Union workhouse authorities, in order that he might receive the relief due to him.'[18]

The zeal of overseers in preventing people—particularly those who had no one to defend them—from receiving that to which they were entitled, casts its punitive shadow on the present, where 'sanctions' and refusal of benefits (our version of relief) are regularly imposed, today in the name of the 'taxpayer', the equivalent of the payer of the poor-rate, and one deemed to receive no support from the contribution (in the iconography he is always male) received from the state.

Mayhew's orphans

As the nineteenth century progressed the subjective world of the children of poverty opened up. Children dominated the urban landscape: by the 1850s more than a third of the population of Britain was under fifteen. As the well-to-do began to restrict family size, the poor showed no such inclination. A restrained panic underlay fear that the numbers of the poor would increase indefinitely. If 'breeding' was what the upper classes possessed, breeding was what the lower classes did.

Many descriptions of street-children survive. Their orphaned state is often mentioned in passing, rather than as the central event of the child's experience. Of the street-people Henry Mayhew interviewed for his *London Labour and the London Poor* many orphans found themselves on the streets or in cheap lodging-houses after an irregular or disrupted childhood. Among them were two flower-sellers.[19]

Particular commodities were associated with various child street-sellers. Girls and women sold comestibles, especially fruit and vegetables, while boys and men dealt in harder objects— wood, scrap metal, glass and paper, bones for industrial use. Both boys and girls were 'rag-pickers', a word still used in South Asia for those who recycle waste materials. Flower girls were ambivalent: men bought flowers for sweethearts and lovers, at the time of assignations, not all of them innocent. On the other hand, flowers, symbols of purity and of contact with a fast-vanishing countryside, brought a whiff of innocence and rural simplicity to city streets. Mayhew insists on the respectability of his girls.

Mayhew observed that Sunday is the busiest day for flower-selling. Girls outnumbered boys by about eight to one, the age of girls varying from six to twenty for flower-selling, while most boys are under the age of twelve.

He evokes two orphan flower-sellers, the elder fifteen, the younger eleven:

> Both were clad in old, but not torn, dark print frocks and they wore old broken black chip bonnets. The older had a pair of worn-out shoes on her feet, the younger was barefoot, but trotted along in a gait both quick and feeble—as if the soles of her little feet were impervious, like horn, to the roughness of the road.

They lived in a street near Drury-lane, a lodging-house inhabited by street-sellers and street-labourers:

The room they occupied was large, and one dim candle lighted it so indifferently that it seemed to exaggerate the dimensions. The walls were bare and discoloured by damp. The furniture consisted of a crazy table and a few chairs; in the centre of the room was an old-fashioned four-post bedstead of the larger size. This bed was occupied nightly by the two sisters and their brother, a lad just turned thirteen. In a sort of recess in a corner of the room was the decency of an old curtain—or something equivalent, for I could hardly see in the darkness—and behind this was, I presume, the bed of the married couple. The three children paid two shillings a week for the room; the tenant, an Irishman out of work, paying two shillings and ninepence, but the furniture was his, and his wife aided the children—their trifle of washing, mended their clothes when such a thing was possible, and suchlike.

The elder girl said, 'I sell flowers, sir; we live almost on flowers when they are to be got. I sell, and so does my sister, all kinds, but it's very little use offering any that's not sweet. I sell primroses when they're in, and violets, and wall-flowers and stocks, and roses of different sorts, and pinks and carnations, and mix flowers, and lily of the valley, and green lavender and mignonette (but that I do very seldom) and violets again at this time of the year; for we get them in both spring and winter…The best sale of all is, I think, moss-roses. We do best of all on them. Primroses are good, for people say "Well here's spring again for a certainty." Gentlemen are our best customers. I've heard they buy flowers to give to the ladies. Ladies have sometimes said 'A penny, my poor girl, here's three half-pence for the bunch.' Or they've given me the price of two bunches for one; so have gentlemen. I never had a rude word said to me by a gentleman in my life. No, sir, neither lady nor gentleman ever gave me six pence for bunch of flowers. I never had sixpence given to me in my life—never.

I never go among boys. I know nobody but my brother. My father was a tradesman in Mitchelstown, in the County Cork. I don't know what sort of tradesman he was. I never saw him. I was born in London. My mother was a chairwoman and lived very well. None of us ever saw a father. [It was evident that they were illegitimate children, but the landlady had never seen the mother, and could give me no information].

We don't know anything about our fathers. We were all "mother's children." Mother died seven years ago last Guy Faux day. I've got myself and my brother and sister a bit of bread ever since, and never had any help but from the neighbours. I never troubled the parish. O yes, sir, the neighbours is all poor people, very poor some of them. We've lived with her [indicating the landlady by a gesture] these two years, and off and on before that. I can't say how long.'

'Well I don't know exactly', said the landlady, 'but I've had them with me almost all the time, for four years, as near I can recollect, perhaps more. I've moved three times, and they always followed me.' In answer to my inquiries, the landlady assured me that these two poor girls were never out of doors all the time she had known them after six at night. 'We've always good health. We can all read.' [Here they somewhat insisted upon proving to me their proficiency in reading, and having produced a Roman Catholic book, 'The Garden of Heaven', they read very well.]

'I put myself' continued the girl, 'and I put my brother and sister in a Roman Catholic school—and to Ragged school—But I could read before my mother died. My brother can write, and I pray to God he'll do well with it.

I buy my flowers at Covent Garden…I pay one shilling for a dozen bunches, whatever flowers are in. Out of every two bunches I can make three, at a penny a piece. Sometimes one or two over in the dozen, but not so often as I would like. We make the bunches up ourselves. We get the rush to tie them with for nothing. We put their own leaves around the violets. The paper for a dozen costs a penny, sometimes only a halfpenny. The two of us doesn't make less than sixpence a day, unless it's very ill luck. But religion teaches us that God will support us, and if we make less we say nothing. We do better on oranges in March and April I think it is, than on flowers. Oranges keep better than flowers, you see, sir. We make one shilling and ninepence a day on oranges, the two of us. I wish they was in all the year. I generally go St John's Wood way, and Hampstead and Highgate way with my flowers. I can get them nearly all the year, but oranges is better liked than flowers, I think. I always keep one shilling stock money, if I can. If it's hard weather, so bad that we can't sell flowers at all. And so we've had to spend our stock-money for a bit of bread, she (the landlady) lends us one shilling if she has one, or she borrows one of a neighbour, if she hasn't, or, if the neighbour hasn't it, she borrows it at a dolly-shop (the illegal pawnshop). There's two pence a week to pay for one shilling at a dolly, and perhaps an old rug left for it; if it's very hard weather, the rug must be taken out at night-time, or we are starved with the cold. It sometimes has to be put into the dolly again next morning, and then there's two pence to pay for it for the day. We've had a frock in for sixpence and that's a penny a week, and the same for a day. We never pawned anything; we have nothing they would take in at the pawn-shop. We live on bread and tea and sometimes a fresh herring at night. Sometimes we don't eat a bit all day when we're out; sometimes we take a bit of bread with us, or buy a bit….I think our living costs two shillings a week for the two of us; the rest goes in rent. That's all we make.'

The brother earned from one shilling and sixpence to two shillings a week, with an occasional meal, as a costermonger's boy. Neither of them ever missed mass on Sunday.

Among inmates of the workhouse Casual Ward, Mayhew observed of a boy of thirteen:

I can hardly say that he was clothed at all. He had no shirt and no waistcoat; all his neck and a great part of his chest being bare. A ragged cloth jacket hung about him, and was tied so as to keep it together with bits of tape. What he had wrapped round for trousers did not cover one of his legs, while one of his thighs was bare. He wore two old shoes; one tied to his foot with an old ribbon, the other a women's old boot. He had an old cloth cap. His features were distorted somewhat with the cold.

'I was born', he said, 'at a place called Hadley in Kent. My father died when I was three days old, I've heard my mother say. He was married to her, I believe, but I don't know what he was. She had only me. My mother went about begging, sometimes taking me with her, at other times she left me at the lodging-house in Handley. She went in the country, round about Tunbridge and there, begging. We had plenty to eat then, but I haven't had much lately. My mother died at Hadley a year ago. I don't know how she was buried. She was ill a long time, and I was out begging; for she sent me out to beg for myself a good while before that; and when I got back to the lodging-house, they told me she was dead. I had 6d. in my pocket, but I couldn't help crying. I cry about it still. I didn't wait to see her buried, but started on my own account. I met two navvies in Bromley and they paid my first night's lodging; and there was a man passing and going to London with potatoes; and the navvies gave the man a pint of beer to take me up to London in the van, and they went that way with me.

I came to London to beg, thinking I could get more there than anywhere else, hearing that London was such a good place. I begged; but sometimes could not get a farthing all day; often walking about the streets all night. I have been begging about all the time till now. I am very weak, starving to death. I never stole anything. I always keep my hands to myself. A boy wanted me to go with him to pick a gentleman's pockets; but I wouldn't; I know it's wrong, though I can neither read or write. The boy asked me to do it to get into prison, as that would be better than the streets. He picked pockets to get into prison. He was starving about the streets like me. I never slept in a bed since I've been in London, I am sure I haven't. I generally slept under the dry arches at West-street, where they're building houses—I mean the arches for the cellars. I begged chiefly from the Jews about Petticoat-lane, for they give away all the bread that their children leave—pieces of crust and such-like. I would do anything to be out of this misery.'[20]

Baby-farmers

Farming of the poor was a concept familiar in the eighteenth century. Sidney and Beatrice Webb quote a newspaper advertisement announcing 'The Poor to Let.' They could be contracted from the parish to an entrepreneur willing to maintain them at so much a head, or for a lump sum. In the first case it was in the interests of the contractor to keep people out of the workhouse by allowing them a niggardly allowance; in the second he sought to cram as many as possible into the house. The Quaker John Scott deprecated the statute, by means of which, 'the parochial managers are impowered to establish a set of petty tyrants as their substitutes who farming the poor at a certain price accumulate dishonest wealth, by abridging them of reasonable food and imposing upon them unreasonable labour.'[21]

'Baby-farming' was a more specialised version of this. The expression was first used in an article in the *British Medical Journal* in 1867 about the dangers of infanticide caused by mothers leaving their children with nurses, who, for a modest fee, undertook to care for them. Outdoor relief was prohibited to mothers of illegitimate children under the Bastardy Clauses of the 1834 Poor Law, yet they were responsible for maintaining them until they were sixteen. The principal occupation for women was domestic service. They were required to live in attics or basements of the houses where they served. It was impossible to keep their children with them. It became the practice to place the newborn with anyone who would look after them. Over these transactions hovered unspoken bargains between desperate mother and often unscrupulous nurse. Although many nurses were honourable, driven to look after children by poverty; if they did their best, this was often limited by the conditions in which they themselves lived. Others could be trusted to ensure the child would fail to thrive and die.

Infant mortality remained high in the mid nineteenth century: Lionel Rose reports 276 infants found dead in the streets of London in 1870 alone. Women who killed their own children were viewed more leniently than 'baby-farmers' in whose care they expired: the former, seduced and abandoned in a state of what would later be called post-natal depression, while women who murdered the children of others were motivated by greed.[22] It is to be doubted that all Victorian 'baby-farmers'—even some who went to the gallows—were indeed criminal. When rearing children 'by hand' involved the use of dirty bottles and spoons, the onset of diarrhoea, subsequent dehydration and death of the child, were common. Certain notorious baby farmers sentenced to death for the decease of children in their care may have been women trying to survive in circumstances similar to those of the women whose infants died in their custody.

There was no legislation to control the practice. Women advertised in the press, offering to nurse or even adopt an infant. Infants were sometimes slowly starved or dosed with laudanum, their milk watered or mixed with lime.

Although amendments to the Bastardy Clause in 1872 gave mothers a theoretical opportunity to pursue putative fathers, proof of paternity was also required, a condition which made the legislation ineffective. Despite organisations like the Association for the Preservation of Infant Life, the principal influence on public opinion was newspaper reports of sensational examples. Following the case of Margaret Waters who had drugged and killed at least fifteen infants, the Infant Protection Bill was introduced in the House of Commons. It failed, since MPs saw in it an encroachment of the state upon parental responsibility.

Illegitimate children were stigmatised, as though the 'depravity' of the mother was both heritable and contagious. Some orphanages refused them, although a large proportion of orphans were illegitimate. Muller's Orphan House in Bristol—founded by a Prussian immigrant who came to Britain in 1829 to train as a missionary—barred such children.[23] The institution eventually consisted of five barrack-like blocks at Ashley Down, through which more than fifteen thousand orphans passed. It was run solely on Christian principles, and all the workers offered their services freely. The last building closed only in 1958.

Parental responsibility

In 1872 putative fathers were made equally responsible with the mother for the support of bastard children up to the age of sixteen. But the scandal of unregulated care continued. Amelia Dyer became a focus of popular hatred after her conviction and execution in 1896.[24] She had 'adopted' a number of illegitimate babies from their mothers for a fixed sum. She neglected them, and when they died, she threw their bodies into the Thames. In the mid nineteenth century children under a year old made up more than half of murder victims.

The dilemma of the mothers of illegitimate children is illuminated by George Moore's novel, *Esther Waters*, 1894. Abandoned by the baby's father, she hears from the lying-in hospital of a place as wet nurse for a well-to-do family. To do this, her own child must be lodged with a nurse. Esther has to pay for inferior treatment of her own child, while she feeds the rich woman's baby. She learns that the babies of the two previous wet-nurses employed by the household had both died, and she retrieves her child from the baby-farmer, determined not to face the world without him.

Such a situation is common worldwide. Poor women must leave their own children in semi-orphaned neglect to take care of the children of the rich.

Jehanara

Jehanara lives in Lucknow. Her house of jute and wood was in a slum on land belonging to the railway department, under constant threat of demolition. It was, however, convenient for her husband, a cycle-rickshaw driver, to rent the vehicle by the day, and for Jehanara to reach her place of work as a domestic in a nearby well-to-do colony. They had four daughters.

The man became sick, unable to work. Diabetes was diagnosed. Since they could neither afford medicine nor sacrifice the money he earned, he continued to work. Within two years he was dead.

Jehanara's oldest daughter, Asma, was married at the age of fifteen. The others were eleven, seven and four. Income fell to a quarter of what it had been. With no male to protect her, Jehanara felt exposed, and the community, where she had been secure, was now fraught with menace to herself and her girls.

Government was building new houses for what are euphemistically called in India 'the weaker sections' of the population. Eating into old wheatfields on agricultural land the single-storey, one-room houses are isolated. Each has a small kitchen and bathroom. They are not normally within reach of the poorest.

Jehanara, now a widow with three girls, was offered money by her employers towards buying one of these houses. The rest came from the parents of her dead husband who gave their life savings. Few employers of domestic workers take an interest in them once their duties are over. But this non-communal, liberal family wanted to help. Their charity had repercussions of which they knew nothing.

The new house is in a row of ten. Only two or three are occupied. Most residents go out to work, so in the daytime, the rooms are padlocked and appear deserted. The water supply is erratic and the toilet not working. One house was bought by a private doctor, who anticipated a future clientele in the neighbourhood.

We reached Jehanara's house one hot afternoon. The two youngest daughters, aged nine and five, sat in the dust outside the front door, playing with stones. The older, Zubaida, says 'We have no friends here.' Her work is to look after and play with her sister, Farida, keep the house clean, wash the vessels. Jehanara is thirty-six, but looks older; thin, energetic with dark hair and bright mobile eyes. She goes out early, leaving the girls at home all day. There are no schools nearby, and no one supervises them. In the slum Jehanara took them to her work, where she could keep an eye on them. This is now impossible. Jehanara takes two Tempos—(jeep-like shared taxis)—and then walks three kilometres. Her fares eat into the 700 rupees she earns; her employers give leftover food and clothes their own daughters have outgrown. Without this she would find it difficult to survive.

Jehanara takes Esha, the oldest daughter, with her. She claims to do this so she may acquire some domestic skills—cleaning, swabbing and cutting vegetables. This is not the real reason. Esha is at risk where they live, for Esha is now thirteen, at puberty, and approaching marriageable age.

The mother has a bitter choice: she cannot leave Esha at home, because of predatory men who may be around. It is better to leave the two younger ones, because although they, too, are vulnerable, Jehanara imagines—perhaps falsely—they will not attract males roaming the neighbourhood. This new settlement has not yet become a community. Jehanara must also pay Esha's fare to the—now distant—home of her employer.

The poignancy of her position is unbearable: chaperone to the thirteen-year-old, while the two young ones are left alone ten hours a day. In the single room are two plain wooden bedsteads, a TV set, an old sewing-machine, with which Jehanara increases her income when the girls are sleeping. On the bed an orange-coloured bolster and thin bedroll. There are cooking utensils, metal plates and tumblers in the kitchen. A change of clothing hangs on a string between two nails in the brick wall. There are no other possessions.

The younger girls are patient and obedient. They do not open their door to strangers. A neighbour promises to keep watch; but she has a daughter with a disability and her husband drinks, so she has little time from her own sorrows. Jehanara leaves midday food for Zubeida and Farida. The girls do nothing. The environment is a study in sensory deprivation: stone and dust; wheat ripening in the fields, an occasional flash of plumage of a bird from the few trees that remain. Zubeida takes the care of her sister very seriously.

Jehanara is like poor women all over the world, whose desire to look after their children is disturbed by the superior money power of the family she serves. These are kindly and considerate: the husband a lawyer, but his wife is called away to attend kitty parties and meetings with her friends, which make it impossible for her to care for the three young children Jehanara serves. They pay Esha a little money for the help she gives her mother.

But all suffer from their mother's unchosen desertion: the needs of wealth have priority over Jehanara's love for her children, who are alone while she earns the money so they may eat twice a day. Domestic labour is by far the greatest employer of poor women worldwide; but this imposes heavy burdens, which they alone bear. The little girls survive only at the cost of an orphaning inflicted by the most loving of mothers.

Reformers and others

Reformers in Britain castigated the cruel treatment of children of destitution. Their efforts fell short because they were locked within the conventions of their time. Frances Power Cobbe, Christian reformer, addressing the Social Science Congress in Dublin in 1861, advocated a proper training as domestic servants for 'friendless girls' in the workhouse.[25] Sympathetic to those she wished to help, she deprecated the tyranny, less of the mistresses of the more gracious classes than that of a humbler stratum, who are 'as varied in character, for good or evil, as any other human beings, but the possession of such irresponsible power as they exercise over their poor drudges is too often a temptation to great and grievous wrong.' She cites the work of the Bristol Female Mission, which registered and inspected workhouse girls in their place of work; while girls 'never suitable for service' were directed to a cotton factory 'managed by very good people, and where the general morals of the "hands" is unusually high.'

She continues:

> The poor workhouse girl is the child of an institution, not of a mother of flesh and blood. She is nobody's 'Mary' or 'Kate' to be individually thought of—only one of a dreary flock driven about at certain hours from dormitory to schoolroom to workhouse yard. The poor child grows up into womanhood, perhaps without one gleam of affection, and with all her nature crushed down and carelessly trampled on. She has had no domestic duties, no care of a little

brother or an old grandparent, to soften her; no freedom of any kind to form her moral nature. Even her hideous dress and her cropped hair are not her own! Yet she is expected to go out inspired with respect for the property of her employers, able to check her childish covetousness of the unknown luxury of varied food, and clever enough to guess at a moment how to light a fire and cook a dinner and dress a baby and clean a house for the first time in her life.

Whatever tender thoughts were kindled in this observer, it did not occur to her that the workhouse child might be capable of anything other than servitude: social convention had numbed her as completely as it had sunk the child into mute acceptance of the fate foretold in her stigmatised uniform and shorn hair.

In 1869 Ellen Barlee depicted lives of the poor, many of whom were without relatives.[26] In 1862, she records, 359,653 persons received parochial relief in London. There were nearly 5,000 in state asylums and a vagrant population of about 70,000. 'In the year to Lady-Day 1861,' she wrote, '£5,000,000 was spent on the Poor Law system. Of this £2,023,394 was spent on relief. The remainder went on establishments erected for the benefit of the pauper population.'

Barlee visited a refuge—closed shortly after her visit—where she met a woman who:

...at the age of twelve was left an orphan and sent to the Union. Thence she went as maid-of-all-work into a low lodging-house. Young as she was, she discovered, before she had been there a month, that it was no fit place for an honest child. She ran away. Having no home, she passed two or three nights on the streets, and applied for a situation she knew was vacant. They would not take her without a character, so she again wandered about, begging for food. She was recognised by a person who had seen her at her former place, and belonged to the same class of householder; this woman, requiring a servant-girl, offered her the situation, telling her at the same time that it was folly to hope to get into a different kind of place after she had been in the first lodging-house, for no respectable family would take her. She entered this woman's service, without even wages, for the sake of food and shelter....The consequences may well be imagined—for twelve long years she dragged on her life, sharing in and witnessing scenes of the lowest depravity, hating, as she told me, her very existence, and longing to escape from her employers, whom she loathed. It was a useless attempt; she was fettered by the circumstances, that in her outset in life she had been, as a pauper child, heedlessly placed, without sufficient enquiry, by parish Guardians in the hotbed of crime, and that, in her isolated condition, proved the barrier to her after-emancipation. I do not believe the poor wretched girl had ever, during her life, had a kind word addressed to her. I mentioned that I would try to get her into a Home, and she clung to the idea with the grasp of a dying person. She called on me, wrote me the most imploring letters, begging me to redeem my promise, and when I succeeded in obtaining for her admission into a hospital, wrote again to thank me, but to remember The Home I had named. At the last stage of her life, for she was dying, she seemed realize what the *word was meant to be*, and to crave that, in some shape, its influence might be extended to her before she left a world which had brought her so much misery.

The difficulty of placing a girl 'from the Union' came, not only from the want of employment apart from mantle-making, stay-making, glove-making and millinery, but from her 'unfitness' for domestic service. Only people who wanted drudges would accept a workhouse child. Barlee wrote:

We find the brand which stamps the workhouse orphan, commencing in the Union nursery, with bare walls and sunless atmosphere, where infancy is snatched from maternal arms to be consigned to the care of cross, unlovable pauper women. In the workhouse school, the same want of kindliness prevails, till the dull, lethargic mind is unable to receive the promiscuous learning thrown at the doors of the child's frozen heart. We find it following her to the situation in which she is compulsorily placed, when considered of an age to bear the burden of life…In vain does the State foundling look around for affection; there is no eye to respond to its first yearnings for love no bosom in which to nestle, and none to breathe over it the heart's prayer or the pitying sigh.[27]

Domestic service was beyond many workhouse girls. Even if trained to 'habits of sobriety and industry', they were unfamiliar with the utensils and implements used in well-to-do households, were slow to learn, maladroit and 'sullen.' This word recurs frequently in describing workhouse children: from Anglo-Norman French, it means 'solitary' or 'averse to company'; qualities believed to be inherent to the children, but acquired as a result of loveless incarceration.

Boarding-out

Orphan children are described as lost property: unclaimed, reduced to mislaid belongings, scarcely animate, with their doughy face and unresponsive gaze.

Davenport-Hill wrote of the advantages of the boarding-out system.[28] In 1899, she tells the story of Little Dicky, who 'was a queer little chap when he first came', according to his foster-mother:

> ...with sore eyes and so rickety and sickly he couldn't walk no distance, and he was so funny, too, in his ways, running in and telling all the neighbours what we'd got for dinner, and shouting out when my husband came home that *he'd* got a father now. Anyone could see he hadn't been brought up like other children, but he came all right in a year or so. Little Dicky is now second gardener in a nobleman's establishment, having worked himself up to that position. He spends his annual week's holiday at his adopted home like a son of the house.

Even more poignantly, she tells of the ability of boarded-out children to earn their living earlier than they would have done so in an institution, as a result of which they can save money. 'One of Mrs Preusser's girls in Cumberland (taken from Bethnal Green), withdrew her a few weeks before she died of consumption, as she wished that her funeral might be paid for with her own money, bequeathing the remainder to her only brother.'

ORPHANS

Street-arabs of Victorian London

Child labour in the countryside had little of the pastoral or idyllic; indeed, straw-plaiting, lace-making and working in the fields as human scarecrows or picking stones was scarcely less damaging than factory-work. But grim conditions in stony cottages and freezing farmyards did not attract the attention that mills and mines did.

Urban areas were the focus of concern. Throughout the nineteenth century, 'street-arabs', vagrant and unoccupied children were a ubiquitous part of a disturbing city pictography; a frightening incipient criminal class which took its tutelage from 'denizens' of courts and alleys in city slums.

The 'street-arab' sounds exotic, foreign kinship with the disinherited of Empire. The attribution of 'alien' characteristics to wayward children went deep. When I was a child in the 1940s, it was still common for working-class parents to call a badly behaved child a 'little Turk'.

The street-children of Victorian London evoke casual labour, petty crime, rooms sublet to lodgers, a landscape of smoky fog and slimy cobblestones, wharves where the water lapped at rotting wooden piers, scavenging, occasional work in the hop-fields or fruit-picking in Kent, health ruined by lead-works or match factories, the same garments taken in and out of pawn, a pinch of tea for three-farthings, needlework, envelope-folding and bottle-washing, a diet of potatoes, bread and sugar, street-gambling, sleeping in doorways, attics and cellars.

This floating world has its counterparts today. The same images spring to life among the orphaned and outcast on the streets of cities in the South. The children form substitute 'families', reflecting the values of the dominant society and its hierarchies of power.

Today's 'street-arabs'

Early this century I met many children on the Sadarghat, the landing-stage on the Buriganga River in Dhaka, Bangladesh.

Abandoned, if not always orphaned, they organised into informal groups. Their sentiments and relationships were similar to those of Mayhew's London, despite differences in heat and humidity, the feral odour of tanneries among a different domestic detritus of banana peel, overripe mangoes, air vitiated by fumes from second-hand Japanese cars stalled for hours, packs of semi-wild dogs, improvised bonfires of plastic and rubber and unbreathable acrid smoke; shelters of packing cases labelled Bosch or Siemens. The derelict children reincarnate their predecessors in London a century and a half ago.

Crowds of children live on the river terminal, perhaps two hundred. Many runaway or discarded children inhabit travel termini—railway and bus stations, the river *ghat* (steps leading down to the water), since these sites of arrival and departure promise symbolic destinations for those severed from family, the only source of belonging in Bangladesh. No one is responsible for these damaged—sometimes ruined—children, whose destiny is to be soon swallowed up in an adult status that will rob them of even the shallow sympathy their position briefly earns them.

Ismail is about twelve. His family is from Barisal (south Bangladesh), but he does not know where. He says he was born on the terminal. He has one sister but never sees her. He lives and works on Sadarghat as a coolie, earning between twenty and twenty-five *taka* a day (twenty-five cents). He sleeps on the concrete benches and has no other clothes than his black trousers, shiny with wear. Ismail eats twice a day, bread or rice from a stall outside, and works from seven in the morning until ten o'clock at night. The police sometimes beat the children and take from them the small money they earn.

Many children carry plastic bowls which they use for begging. Some wear the empty upturned container on their head. Yusuf Ali is eleven. He has no family. He was studying in a madrasa, but when his mother died, his father abandoned him. He came here three months ago, because he knew other children live here. He sometimes works as a coolie, and begs if there is no work. Even in these impoverished places, crowds are so dense there is always someone who will give the necessities for survival—a *chappati*, a dish of unfinished rice, some fruit, a few *taka*. Yusuf Ali wears a checked *lunghi* and a blue shirt. He is very thin. His eyes are insistent, appealing.

Beauty is ten, a small girl with close-cropped hair. She wears a faded ragged dress, and recalls the street-waifs photographed by Dr Barnardo in the 1870s. Her parents are dead, and she has lived on the *ghat* for three years. She helps the owner of a vegetable stall, earns twenty or thirty *taka* a day, and sleeps on the stone surface of the floor of the terminal. She eats at a stall outside. Beauty has no relatives, but says the children look after one another. With a simple gesture, she says, 'These are my family.' Although the children are competitive in their search for survival, there is also a protective network; and the readiness with which Beauty uses the word 'family' suggests even the outcast reconstitute themselves in the image of the dominant institution. The children recognise in each other the only resource they have. Beauty came to Dhaka with her parents, but both died within a few months. She has no brothers or sisters. She would like to work in a house; she has heard of girls who work as housemaids and have a mat to sleep on under a roof—a modest ambition for exploitative work, but to her, a child lost in the menacing presence of travelling strangers, most of them men, it seems like deliverance.

Similar scenes are found on the railway station at Kamalapur. The dingy station children are part of the landscape. No one looks at them. Even those whose bags they carry scarcely give a passing glance, but hold out two *taka* at arm's length. Here, too, the children have no one but each other; epithelial marks of cuts, knocks from heavy cases, cropped hair, faded garments; silver teeth between dusty lips, mineral eyes of copper or bronze.

Kokon is twelve. He wears a striped shirt and a rough cloth around his shoulders. A bandage covers the lower part of his leg. Two days earlier, a fish barrel fell on him as he was unloading it from the train. He came to Dhaka a year ago and is alone. He has no brothers or sisters. His parents are dead. He sleeps on the station. Today he has so far earned nothing (it is noon). He expects fifteen or twenty *taka* a day, and eats from the stalls outside the station. In the morning he pays three *taka* for *roti* and tea. In the evening rice and vegetables cost five *taka*. Kokon's father fell sick and died, and his mother died in childbirth soon after. He has no clothes other than those he wears. He washes himself in the river.

Alamgir, seven, works and sleeps on the station. From Sylhet, he was brought to Dhaka by a stranger and abandoned on the station; was the stranger paid to rid the family of one mouth to feed? Alamgir has two sisters and four brothers at home. He gets a little money by begging. He eats *roti* with vegetables, but on days when he gets no money he will eat rotten food and discarded fruit. He wears dark grey short pants with an elasticated top. He has no shoes, no shirt; as bereft of belongings as it is possible for a human being to be.[29]

These are a melancholy resuscitation of figures from a Victorian landscape: the same outstretched hands, the supplications of waifs five or six generations ago. There are, of course, other than material differences: not only the colour of their skin, but also, their consciousness of religion. They exhibit, not the 'stolid inexpressive countenances' of Mayhew's children, but the ubiquitous smile of the poor of Bangladesh, the more inexplicable since theirs are also the miseries which afflicted rejects of the casual ward and the dripping arches of London.

The great difference between the forlorn children of Bangladesh and Victorian London is that nineteenth century England saw an army of reformers, philanthropists and social workers, as well as governments anxious about the disruptive potential of youthful vagrants. Governments of the 'developing' world, having observed the successful assimilation by Western countries of threatening populations, have little to fear from them; and accordingly show little interest in their lives. Foreign aid, NGOs and economic growth are the only instruments of their emancipation.

Outcast children

Later in the nineteenth century it was thought necessary that neglected and mistreated children should be removed from their environment, protected against vicious or drunken parents and associates. That pauperism could be eliminated by separating the young from their families was not new; but the nineteenth century inaugurated a great epic of orphan-creation. If parents could not school them to a life of regularity, discipline and Christian morality, others would have to do so, interposing themselves between one generation and the next to reform—and re-form—them in ways in which their biological parents were incapable.

Institutions for abandoned children and for incorrigible youth already existed. In a predominantly agrarian society it was easy to isolate them from families unable to provide them with sustenance. But the early industrial era was the Age of Orphanages, just as it was for the detention of other deviants—lunatics, paupers and criminals, human by-products of the gospel of wealth-creationism.

Orphanages were far from asylums for those without parents. Indeed, the word 'orphan' was treacherous, piously manipulated, less to replace dead parents than to substitute for them the more effective parenthood of charitable institutions and the state. Most children in nineteenth century orphan institutions—up to 80 per cent—had at least one parent living.

Parish children

For a majority of children whose parents had died or deserted or were unable to maintain them, the workhouse remained the first asylum. By 1840 almost half the residents in workhouses were children.

Although the workhouse was supposed to educate its child captives, this was largely ineffective. Teachers were often paupers, illiterate and ill-informed. In the 1840s, unions of parishes were allowed to combine to create District Schools, in which children would be boarders. This would turn boys into diligent workmen and girls into tractable domestic servants. Some schools held a thousand pupils. They became a source of infection, particularly ringworm, other skin diseases and ophthalmia. Mr Drouet's establishment at Tooting was a district school; and although some continued into the 1890s, by the 1970s, Boards of Guardians increasingly relied on cottage-homes for accommodating pauper children, in a 'family-group' system. These were described as 'pretty country villages,' with schools as part of the environment. Cottage-homes would offer children the chance of a healthy family life. Not their own family of course. They would be tutored by their social superiors in the sanctity of an institution their own parents had profaned, and removed from baleful relationships with their own blood-relations. Physical improvement, moral instruction and vocational education would transform their lives; they would even receive personal affection.

This also proved less than satisfactory: the communities were disconnected from the world where children would have to live. A solution was the 'scattered homes' system, pioneered in Sheffield in the 1890s, where children would live in houses in a wider community and attend local schools, together with those not subject to the Poor Law. This would provide a more realistic preparation for the outside world. Boarding out of poor children was also revived in the 1870s, including placement beyond the boundaries of the parish unions. These were principally orphans, illegitimate or deserted children, whose parents were undergoing penal servitude or were out of the country: their contact with kin had already been severed.

Reformatories and industrial schools

The fate of the orphaned, the illegitimate and the 'criminal' child were closely interwoven. In 1851 Mary Carpenter published *Reformatory Schools for the Children of the Dangerous and Perishing Classes and for Juvenile Offenders*.[30] Daughter of a Unitarian Minister, Carpenter had opened a Ragged School in her native Bristol 1846; in 1851 she established Kingswood Reformatory in a building that had been used as a school by John Wesley. She influenced the 1854 legislation, Reformatory Schools Act, designed to separate child offenders from adult criminals. (These were children of the 'dangerous classes'.) The Industrial Schools Act of 1857 could order vagrant, destitute or disorderly children to boarding schools to forestall their entry into the penal system (the 'perishing' classes). Such children, between the ages of seven and fourteen, spent fourteen days in jail before being directed to the appropriate school. Industrial Schools remained until 1933. In the mid 1880s, they housed about 5,000 children.

When children left the reformatory, industrial school or orphanage, they were usually on their own, unless parents, previously unwilling to acknowledge kinship, came forward; which they sometimes did, not always to take advantage of their earning capacity, as their institutional guardians suspected.

The departure of pupils, with the Spartan dower they were provided with, is evoked by Gertrude Tuckwell:

A boy's outfit will vary to some extent with the school to which he has been sent, but he may well in any case be furnished with a sound tin or wooden trunk, containing probably two suits, two pairs of boots, shirts, handkerchiefs, socks, collars, brush and comb and a Bible; and possibly an overcoat. A girl's outfit would correspond with the boy's: she would have dresses, aprons and a certain amount of underclothing.' By this time, a majority of boys expected to become labourers (the trade in which they had been instructed bore little relationship to the actual labour market), while girls found employment in service, not always in a particularly well-to-do household.[31]

Of course, boys were always the principal object of salvage, if not salvation, since boys tended to congregate in intimidating numbers, to defy authority, to organise theft and robbery. Girls endured a milder form of rescue, since they had to be saved from prostitution; but with adequate training, they could be groomed for domestic service. The Workhouse Visiting Society proposed a Home for Young Women to the Poor Law Board in 1860. 'The exact number of "able-bodied" young women has not been precisely ascertained who, instead of benefiting their country, are burdens upon their parishes, leading useless lives, while servants are wanted everywhere, not only at home, but in every quarter of the world.'

The Society proposed to free from permanent pauperism the most hopeful among the young women. 'We may suppose that there are many who, having been educated in pauper schools (two-thirds of whom are orphans), find themselves at times homeless and friendless from sickness or other causes.' To such women a home would be offered, where she might learn the household work she never had the chance to acquire, and from where she might be able to start once more in life 'uncontaminated by the promiscuous assemblage of the workhouse.' They would be trained 'for service whether at home or in the colonies, by teaching them household work in the kitchen and laundry as well as sewing work.'

If these ambitions for pauper girls were modest, they were at least an improvement on the principal activity in the workhouse—oakum-picking and hair-picking. This latter consisted in, 'separating and pulling out hairs from the twists into which they were made by machinery, to create the curl which gave it the necessary elasticity for use as stuffing for mattresses or furniture.'

The Poor Law Board appreciated the benevolent intentions of the Society, 'training them for servitude' but the request for a separate home was declined: 'Because the Guardians would have no legal authority over such persons, nor to restrain any disorderly or misconducted inmate, the existing law does not justify the Guardians in applying poor rates to the establishment.'

The charitable impulse

In 1862 Parliament allowed Poor Law children to be sent to voluntary institutions, if these were certified by the Poor Law Board.

Dr Barnardo's philanthropic work from the 1860s also detached poor children from their kin. Children were to be 'saved' from their families because of the greed and irresponsibility of parents who compelled them to labour. The immorality of mothers and fathers, not misery, hunger or social pressure forced children to labour, crime or prostitution.

Barnardo's nocturnal sorties into the underworld, 'amid scenes repulsive to all but the Christian philanthropist—drunks, ferocious and besotted, women, with nothing womanly or even human about them'—were unlikely to be called into question by contrary evidence, not least because his lurid prose deterred others from venturing into such sites of desolation.

Barnardo started a Ragged School in the 1860s. Jim Jarvis, who ran away from the workhouse after his mother died, took Barnardo to a rooftop, where he counted eleven boys sleeping. Barnardo wrote:

> Just then a cloud passed from the face of the moon, and as the pale light fell upon the upturned faces of these sleeping boys, I realised the terrible fact that they were absolutely homeless and destitute, and were almost certainly samples of many others; it seemed as though the hand of God Himself had suddenly pulled aside the curtain which concealed from my view the untold miseries of forlorn child-life on the streets of London'.[32]

Barnardo's Home for Destitute Boys opened on Stepney Causeway in 1870. A similar initiative with girls failed, because of what Barnardo called 'the degraded behaviour of girls'. Realising that barrack-style institutions were unsuitable, he opened the Barkingside Girls' Village Homes in 1876, which became a model for both charitable and state-run institutions.

National Children's Homes, the Waifs and Strays (Church of England) Society also opened orphanages. These received many bereaved or abandoned children in the early industrial era. The word 'orphanage', originally an abstract noun meaning the condition of being an orphan, came to signify a structure of stone and brick, part funerary monument to dead parents, part prison for those who had lost them.

Throughout the nineteenth century, the rhetoric was of 'conversion', 'salvation', 'evangelical transformation'. 'Learning to forget,' was part of the training of Barnardo. 'After 12–18 months', he said in *Once a Little Vagrant, Now a Little Workman*, even 'their physiognomy changes'.[33] Visitors to the Metropolitan Association for Befriending Young Servants (formed in the mid 1870s) also expressed revulsion at the 'evil influence of their own relatives' upon the girls.

International orphans

This spirit has not deserted the world, as cross-country adoptions in the recent past clearly show, although inflected now by sophisticated commercial considerations. African and Asian orphans became traded goods, acquired for the formerly childless or the philanthropically-inclined of Europe and America. More recently this practice has come under scrutiny.

The story of an 'orphan crisis' in the world originated in a UNICEF report in 2005, which estimated 132 million orphans in sub-Saharan Africa, Asia, Latin America and the Caribbean. Most of these children were cared for by their own relatives and a majority were over the age of five (which is the upper limit for potential Western adoptive parents). The search for orphans for well-to-do childless Westerners led, in some cases, to the theft or purchase of children from parents in the principal countries from which adoptees came—China, Russia, Brazil, Ethiopia, Belarus and Honduras.

This has now decreased substantially, but was for a time a lucrative form of sundering children from their parents: a globalised version of Dr Barnardo's benign seizure of the children of poverty in nineteenth-century Britain. In the USA, international adoptions fell from about 23,000 in 2004 to 6,441 in 2014.[34]

The trade in orphans is not a new development. In Dickens' *Our Mutual Friend*, the search by Mrs Boffin, childless wife of the 'Golden Dustman' for an orphan is an occasion for satire. The Rev and Mrs Milvey are charged with finding one suitable; no simple undertaking:

> Either an eligible orphan was of the wrong sex (which almost always happened) or was too old, or too young, or too sickly, or too dirty, or too much accustomed to the streets, or too likely to run away; or it was found impossible complete the philanthropic transaction without buying the orphan. For, the instant it became known that anybody wanted the orphan, up started some affectionate relative of the orphan who put a price upon the orphan's head. The suddenness of an orphan's rise in the market was not to be paralleled by the maddest records of the Stock Exchange. He would be at five thousand per cent discount out at nurse making a mud pie at nine in the morning, and (being inquired for) would go up to five thousand per cent premium before noon. The market was 'rigged' in various artful ways. Counterfeit stock got into circulation. Parents boldly represented themselves as dead, and brought their orphan with them. Genuine orphan-stock was surreptitiously withdrawn from the market. It being announced, by emissaries posted for the purpose, that Mr and Mrs Milvey were coming down the court, orphan scrip would instantly be concealed, and production refused, save on a condition usually stated by the brokers as 'a gallon of beer'. Likewise, fluctuations of a wild and South-Sea nature were occasioned by orphan-holders keeping back, and then rushing into the market a dozen together. But, the uniform principle at the root of all these various operations was bargain and sale; and that principle could not be recognized by Mr and Mrs Milvey.

6

PHILANTHROPIC ABDUCTION

The erasure of birth families

Children portrayed as waifs and strays, urchins or guttersnipes were ready for removal from parental influence. After the Second Reform Bill of 1867, more adults were enfranchised. Partly to justify withholding the vote from the rest, the unpropertied, these were depicted as a neglectful or worthless humanity, unfit even for the duties of parenthood, let alone the responsibilities of those who had a 'stake' in the nation.[1] In this context, Barnardo was a pioneer of what he later referred to as 'philanthropic abduction' of children, a middle class Pied Piper, who would call them away from an impure, corrupt heritage. He defended the principle in 1889 in a case when he refused a request from parents for the transfer of their children to a Catholic institution.

Barnardo also employed the language of colonial exploration, referring in one promotional pamphlet to the 'terra incognita of our modern Babylon.' For this he visited Hotwater Court, where, in one building he saw:[2]

> ...a pile of cast-off rages unworthy of a beggar's notice... I felt beneath the rags and soon grasped the thin spare arm of a boy...

Behind him another boy, about nine, two or three years younger. The older lad, Arthur, was really the guide and protector of his younger brother, whom he called with a simple pathos that was very touching, 'Little Bobbie.' The two boys, alone and without a relative in the world, except one older brother, who was a thief and had been frequently sentenced to imprisonment. This man had kept his two little brothers in servile bondage, making them do his work as accomplices. At last, from a tramp's kitchen in Brighton, where they had all sought shelter, the two boys crept forth early one morning, and trudged to London. Here they lived that awful time of famine and wretchedness which so many of these poor children of our streets know: begging from door to door, feeding on garbage when all else fails.

Barnardo took them to his Boys' Home in Stepney. They were delighted to be sheltered, clothed and fed. But Big Bill, the brother, traced them. Arthur begged to be allowed to leave the Home to escape his attention. 'The previous day', Barnardo wrote:

> I had had an interview with a gentleman about to leave for one of our Colonies. And he had suggested that if I were disposed to send boys to Canada, he would gladly undertake their care, and do what was possible for them. The child, when asked if he desired to go, asked 'Is Canada down Wapping way?'

Dr Barnardo accompanied them to Liverpool, and they sailed for Montreal, where they were adopted by a well-to-do farmer who had no family of his own. Arthur did well and went into the church.

All the elements of nineteenth-century melodrama are here: guileless children oppressed by evil adults, their kin and nominal protectors; the saviour who finds them and offers them succour; pursuit by the tyrant; escape to the Colonies, where the children of misery are metamorphosed from street-rats into exemplary citizens of Empire.

The folklore of parental cruelty

The horrors are stressed to justify breaking and entering the dilapidated ruin of the family relationships of the poor. Gertrude Tuckwell visited Barnardo's Barrack School in Stepney, where all prejudices against the poor were confirmed:

> One finds hideous testimony in favour of all the sinister views as to the lowest stratum of parents. These children had excited the sympathy of credulous passers-by as they lay in their mother's arms— the one by reason of his blindness, the other by his hideous deformity. In one case, the mother had run needles into the child's eyes, in the other, she had strapped its tiny legs across its chest in order that its condition might aid her success in begging. There they are, living object lessons to that worse than foolish section of the public which insists on dispensing indiscriminate charities in the street.[3]

The emergence in present-day Mumbai, Dhaka and Jakarta of identical stories to those which circulated in nineteenth-century London is intriguing. Does this record a lasting characteristic of cruelty among the very poor? Is it an export of middle class demonology and folklore to former imperial territories? Is it a transmission across cultures of reasons for the rich not to relieve the misery before their eyes? Or is it testimony of the constancy of the worst of human nature?

Charitable enterprises often exaggerated the condition of those for whom they collected donations. They were not averse to degrading further the lowly position of their objects of pity. In 1874 a girl, Florence Holder and her sister, posed for publicity photographs for Barnardo's, one as a servant girl, the other as a newspaper vendor. Florence appeared on collection boxes as 'a little waif of London, rescued from the streets, six years old.' Two years later, the mother recognised her daughters and complained to Thames Police Court of 'a cruel fraud.' Neither had sold anything in the streets. The mother claimed she had left them at Barnardo's so they would be educated. The case

was dismissed, but Barnardo was censured for 'fictitious repre-
sentation of destitution'.[4]

Even the most sympathetic observers were affected by an
ideology of the inferior humanity of the poorest. Ellen Barlee,
describing in 1869 Brockham House, a private initiative run by
the Honourable Mrs Way of Wonham Manor, records the usefulness of 'unpauperizing the pauper child', by 'converting the
surplus number of untutored pauper children into useful
domestic servants.' Of fifty girls who passed through the establishment, eleven were illegitimate, deserted or of unknown origins. 'These had been so long in the workhouse that in the
various changes connected in the place, their original history
had been lost sight of, a melancholy fact which is of frequent
occurrence; indeed with many children, their identity is lost.'[5]

Separations

When children left reformatories and industrial schools, 'in
most cases, great care is taken that the boy shall not return to
his parents'. Tuckwell estimates 'vicious parents' to represent
half, fewer than the 85 per cent previously thought to be unco-
operative, but they:

> ...object strongly to paying the sum imposed upon them by the
> Magistrates, they will move from place to place to evade payment,
> and hide to escape the officer who collects their fees, but they
> always bear in mind the date at which the boy's detention is over,
> and appear usually to claim him, and to utilise for their own
> advantage his wage earning powers.'[6]

This view persisted into the twentieth century. Some children requested removal from their tainted heritage. In 1917,
W. Clarke Hall in *The State and the Child*, claimed many poor
children recognised the danger to their morals if left in their
home environment.[7] As a magistrate in the Children's Court,
he describes 'the brightness of the children who come before
us. Many say, "I think you had better put me away, sir";

because they know that the home and environment are conducive to crime.'

Reform of the reformatory

In the nineteenth century reformers consistently denounced the joylessness of depositories for the unwanted and 'wayward.' Reformatories had been set up following legislation of 1854, to separate juvenile offenders from the corrupting influence of mature delinquents in prisons, although there had been a recognised need for such places at least a century before: training ships had been dedicated to the same purpose. Gertrude Tuckwell, Christian socialist and the first female magistrate, gave an account of a child's prison experience before his removal to a Reformatory:

> In the boy's little room is a narrow bed with a plank for bedstead, there is a little table at which he takes his meals, and a stool to sit on. In the corner there are three shelves on which rest his mug, his Bible and his brush and comb; against the wall leans a brightly polished basin, with a can beside it. His day is spent in picking rope into oakum, but meal times, chapel, school and exercise vary the employment. Every morning the prisoners assemble in chapel, and here in the front seat the boys sit together. Talking is forbidden, but now and then a surreptitious whisper is overheard 'I say, Jim, how much longer have you got?' Exercise lasts for an hour each day, when the boys walk up and down the prison yard...The schoolroom, a large bare room, with long tables and niches on either side, has little in common with the Board School which our boy probably previously attended, full of pictures, apparatus and diagrams. It is innocent of decoration except for a very large table of the Ten Commandments, which with poetic justice forever faces the poor little law-breaker. And the teaching differs from ordinary teaching as does the School. The boys' lessons are confined to reading and writing; blackboard illustrations and object lessons are conspicuous by their absence. His food, though plain, is plentiful: it consists principally of bread, potatoes, oatmeal and soup, with meat once a week at least...[8]

These are studies in deprivation for children from whom so much had already been withheld. Their reformative power was exaggerated, and their capacity to depress further the condition of their victims largely disregarded.

If the interior of the reformatory is bleak, children who remained in the workhouse were even worse off—children of widows unable to provide for them, orphans and children of adult inmates, some infirm, some vagrant. There were also the 'in-and-outers'—admitted and discharged several times a year. Tuckwell described them:

> Their bodies clothed in workhouse livery, their minds cramped by its dull routine, they are helpless, when at the expiration of their childhood they are sent into situations and thrown more or less on their own resources in a world where something more is required for their success than a limitless capacity for scrubbing stone passages. It is not surprising that such children should, in most cases, return eventually to the workhouse, the only place for existence in which their training has fitted them.[9]

Survival of the punitive sensibility

Palliatives extended to the most wretched children were not conceded without resistance. The Poor Law Board Order of 1869, which promoted the boarding out of the poorest was contested, since 'a man would receive as much support of two pauper children as he would be able to earn by hard toil.'

'Pauperism', wrote Henry Fawcett in 1871, 'is therefore a desirable profession.' An unforgiving spirit animated even some reformers. Fawcett insisted that 'a man who incurs the responsibility of causing children to be born is not only bound to maintain them while living, but also to make provision for them in the event of his death'; as though the instantaneous pleasures of sex—however strenuously prohibited—are going to prompt the participants to consider life insurance in the event of conception. He also considered boarding out an inducement to mothers to desert their children, if the father had already departed. He went further, and claimed that both parents might feel 'a duty to desert' to promote the welfare of their children. Parents were accused of orphaning their own children: a course of action increasingly undertaken by the state.[10]

Such observers shed light on the history of feelings, a complex and somewhat neglected study; for however constant human sentiments, these are always tempered by the dominant values of the age in which they are expressed. Fawcett reprobates what he calls 'spurious philanthropy and mischievous benevolence;' and betrays what now appears a strange insensitivity to the children themselves, whose principal function was to serve as scourge to those who had 'caused them to be born'.

A desire not to 'reward' morally culpable adults by the state or charity taking care of their children has proved extraordinarily tenacious: these creatures of sin should on no account be brought up under conditions more conducive to health than the rest of the children of the working class. Punishing the consequence of adult wrongdoing (children) was a means of preserving hierarchies of moral merit. A whiff of this lingers in our time, where 'benefit caps' and limiting allowances to couples with more than two children have made a not insignificant contribution to an increase in child poverty.

Other threats

There were other threats to the safety of children than cold Poor Law functionaries: in nineteenth-century schools and homes, fire—as well as disease—claimed children's lives. The Grenfell Tower catastrophe in 2017 was a grisly reminder of how official neglect and indifference towards poor people survives the reforms, improvements and progress of which we are all theoretical beneficiaries.

It is astonishing that fire could find anything to consume in the hard mineral structures of nineteenth century institutions. The Forest Gate Industrial School fire of New Year's Day in 1890 killed twenty-six children 'belonging' to the Whitechapel

Union, mainly through smoke inhalation. The fire started in the store where blankets and woollen clothing were kept. Most deaths occurred in the upper floor. The staircases outside the building were locked.

Reports from the neighbourhood were factual and detailed, but as the event was described by newspapers further afield it acquired embellishments that suggest an irresponsible and tendentious press is no new thing. In the *Northampton Mercury* of 1 January 1890 the report ran:

> Hardly had the merry pealing of the bells ceased on Wednesday when death overtook twenty-six inmates of the Forest Gate Pauper School, Essex. With appalling suddenness they were asphyxiated by reason of a fire which, in itself, was out of all proportion to the gravity of its results. There were 58 boys in the ill-fated rooms, and of these 26 fell a prey to the smoke. If we may take consolation in this grim episode of the young year, it is to think that the unfortunate little fellows died calmly, probably without ever being conscious of their approaching fate. The faces of all bear a peaceful happy expression. They went to bed all with joyous hearts, for the superintendent had promised them that on the morrow each should receive a toy and such good cheer as delights the hearts of juveniles. Wednesday, in fact was to be for them, had not Providence ordained otherwise, the jolliest day of the year. The generosity of the Poplar and Whitechapel Guardians, under whose auspices the school is conducted, is even at this sad moment testified in some measure by the ELABORATE CHRISTMASTIDE DECORATIONS of the dining-hall and of the corridors. No little praise is due to the superintendent who only began to think of his own injuries when he had more time. In falling down the stone steps one of his arms received a severe blow.

In the same issue it was recorded that Henry Hobbs, a lad, was charged with stealing two live tame rabbits. The boy pleaded guilty. He also admitted having been convicted and punished at Wellingborough petty sessions in July 1887, when he was birched for stealing three bottles of scent. He was sentenced to 14 days imprisonment and four years in a Reformatory.[11]

Out of sight: orphans by migration

In another ingenious mutation of official orphanage, large-scale emigration of pauper children—the sound in mind and body—further drove apart generations of the poor. Although this affected fewer children than were placed in workhouses, it was symbolic of something more than the numbers involved.

The Act of 1834 permitted parishes to raise money to send adults abroad. An Assistant Commissioner claimed 'workhouse children had few ties to their native land, and such as there were could be broken only to their profit.' In 1848 Lord Shaftesbury advocated migration for slum children, and recommended sending them overseas 'right away from their depressing and demoralising surroundings, and far out of the reach of their parents, often the chief cause of their misery'. These visions were realised on a significant scale in the 1860s.

Such schemes were constrained by the fact that until 1853, 'transportation' remained a punishment for children under fourteen. They also encroached upon the work of the Society for the Suppression of Juvenile Vagrancy which, by 1840, had sent 440 children to the Cape; mostly boys, apprenticed to Boers who knew little English. Of their labour—as cattle-herders—one magistrate observed, 'In this employment his time is passed, during the heat of the day, either sleeping under a bush or in strolling, sluggard-like, after he cattle; his only association is a stray Hottentot, and his only attainment indolent, slovenly habits.'[12] A further complication was that the Governor of Parkhurst prison made it a privilege for delinquent boys of good behaviour to be sent to Australia. Between 1842 and 1852 1,498 boys were despatched in this project, a curiously punitive recompense.

Some children from the St Pancras Workhouse—that persistent pioneer in disembarrassing itself of unwanted children—went willingly to Australia in the early 1850s; but this was found not to have been within the terms of the 1850 Poor Law Amendment Act. The Poor Law Board found that although the children had been apprenticed as servants to the age of eighteen, and the shipment had been conducted 'with regard for their welfare', it was nonetheless illegal.

An early initiative was taken by Annie McPherson, who established a child emigration society as a voluntary body in the 1860s. Born into a Quaker family in Stirlingshire, she moved to London in 1865 to teach at an institute run by the Society of Friends. With some wealthy Evangelicals, she worked in the East End, 'where Satan reigns openly.'[13] She opened a House of Industry in Commercial Street for boys under ten, a home for girls, and finally, a home for boys between ten and thirteen. Among the children she received was a girl who was literally kicked by other children till she yielded to them the doorstep on which she slept, and a boy who made a living performing acrobatics in the gin-palaces; an occupation found today among migrant tribal children turning somersaults at traffic lights on the burning roads of Dhaka and Delhi.

After the last cholera epidemic in 1866, there were other reasons to relieve the city of noisy and troublesome street-children. Emigration appeared a panacea for abandoned infants, referred to euphemistically as 'imps', 'urchins' or 'cubs' by those who wished to avoid pejorative terms, since their removal to the dominions not only transferred them to a place of safety, but also relieved both the minds and the purses of the rate-payers. In 1870, Annie McPherson accompanied 140 boys to Canada, children she described, ominously, as 'orphans, or *worse than orphans.*' McPherson was thankful that four out of every five infants died before their fifth year, to spare them the gruesome fate that their gin-sodden mothers and violent fathers reserved for them.

This disposal of children was often unsatisfactory, particularly those sent by Maria Rye, who accompanied her first party of children to Canada in 1869, children who were under the care of the Poor Law Boards of Guardians.[14] Older children were often sent to exploitative homesteads, where they were overworked and neglected. It is difficult to understand adults sending to an alien environment children who had known only brick East End tenements, throngs of infants in the gutter, noisy beer-houses and music-halls vying with gloomy half–deserted chapels for the attention of the people; starvation-labour of running errands, selling herbs, paper bags, matches or scrubbing doorsteps. The emigrants were unprepared for long harsh winters, the isolation of the prairie under immense skies, icy barns, sleeping on straw and eating unfamiliar food, with only the warmth of the bodies of horses and cattle as protection against freezing to death, denied the closeness of other children in the city streets that had previously sheltered them. Girls were up at dawn, washing mud-encrusted clothes, scouring and sweeping, cooking, responsible for children only a little younger than they, before retiring, exhausted, to a garret, chill or stifling according to the season, a thin straw bed, a chamber-pot and a text on the wall.

The Local Government Board replaced the Poor Law Board in 1970. Four years later inspectors went to Canada, and reported that many children had been distributed without proper regard for their fate. Andrew Doyle published his report in 1875, criticising the very system of emigration, since it was the function of the Board of Guardians to train pauper children for work.[15] He was fiercely attacked, not least because he was a Catholic and had questioned the integrity of staunchly Protestant initiatives.

Barnardo also sent children with Annie McPherson's organisation until his own emigration programmes began in 1882. In the following twenty years he sent over 24,000. His schemes were better organised; most children were boarded out and received proper wages for work. Emigration was interrupted by World War One, but similar schemes for dealing with—as opposed to caring for—unwanted children lasted well into the twentieth century.

About 150,000 children were 'emigrated' from Britain from the seventeenth century until the mid 1960s; about 80,000 to the Dominions between 1870 and 1920. This form of 'rehabilitation' also helped populate the Empire. Some were orphans, others reformatory and industrial school children, some street children taken into voluntary homes, as well as adolescents from workhouses. Although in theory their consent was necessary, few resisted arbitrary deportation. One-third of residents in voluntary homes were orphans; many more the offspring of destitute parents, especially widows. For a majority no contact with families and relatives was maintained; it was assumed such attachments were damaging and wanting in emotion. Relationships may have been difficult and unfamiliar to the submissiveness of middle-class children; but there is no reason to doubt that they were any less profound than those of the most privileged.

Denis Crane referred in 1915 to 'John Bull's surplus children'.[16] He described in lyrical terms their arrival in Canada:

> ...thinking of these pleasing acres, soon to flourish with barley, oats, roots and corn; of the orchards already adorned with blossom; of the brilliant sky; of the fading hills behind us, and that great inland sea Lake Ontario, 180 miles long by nearly 50 miles wide, away to the south. We feel that to have exchanged the back streets and the grimy workrooms of an English city for a prospect as wholesome and agreeable, with the still larger opportunities beckoning from the West, is for these youngsters the wisest bit of good fortune that could have befallen.

Denis Crane was writing when a quarter of a million children under the age of sixteen were receiving Poor Relief, more than 70,000 of them as 'indoor paupers'; while industrial schools and reformatories accounted for another 29,000; and about 5,000 were 'on the tramp' in Britain.

Calculations were made to the last penny. The average cost of keeping a child in London was twenty-eight pounds eight shillings and tuppence in a year; twenty-four pounds to twenty-five pounds if boarded out; forty pounds or more in cottage homes. An average stay of eight years would cost the ratepayer £160 per child.

A single payment of twenty pounds to one of the Emigration Societies would cover the cost up to the age of thirteen.

No wonder the advantages to the child of removal to new worlds were enumerated:

> As to the work on farms, it is of that kind that most appeals to a boy's heart, provided he has not already become too deeply corrupted by the vicious amusements of great cities. It is more natural for the normal boy to love horses and engines rather than office stools, and to take pleasure in fields and barns than in warehouses and shops.

This bucolic idyll for the offspring of industrial exhaustion had other purposes. 'The farmers who take a boy or a girl to live with them are generally actuated by humane and even parental instincts, but they do not engage a child for fun. They expect him to work and have no use for idleness.' The line of descent from the Elizabethan Poor Law is clear: the stigma of pauperdom would be overcome by expiatory labour. 'The changed man begins to realize God, and is amenable to religious motives and to spiritual quickenings.'

Compulsory migration in the twentieth century

This was not the end of coercive migration, although over time, the emphasis changed from getting rid of 'guttersnipes' to providing British 'stock' to populate the Empire. From the 1920s children from Britain were sent to Australia under the Fairbridge scheme (named after Kingsley Fairbridge, a South African who initiated the resettlement of slum children to Rhodesia, South Africa and Australia). This continued until 1967: many children were duped into believing they were embarking on a great adventure only to discover they had been irreversibly *emigrated*. In 2010 Gordon Brown, Prime Minister of Britain, apologised for this abuse of children who, for no reason intelligible to the contemporary sensibility, had been sent to Australia. (Actually, the racist purpose was to help preserve 'the race'.) The majority of children, under the aegis of charities, religious institutions or local authorities, were from poor families. Some were orphans, but many had at least one parent living. Some were told they were going 'away for a holiday.' Most lost all contact with their birth families, and many were separated from their siblings. Many went to servile and labouring farm work. The absence of any sense of who they were, the taunts of peers and the indifference of those who employed them made them lost children, 'dead souls', punished in a hauntingly clear continuation of the policy of 'transportation', when convicted children as young as seven or eight were sentenced to punitive exile which usually became permanent. Philip Bean and Joy Melville collected the reminiscences of these in *Lost Children of the Empire*. This scheme falls within the remit of the present investigation into Child Abuse in Britain.

Voices of the children themselves were recorded in *Lost Children of the Empire*. One child said:

> When I was about ten, three serious-looking men visited the Home. The children were all lined up in the hall and asked 'Who wants to go to Australia?' 'Me! Me!' we all shouted, putting our hands up into the air. We thought it was an outing and we didn't go on many outings. A number of the girls were picked, I don't know why we were chosen, and we were told some more about the trip. The men made it sound like fun, there would be lovely fruit on the trees which you could pick out of the windows, and we'd get 'aunties' and 'uncles'. We went for our medicals, had our tonsils out, and were put on a train to Southampton and then on to a boat.[17]

It can be seen how a malignant Poor Law ideology was exported to 'the dominions', along with institutionalised childhoods and a wilful orphaning, in an extreme example of unintended irony, by what was referred to as the 'mother country.' If countries do indeed assume such roles, they clearly suffered a severe deficiency in what are now called 'parenting skills.'

Orphans of the living

Joanna Penglase observes that children have always been victims of 'adults' idealised notions of childhood.'[18] This has involved, not only a class-based intolerance of poor families in industrial society, but also the suppression of children's voices. It was a matter of principle that they should not be listened to, since adults invariably 'knew best'. Everything they did was in the child's 'best interests'. The same mind-set kept the peoples of Empire subordinate to the superior wisdom of their colonial overlords; and Hugh Cunningham draws attention to the rhetoric that assimilated children to subjects of Empire.[19] Both were in need of tutelage, because they were 'ignorant' and 'savage'. Indeed, missionary tracts evoking the barefoot *marmaille* (brats) of London 'infesting' the streets, threatening the citizenry with dirt, disease and crime, differed little from those that pleaded that the heathen feet should be shod, that they might walk sedately from the immemorial darkness in which they had languished into the clear light of Christian compassion.

Joanna Penglase, whose own mother 'voluntarily' placed her in care, because she had no choice if she was to work, has a keen ear for the self-deluding platitudes of adults that justify mistreatment of children. There is nothing like linguistic analysis for uncovering the self-seeking prejudice and bullying of authority. Children 'ran wild', 'got out of hand', were in 'moral danger', came from 'broken homes', were 'wayward', required 'moral and spiritual training', were 'better off' in a home. They were 'incorrigible', there was 'bad blood', they were 'common', 'devil's spawn', 'trash', 'worthless'; they would 'never amount to anything' and would 'come to a bad end'. Their parents were 'irresponsible', 'hopeless', 'drunken', 'wanting in character', feckless', 'unfit'. A litany of moral defectiveness is always available to those whose calling is the suppression of the powerless. When I was a social worker in the 1970s, the dread of many women was that they would be judged 'an unfit mother', an unappealable reason for seeing the child taken from them.[20]

225

The 'best' which adults knew also led to the manufacture of fables about the child's orphaning, and lies supposed to comfort children, served principally to reassure their carers. These often suppressed the truth in order to deflect awkward questions. Just as ignorance of their parentage left room for abandoned children to weave their own fantasies about them, so their minders created fictions, even if these added to the child's confusion and aroused further anxiety and suspicion.

A woman born shortly before World War One was told her parents had died in a car crash when she was a baby. This tale might have alerted her to the unlikelihood of such an occurrence—road deaths being rare at that time—but she accepted the story. Brought up by an aunt, she was sent to boarding school at seven, and transferred to a convent in Belgium when she was twelve. Her orphaned condition was an invention, designed to maintain the respectability of the 'aunt' who was, of course, her birth-mother. The stigma of illegitimacy was worse than the taint of orphanhood, at least for the mother; and this must have justified the falsehood she created for the girl. When the 'aunt' married, her husband insisted that the child be sent away; hence her removal to the penitential retreat of the convent—a place where she might also, perhaps, expiate the fault of her mother. She and the 'aunt' are buried in adjacent graves, and no whisper of their true relationship disturbs them even in death.

Children remember with resentment deceit practised upon them. Eileen Simpson's mother died when she was less than a year old and her sister Marie a year older. They were sent to a convent 'boarding school' outside New York, a loveless place, which she discovered as an adult, when it was being demolished, was actually an orphanage. She derived some consolation from this: after all, 'An orphan who goes to an orphanage is far more orphaned than one who goes to a convent boarding school.'[21]

Unimpeachable carers

Just as a pejorative vocabulary was applied to the fallen, low and degenerate—children and adults—so it was also assumed that those charged by society for their 'reform' or betterment were 'irreproachable', 'respectable', of 'the highest integrity. Institutions for their 'rehabilitation' (another interesting word, since no one has ever defined what 'habilitation' might have been) would be superintended by people of the highest calibre, individuals who sometimes assumed labels of false kinship— Aunties and Uncles—of sound religious principles and unquestionable morality. The consequences of this faulty distinction between children of 'bad stock' and those into whose disinterested care they passed, has been revealed in recent years, in stories of abuse, sexual, physical and emotional, which emerged from asylums and retreats designed to preserve the young from their heritage of evil; but which often exposed them to treatment far worse than anything they would have experienced, if left to their own 'defective' families. The phrases which resound down the centuries—the virtues of time-keeping, thrift and sobriety; humility and resignation—suggest the treatment of human misery with piety that rarely became pity.

Reform

In 1889, Parliament passed the first of a number of what would be hailed as 'Children's Charters'. Wilful cruelty to children became a crime. A wife could give evidence against her husband, and the testimony of a child was admissible. Houses could even be searched, where there was 'reasonable cause' to suspect the ill-treatment of a child. This late departure from respect for the privacy of family life was radical, since until then, it had been possible to get a search warrant for stolen goods—a spoon or a length of muslin—but no one could search for an abused or injured child. In 1894 the law was changed, to protect both boys and girls until the age of sixteen.

The Charity Organisation Society dates from 1869. This conservative organisation was intended to address indiscriminate alms-giving and the 'dependency' it engendered. By the end of the century, this tradition was striking against two developments. First of all, Booth and Rowntree had conducted more 'scientific' studies of poverty, and found that low wages, sickness, unemployment and the death of the main family earner were major factors, and that poverty was a socially structured rather than a moral issue. At the same time, the low physical standard of recruits for the Boer War raised fears for the efficiency of the nation: public health, racial hygiene, the maintenance of Empire became matters of urgency. Children, even the most humble, 'belonged to the nation.'[22]

The Children Act of 1908 declared it the duty of the state to maintain the life and wellbeing of its young. The feeding of children at school, medical inspections, juvenile courts as instruments of reclamation rather than punishment, supported this view. The majority report of the Poor Law Commission in 1909 was a timid document, but the minority report, written by Sidney and Beatrice Webb, a radical departure from the administration of the poor law, proved far more influential in the long run.

After World War One, efforts to mitigate the stigma of illegitimacy by increasing adoptions led to the first Adoption Act in 1926. The number of children in workhouses was reduced. By 1918 half of 'indoor child paupers' were in institutions separate from adults. The Poor Law Act of 1930 created Public Assistance Committees run by local authorities, while the Children and Young Persons Act of 1933 provided a degree of welfare previously unheard of. In the 1930s, returning children to their families was not yet widely practised, given the high levels of unemployment and poverty. The local authority or voluntary bodies remained 'fit persons' to whom neglected or mistreated children would be entrusted. This changed only after World War Two.

In 1939, a child, Dennis O'Neill, aged seven, and his two brothers and sisters, were taken from their parents for neglect.

The girl went to her maternal grandmother and the three boys were under the supervision of the local authority. They went to a series of foster-homes. Dennis was sent to a remote Shropshire farmhouse where, in 1945 he died as a result of beating and malnutrition.[23]

A Committee under Myra Curtis, set up to look into the care of children deprived of parents or home life, found responsibility was too diffuse—the Ministry of Health, the Home Office and the judicial system failed to co-ordinate, while existing institutions could not offer the personal affection and individual care children required. Child Care Offices were appointed to oversee the work of local authorities and voluntary bodies, and to ensure that boarding out took place where possible, while small family group homes catered to the rest. The Children's Act of 1948 also legislated for the return of children to the parental home wherever possible, and individual casework with families would work to this end. This was reinforced by the 1963 Act, which definitively rejected the segregation of neglected, deprived or 'delinquent' children, and those beyond parental control, and sought to integrate them, if not into their own families, at least into as close an approximation of them as possible.

Leisurely legislation

When we survey the antiquated and unrepealed litter of legislation that trails through the centuries, we are surprised, not so much by the eagerness for reform as by the indolence of those who professed to improve the lot of the poorest of the young. In 1839 the custody of infants under the age of seven was awarded to the mother in case of marital separation, but the age of consent remained at twelve until raised to sixteen in 1881. That same year, responding to concerns about the physical chastisement of children by their parents, Lord Shaftesbury—prominent reformer of factory legislation against child exploitation—said, 'The evils you state are enormous and indisputable, but of so private, internal and domestic to be beyond the reach of legislation, and the subject, indeed, would not, I think, be entertained in either House of Parliament.' The National Society for the Prevention of Cruelty to Children was founded in 1884, sixty years after the Royal Society for the Prevention of Cruelty to Animals. Sexual abuse by members of a child's family was made a crime in 1908; in the same year the Children Act finally made all foster-mothers liable to official supervision. Juvenile Courts were set up in 1908, but it was only in 1937 that the age of criminal responsibility was raised to eight. The school-leaving age rose to fourteen under the Fisher Education Act in 1918, but it was 1947 before it reached fifteen. Under the 1933 Children and Young People Act, no one under the age of eighteen could be sentenced to death. 'Illegitimacy' gradually became 'bastardy' in the twentieth century; but destitute pregnant women could be detained indefinitely in mental institutions as 'moral imbeciles' according to an Act of 1913. The 1872 reform of the Bastardy Laws remained the basis for the financial arrangements for illegitimate children until 1957. The First Adoption Act was passed in 1926: there was no regulation of adoption agencies. In 1929 Boards of Guardians could offer relief to unmarried mothers outside the workhouse for the first time since the 1834 Poor Law Amendment Act. Only in 1949 in England and 1963 in Scotland could children inherit as a right from their adoptive parents. In 1963 the age of criminal responsibility was raised from the age of eight to ten. In the 1970s Barnardo's abandoned institutional care for fostering; and in 1975 adopted children were able to discover as of right the identity of their birth-parents. The Children (Leaving Care) Act of 2000 made local authorities responsible for the support of care leavers until the age of twenty-one.

The shadow of the institution

The nineteenth-century institution casts a long shadow over posterity; and testimonies of the living recall its baleful effect upon childhoods up to and beyond World War Two. Despite advances in child care, the last to benefit were children without emotional family ties. Even those whose parents still lived, but were compelled to use asylums, schools and institutions to look after their children (particularly widows or lone mothers, who had to work), were often treated by the establishments that cared for them as a burden, in need of severe discipline and control; to be chastised into good behaviour and decent citizenship.

A clear picture emerges from the experience of such children; now themselves old, often sad, sometimes embittered by formative years spent in elaborate Gothic buildings. These would have extensive grounds, but would often be cold and loveless, with echoing walls, high ceilings and windows; tepid radiators which failed to compensate for draughts, stone staircases, long dormitories ('sometimes you couldn't see the other end because of the fog'), hard beds, stony ablution blocks with plaster sinks and unheated water, runny noses, chilblains, constant coughs, chapped knees and clothing that irritated the skin. It was a time of punitive eating, not healthy but filling, suet pudding and sago, boiled potatoes and greens washed white by boiling, hard bread and watery cocoa; with occasional disasters ('there were maggots in the meat one day, so we refused to eat it'). Eileen Simpson said 'For the fasting child, there was a secret pleasure to be had in chewing the celluloid cover of a missal. It was sweet and crisp and more satisfying than anything there would be to eat later in the day.'[24] There was regimentation, activities that inspired neither initiative nor creativity, under constant supervision, where close friendships were forbidden or broken up, and sexuality prohibited ('hands outside the bedcovers to show we were not playing with ourselves'). Chambers for sleeping were maintained at low temperature, to refrigerate desire and freeze emotion. The beds—iron cots with flock mattresses—invited no relaxation, provided little warmth; even so, getting up from them in half-light of a winter dawn was an added penance. Mattresses turned and aired every morning, and the bed made with no wrinkle in the sheets, as the children stood to attention for inspection. Those who had wet the bed were humiliated and sent to wash the soiled covers, sometimes forced to make the bed immediately afterwards, so the next night was spent in damp bedding. Repeated 'offences' were liable to physical punishment. Systems of chastisement were unimaginative and predictable—deprivation of inedible food, being locked in a broom-cupboard, or made to stand on the table at meal-times, exposed to the mockery of other children, withdrawal of meagre privileges, the imposition of silence.

Above this perpetual superintendence was the presence of a God who was invoked to bless miserable fare, joyless activity and the goodness of those devoted to the service of children unwanted and unloved. The march to chapel, numbing pews, incomprehensible sermons and hymns that re-affirmed that 'God made both high and lowly, And ordered their estate.' Lessons in obedience, docility and acceptance were absorbed ('we had never known anything else'; 'we didn't know how to rebel'), and the small acts of revolt by hardy individuals resulted in mass punishment. Many children made up fantasies about being 'rescued', of fathers who returned unexpectedly from South Africa or America where they had made their fortunes, or of mothers in fur coats and scented silk scarves who came to scoop them up and carry them away from the desolation of flint and granite. Personal possessions were confiscated, dolls had to be placed on the windowsill at night, toys disappeared and were never seen again. It was a study in sensory as well as emotional deprivation, 'there was grass outside, but we were never allowed to play on it'; schoolrooms without pictures, only a globe and a blackboard, windows so high you couldn't see out of them ('I used to watch the sky, and wonder where the clouds went'), nothing to rouse the imagination or delight the spirit. Above all, the rigorous timetabling, ('it was living by numbers'), and long-ing to be ill, because routine was interrupted, the infirmary warm, the food different, even though illness was suspect, and you had to be really sick before you were admitted, ('I complained of feeling unwell, but I was told to go out to play. I fell down and lost consciousness. I had jaundice, which I must have picked up from infected food, but of course, you knew nothing of that.') There were friendships, all the sweeter for being frowned on, ('I was separated from the one person I loved'); and some staff members were kindly or broke the rules; while others had favourites, which created great animosities and jealousies. ('I wondered what the nuns used to feel. They had so much love for Jesus and none at all for us.') The Home, the Asylum, the School—by whatever name it was known—was an enclosed world; and the outside, shadowy and mysterious, an object of longing and also of fear, since the institution provided certainty, its solid structure and its impermeable time-table not subject to alteration or change. Only on great national occasions, the children were paraded, to hear of the outbreak of war, the signing of peace, the Abdication, the death of the King, the Coronation; and almost always, Empire Day, ('The king dying was a holiday for us. We wished it would happen more often.') Otherwise, the battle against cold and hunger, the small barter and exchange between those who had almost nothing, punctuated by the occasional escape, ('I was brought back and beaten in front of all the children. It hurt, but I knew I had everybody's sympathy.') It produced children who learned to expect little, self-effacing and insecure; and others defiant, their heart hardened against the pain of others; and a lifetime's inability to enter into spontaneous intimacy.

7

WAR AND THE ORPHANS OF STRIFE

World War One

The 1914–18 war interrupted ideas of progress that had begun to emancipate children; and its aftermath created alarm at the loss of a generation of young men, and the consequences of this for women and children.

More than half a million children in Britain lost their father in the 1914–18 war. In the Census of 1921, there were 1.72 million more women than men. The demography of the country, misshapen by war, created tens of thousands of orphans, and distorted the lives of countless others. Women tell of the terse telegrams, Missing in Action, Killed in Action, each word separate and in capital letters, so that it appeared like an anonymous letter from an ill-wisher. They looked at the summer sky, saw the same clouds that had floated over scenes of slaughter in France and wondered how husbands, sons and brothers had died. Grieving but resourceful, they sent their children to queue at the grocer's for margarine, inferior cuts of meat and soap, oppressed little girls with cropped hair, in pinafores, boys' boots and grubby socks, part of whose duty was to wheel the second-hand perambulator with the child their father would never see.

The boys, in flat caps at fourteen in mimicry of working men—
which they were—sent on fools' errands by workmates, a long
weight, a glass hammer or sky-hook. And many men who did
return, some embittered and angry, did not believe the children
were theirs. Stories of privation and horror soon palled. The
human wreckage of World War One were still a presence—an
embarrassing one at that—in our town, even after the end of
World War Two, wraiths with crutches and a trouser-leg sewn
up, around their neck a strap with a tray selling boot-laces or
boxes of matches. Some were harsh to their children, as though
visiting upon them punishments they had received, with the
buckle-end of a belt or a stair-rod kept on the picture-rail for
the purpose. Women, forced to relinquish the war-work they
had done, returned to the barren hearth of rented accommodation when they re-married, sometimes inflicting hostile or
drunken stepfathers on the children.

Alice, born in 1896, showed the scars on her arms that still
remained at the age of ninety-four. She said:

> That was from my step-father's buckle. My father died in the Boer
> war; mother remarried and had nine kids. My brother ran away to
> the Navy at thirteen; his ship was sunk in the War when he was
> fourteen. I worked making tins for the boot polish factory. My play-
> time was stealing cinders from the trucks in the railway-sidings. My
> stepfather said to me one day 'I'm going to show you what married
> life is like.' I knew what he meant, so I ran away. When they wrote
> and told me he was dead I said 'Let's find a union jack and put it
> out in the street.' My mother never stood up for me. I pushed a
> truck loaded with pig-iron, I drove a horse and cart for the railway
> for fifteen years. My horse knew me better than a dog. My husband
> was crippled in the War, a bullet through his jaw and a smashed
> pelvis. He died in 1961. A golden man.
>
> I brought up my five children and fostered seven others. I did it out
> of love, there was no payment for it. I laid out the dead, six in that
> house opposite, two next door. The only thing that upset me was
> having to lay out small babies, and there were enough of those. I've
> got eleven grandchildren. I was married at sixteen, a grandmother

at thirty-three. If our lives weren't destroyed by poverty and unemployment, there was always a war just in time to remind us there were worse things.

For all the piety and sorrow over orphans, there is no record of any society forbearing to create them by a refusal to wage war, that prodigal begetter of bereaved youth. Indeed, human slaughter and the amputation of kindred in the past century by war and ideologies in the name of which it was waged eclipse the casualties of ferocious religious strife of Europe in the previous half millennium. Perhaps only the massacres and famines of imperialism foreshadow the great orphaning of 1914–18, the genocidal frenzy of Hitler, the mass starvation and forced labour of Stalin.

In the twentieth century, a desire to demonstrate human emancipation from the superstition and unreason of religion proved only that secular faiths could replicate its worst horrors—extremes of nationalism, Communism and Fascism; beliefs which, aided by technology, demanded human sacrifice on a scale of which those whose primitive intolerance had nothing but the rack and thumbscrew to assist them, could scarcely conceive.

The Nazi orphan-machine

More than sixty million people died in World War Two; the number of orphans remaining at its conclusion is difficult to calculate, since many children perished with their parents. Orphanage was the price of rescue for many who survived— victims of concentration camps, rescued children, children sent to a place of safety from bombs.

Grazyna was orphaned by the Nazis in Poland. Born in 1936, she was three when the Germans invaded:

My mother was a doctor and my father a chemist. They were the first people singled out by the Nazis, because these were most likely to be social leaders and to help the Jews. A far-sighted uncle (my father's brother, a very handsome man and a wheeler-dealer) managed to hide me with a farming family just outside Lodz. I don't know how he did it. Some Poles concealed Jews for money, some for religious reasons, some as an act of mercy.

I just accepted it. I was part of the family, which had a number of boys but no girls, and I played with them. Whenever there were German patrols in the neighbourhood, they used to hide me under straw in the barn. I didn't go out much. I remember being always cold and I was constantly hungry. There was no food, even though it was a farm—maybe the produce had to be given to the Germans. I had rickets. At the end of the war, I went to a hospital in the mountains, and a nurse whipped egg-yolks to nourish me.

All my family in Poland died in the camps. Only this uncle survived. He was very adaptable and passed for Polish. Of course, many people of the middle class were well assimilated and he had many friends. No one ever denounced him. My father was a well-known chemist, quite famous for some of the medical compounds he made. There is a book about his work in Harvard University. After the war, my uncle took over my father's identity.

When the war ended, and news came that the Russians were approaching, the Germans went. Just like that. Sometimes they just left the tea they were drinking, a half-eaten meal and fled. They were afraid of the Russians. The Russians lost so many million people during the war. The idea that they were going to overrun Western Europe during the Cold War was just propaganda, they had lost too many to want to embark on new adventures, but the West had to keep the myth alive that they were going to start another war.

My mother's brother lived in Paris, and after the War I went there for a time. I was ten. His wife was an invalid, and there were terrible shortages in Paris. There was a Jewish organisation which helped Jewish orphans go to South Africa. My grandmother and her sister had gone there well before the war. The husband of my great-aunt was a watchmaker, very skilled—all he had to do was pick up his tools and go, he had portable skills. The people who suffered most were the poor Jews, people who could not assimilate or alter their identity in order to avoid the attention of the Nazis.

When I went to South Africa, I could not speak a word of English. I knew Polish and French. I had to learn Afrikaans and English. When we got to Cape Town there was some bureaucratic problem, and I spent six months in an orphanage. I think most of the children were from broken families, there were not many true orphans. And then my great-aunt was already a very old lady. I don't think she had much inclination or ability to look after a twelve-year-old girl. I was sent to a superior boarding school in Cape Town, where the children from all over Africa came. I finished my matriculation.

Because I had always been cold and hungry, I started work in catering. I developed a good business in South Africa. I married and had three children, but the marriage broke down and I came to London to make a fresh start. Here I developed my own high-class catering business. I love cooking and I was very successful. My children have also achieved what they wanted. One has worked with Microsoft since the beginning, and I remember him telling me that one day machines would communicate with each other. I thought that was crazy. My daughter is an artist and lives in New York, and my other son is in London.

I am a survivor. I accepted the conditions in which I lived. I don't think it had any very negative effect on me, even though I was not loved as a child. I look on life positively. My second husband suffers badly from depression. Dealing with that is hard, but I have come through worse ordeals than that.

Parents orphan their own children

Britain accepted about 10,000 unaccompanied child refugees below the age of seventeen from Nazi-occupied Europe in 1938. Although the children were unaware of it at the time, many of their parents had some apprehension that they would soon become orphans; as indeed most did within three or four years of their departure. Those saved by this act of charity by the British vividly recalled the parting—tearful faces, handkerchiefs waving, hopeful protestations of a quick reunion, the blur of smoke and the last convulsive hug and kisses. The choice between the pain of separation and the (fairly) certain survival of their children created much heartbreak but little indecision. The extreme sorrow of goodbye contrasted, in the children's memory, with the no-nonsense coolness of their reception in Britain, where embraces were scarce and displays of emotion considered embarrassing. A number of children had already been assigned to families; others went to holiday camps and reception centres and waited to be selected by those who came to inspect them. Some were even taken back and exchanged for others, as though they had been a faulty purchase. Certain parents begged their children to find a place for them also—the British limited the entry of adults to those who were prepared to work as maidservants, gardeners or butlers. A few children did rescue their parents in this way; but the majority were destined to early bereavement through the industrial efficiency of mass murder in Europe.

Many orphaned children developed strong relationships with those who took them in; and since their own families had been, on the whole far-seeing and intelligent, their children grew up to be successful.

Leslie Brent became a member of a team researching skin grafts and tissue rejection, which earned Peter Medawar a Nobel Prize in 1960.[1] Leslie's whole family died, apart from an uncle and a cousin who were outside of Germany at the time. The family were from a small town in Pomerania on the Baltic coast, Koslin, now in Poland and called Koszalin.

Persecuted at school, he was removed to a Jewish Boys' Orphanage in Berlin; a bitter irony, since at that time he was not an orphan, but would soon become one. From there he was selected for the Kindertransport. He says:

> My parents stayed in Koslin. My father lost his job. In 1938, they went to Berlin, because they thought it would be easier to 'disappear' there. They were deported in October 1942. I thought they went to Theresienstadt, and from there to Auschwitz. Once, visiting Poland as a lecturer, I visited Auschwitz. I broke down. There was no grave or date, and I had never grieved for them properly.

It turned out they never went there at all. They were sent to Riga in Latvia, where, three days afterwards, they were taken into the woods and shot. My sister was with them. She was a trainee nurse in the Jewish hospital in Berlin, which remained open throughout the war. Part of it served as a collection point for deportations. She insisted on going with her parents and they died together.

I never felt abandoned. I knew it was in my best interests. When we came to England, we had no idea it would be permanent. Most parents said 'We will see you soon.' I kept up a correspondence with mine till just before they were deported. We were allowed to send messages through the Red Cross. They had to be anodyne, limited words. My last message from them told me they were going on a journey. I had no idea what it meant, but it must have been just before they were deported. It was handwritten by my father— usually he typed the message—and his writing was rather wild. They understood their fate. I had several letters about other members of my family, saying my aunt or uncle 'sind verreist'—had gone on a journey, a euphemism for deportation…

My parents were practising Jews, but they loved German culture, music and literature. Their tragedy was that of hundreds of thousands of people. When Hitler came, they thought 'It can't last.' They made no attempt to get out until it was too late.

Leslie later joined the army, and after the war, had a grant to study Zoology. His Head of Department was Peter Medawar, who offered him a place in his research team. He worked for fourteen years with Medawar on immunological tolerance, and took the chair of immunology at St Mary's Hospital in Paddington in London.

Orphans of war's end

The opening of the concentration camps and the bombing of Dresden did not end the making of war orphans. The A-bomb in Hiroshima took the parents of about 5,000 children. Many children had been sent to the countryside for their safety from conventional bombs. The care of such children wandering in the city, and those who had survived in the countryside, was undertaken by teachers, Buddhists and in Nagasaki the Catholic Church was the lead agency in rescue.

Seiko Komatsu was nine. He was 2.5 kilometres from the epicentre of the bomb:

> The Schoolchildren's Evacuation Reinforcement Guidelines were decided in March 1945. From April to July 1945, national school pupils from the third to sixth grade in Hiroshima City were evacuated in groups to temples and community halls in seven counties. I should have been one of the children safely evacuated. But my parents had both died when I was one year old, and my grandparents, who had raised me since then, did not want me separated from them.

Their love for their grandchild had unhappy consequences:

> On the morning of 6 August I awoke at around 6.30, and with my grandmother, boarded a Hiroden Railway Miyajima Line tramcar. We got off four stops later at Kusatsu Station, approximately 4.5 kilometres from the hypocentre. My grandmother was regularly commuting to a clinic in that area to receive treatment for a nerve problem in her foot, and she used to take me with her. That day four or five patients were ahead of her. I was too hungry and impatient to wait. I took the train home alone to eat breakfast.

> Just after I had grumbled my way through a meal of inferior boiled barley, an intense red flash lit up the window glass, followed by a tremendous roar! I was thrown about five metres and landed violently on the tatami floor. In my mind, all was darkness, and I had no idea what had happened. After a while I came to myself and stood up. Looking around, I saw the window glass shattered to tiny splinters and the chest and dish cupboards falling over. A shard of glass pierced my left knee and I was bleeding. Both my elbows were burned.

> Something hard had fallen from the ceiling on my grandfather's head, leaving a gaping wound about five centimetres long. Fortunately we had some yellow medicinal powder for emergencies, and he sprinkled this on his gash. Then he grabbed my hand and took me to an air-raid shelter located at the foot of a mountain

some distance west of us. People filed past the shelter, many whose deep burns indicated they had been exposed near the hypocentre. Miserably, they trudged on, seeking refuge in the countryside.

In a little while, a middle-aged woman entered our shelter pulling a younger woman by the hand. At first glance I thought the young woman must be a ghost—her deathly features, the hair standing straight up on her head, the ragged and torn clothes. Severe burns spread from her face to her chest and arms. Her skin dangled from her, exposing ripped, red flesh. Drops of oil stood out on her darkened swelling skin. The woman was a truly hideous sight.

There was no medication in our shelter. At the time, mercurochrome was the main treatment for wounds and injuries; most types of lesions were routinely painted bright red with this medicine. I wondered what could possibly be done for this woman. But suddenly the older woman picked up a small basin from the corner of the shelter and proceeded to urinate in it. She then soaked the torn rags in the urine and diligently set about washing the younger woman's wounds with the ammonia from her body. I can still vividly recall that scene.

Later, black rain began falling heavily over the northwest area of the city. That mixture of dirt and dust containing terrible radioactivity came down for nearly two hours. It finally stopped just before noon, at which time my grandfather led me by the hand to our home behind the Nishi-Hiroshima Station.

Ours was a two-storey wooden house standing on a seven-metre stone wall rising out of flat rice paddies. Completely unsheltered, it bore the full force of both the heat ray and blast. The rear of my house facing the epicentre had burst into flame. It appeared that the fire had burned for some time, until soused by the black rain. The blast itself had caused half of the second floor to collapse.

When they found Seiko's grandmother, she was sitting on the floor, dazed and soaked, murmuring 'The rain hurt, it hurt so much I couldn't bear it.' She died the following September. Through poverty, malnutrition and exposure, his grandfather died exactly two years after the blast. Orphaned a second time at the age of twelve, Seiko went to live with an uncle in Osaka.

He suffered for the rest of his life from emphysema and liver damage. To make a living he worked at the Hiroshima Peace Memorial Museum.[2]

Today's orphan-producers

Whatever incentive to success some have found in their condition as orphans, the great majority of the world's estimated 130 million orphans are among the poorest. Global life expectancy is about sixty-nine years; for orphans it is less than half that. In the United States, of those leaving foster-care at the age of eighteen, 25 per cent will become homeless, 56 per cent will be unemployed, 27 per cent will wind up in jail, and 30 per cent of young women will experience early parenthood.

War and civil strife continue to *engender* orphans with machine-like efficiency, in Yemen, Iraq, Afghanistan, Myanmar, South Sudan and Syria, The UN estimates well over a million Syrian child refugees, most of them in Turkey, Lebanon and Jordan. About 70,000 have lost their fathers; of the rest, some are alone in camps. Parents, in an act of heroic self-sacrifice, have sent their children to Europe and beyond, where they strike against the flinty walls of privilege.

Reyhanli is on the Turkish border, on the other side of which is a refugee city. It began, like all such settlements, as rows of tents on a bleak plain, a temporary tent city for a few thousand of the ten million displaced in Syria. It has grown into a town of breezeblock buildings, walls of industrial debris and corrugated metal: a provisional township with ramshackle shops selling falafels, cigarettes and cold drinks to people from Hama, Idlib and Kafra Janna. It is beset by searing winds and stinging dust in summer, while mud, rain and snow leave rough waterlogged tracks in winter. Half the refugees are children, most without education, trying to earn in any way they can. There is insufficient water—brought in daily by trucks—few medical posts with little medicine, and an acute shortage of latrines.

Bread is brought in from Turkey, while kitchens in the camp provide some rice and potatoes. In October 2016, a bomb blast, claimed by ISIL (which has a significant presence) killed thirty people. Death is the most frequent visitor to the malnourished and neglected.

In Reyhanli, early in 2017, there were eight orphanages, insufficient to accommodate all children who have lost both parents. Many have seen fathers and mothers die by gunfire, bombs or the collapse of buildings. One child was reported to be watching over and over again a YouTube video of the death of his father: a generation of children, shocked and embittered, who will grow into adults animated by who knows what vengeful nihilism, and disregard for the humanity of which they have also been robbed.

It is inevitable that those held in such places will look elsewhere for sanctuary. Some, trapped on the periphery of Europe, or on the streets of capital cities, have been thrust into adult responsibility by grief and loss, looking after siblings and friends even younger than themselves.

Farah

Farah, sixteen, saw her home in Aleppo destroyed, with all her family members inside:

> I had gone to fetch bread, and as I was coming back, there was a sudden explosion. I was thrown against the wall and blinded by dust. When I opened my eyes there was just a pile of brick and concrete where the building had been. My mother and father, my two brothers and baby sister were inside.
>
> I couldn't cry. Neighbours came and tried to rescue those inside— there were other families as well—but they could not lift the concrete which had collapsed on them. I had left my mother preparing the evening meal, my father watching TV news, my brothers with their schoolbooks. Then there was nothing. My aunt came and took me to her house, and I lay with her all that night, trembling,

but not crying, because I could not believe what had happened. I thought I would wake up and it would be as it was before, they would all be back in their places. I did sleep, and in the morning, my auntie told me there was nobody left. I saw my mother's body, but then they took me away, because seeing her sleeping and covered in dust made me cry; and when I started I couldn't stop.

After that I was frightened of every noise, and the sky which brought the birds and the sunshine became cruel because it brought us bombs and death. My auntie and uncle decided they could not stay because of what had happened, and they might lose all their children too; so we went by car to Turkey, where we crossed the border. At that time, it was easy. We went to a refugee camp, where we were always cold and hungry. Men came to us who promised they could get us to Europe. They were smugglers and they made a lot of money. They charged whatever people had. If they had two thousand dollars, or one thousand dollars, they would take it.

That was how we came to Greece. Our boat came at night and it was so low in the water, we didn't dare to move. We were told to sit still or we would all be drowned. When we got to the island (Lesbos), there were more camps. There was food but that was all. I met a man there who told me about Italy where we heard there was work and somewhere to live. I became his wife, not legally of course, but for the sake of survival. He left me. I met a family from Syria, who gave me a room in their apartment. Sometimes I beg on the street, but I do not earn much. People offer money to sleep with them. I met another man who says we can go to Sweden. I don't know. I have moved so much, I have no hope in a future.

Riaz

Riaz is twenty:

I was born in Azaz District in Aleppo in Syria in 1996. In 2011 my town was the most beautiful town in the world. Now it is in ruins, dangerous and destroyed.

I don't like violence. I was never rough at school and I still would not hurt anybody. There were five in my family—father and mother, one younger sister and one brother older than I. He was seventeen when he was killed by the army. I do not know what has happened to my sister. When he was killed, my parents sent me to Turkey with many other people from Aleppo. That was in November 2013.

From Turkey I came to Greece. There I knew no one. I had no relative and no friend. In Athens it is hard to find work, because there are so many people, both Greeks and refugees, without home or work. In Greece I passed a very difficult time. I had nothing to eat. No one provided me with any food, and I had to sleep in the park.

When it rained it was a disaster, and I thought I would die of the cold. It was the same as when I was at home, I thought every day 'Today we shall all die from the bombs and explosions.' In Greece I was thinking 'How will I survive the hunger and cold of this day?' I did not know where to go. I have never done harm to anyone in all my life. Why should this be our fate?

I am now in Rome, and have been here for nine months. At least I have a bed to sleep in and can eat. I do not know what has happened to my parents, and I still have no idea where my dear sister may be. For three years I heard nothing from them, I do not know if they are alive or dead.

It was not easy to get here. In Greece, for five euros I would go to bed with another man. This was a great sin for me. After this, many times I thought of killing myself. This world is too cruel, it disgusts me.

By getting some money together I saved 600 euros to come to Rome. I came in a fish truck. Normally they would charge 1500 euros for the journey. I was lucky because I came for less than half the price.

I am fine now. I do not know how long I will be here. Here people leave me in peace, even though there are also people here who are not good. They do not want us here. I am thinking how I can get to Norway. I ask my friend Damba, he is my close friend. He is from Eritrea and I would go with him, because he has a friend who lives in Norway.[3]

Other people's children

Children orphaned by war inspire sympathy because of parental death in defence of their country; but they are also victims of ambivalent attitudes towards war—patriotism in conflict with revulsion against deaths voluntarily inflicted, not by nature but by human will. The orphaned of the Napoleonic wars were more often than not consigned to the workhouse, while those of the later nineteenth century and of World War One found such refuge as orphanages provided. By 1939, these had been renamed 'children's homes', a euphemism that did little to diminish the pain of those they sheltered, since the regime of the institution remained unchanged.

The obsessive concern with our own children, and our eagerness to undo the wrongs of abuse and violence committed against them contrasts strangely with our refusal to succour those whose childhood has been drenched in the blood of those they love no less than we cherish our own. In many ways, the deafness to the suffering of others is a repeat of the indifference of the ruling elites of Britain to the miseries visited upon the children of the poor in our country. Should we see in the refugee camps of Turkey and Lebanon, in Greece and Italy, an equivalent site of forgetfulness to the poorhouses and penitentiaries, the Bridewells and hulks of our own past? The casual randomness with which orphans were made by war and scattered in orphanages, institutions and residential schools in Britain may have been tempered; but the sentiment lingers in the ease with which we can accommodate the grief of others, now that those others are no longer the insignificant of home, but the displaced of 'distant' countries glimpsed only through the solid and distancing windows of TV screens.

Myanmar

Closely allied to war in the indiscriminate destruction of families is the persecution of minorities. Social or religious 'cleansing' are a feature of this newly regressive age, just as secular ideologies performed the same melancholy function in the twentieth century. It seems human communities have difficulty sustaining themselves without some malignant force against which to define themselves: witches, deviants, dissenters, minorities; any 'alien' group will do.

Among the Rohingya Muslim minority in Myanmar, the agents of orphanage have been busy in 2016/17.

More than 50,000 Muslim Rohingya refugees fled to Bangladesh after a violent military crackdown on the minority in Myanmar. Following the death of nine police officers in October 2015, attributed to Rohingya militants, the army has disproportionately attacked civilians. In the bleak stony camp at Teknaf in the far south of Bangladesh, new arrivals bear stories common to all who flee persecution and violence—pillage, the destruction of homes and livelihoods and rape. Among them are hundreds of lone children, who have seen their parents killed, and who themselves have been the victims of physical and sexual assault. Intensification of the attack in 2017 led to the flight of more than half the million or more Rohingyas in Myanmar, a country which denies them identity and belonging.

Anowara

My name is Anowara. I am fourteen.[4]

I am from Naisong Zawmadat in Myanmar. I used to work with my father at the seaside. We fished for prawns and carp, I was happy with my parents, my brothers and sister before the war. We ate well. In the afternoon I could play with friends.

Two weeks ago, the military arrived in our village. They entered every house and rounded up all the young men. When they tried to run away they were shot in the back. Some people got away. I do not know where my parents are.

One of the Burmese soldiers took me behind my house, raped me and left me there. My older sister was taken by soldiers to the school room, where they also raped her and then killed her. They cut her right breast and stuck bamboo inside her. They killed her very painfully. Then they burned our house. I was the only one left.

Next day I escaped from the village with one other girl. We came to Bangladesh. We walked for four or five days in the hills almost without any food. Many of those who walked did so barefoot. Late night we came to Nakhaichori Bazar. I don't know anyone here.

The owner of this house saw us sitting in the cold and wet, and brought us here. I want to go back to my home, my country. Myanmar needs peace. Who wants to be refugees? We are running from the military. Four or five hundred of them came. They shot us in the back, then they took young girls for gang-rape.

Monshon

My name is Monshon Marma. I am eleven.

I lost my father when I was small. I do not know where he is now, whether or not he is alive. The Burmese army shoots the Rohingyas, and the Rohingya Solidarity Organisation [a former militant organisation that later became part of the Burmese Army] kills us. The soldiers came one night and took him away. He did not return.

My mother left me and killed herself. Now the poor people are dying everywhere. I was lucky because before she died, my mother sent me to this monastery, where there are eighty orphans. Here we study our language, Bangla and English. I am happy to study. In the afternoon I play football. During the day we go to plant trees.

The story of all the children here is the same. In order to live I sell vegetable produce. Many people have helped me. I think I am very intelligent, because I am always first in school. I love to study, but I know it is impossible. After we have finished elementary school, who will help us?

I know if my parents were alive I would go to secondary school. But now I am in the hands of God, I shall go wherever he leads me.

Arefa

I am Arefa, and I'm seventeen-years-old.

In Myanmar I had a beautiful family. I had six sisters and two brothers. Four of my bigger sisters were married and lived in other villages with their husbands and children. My two older brothers lived with their wives, and I stayed with my little sister, my mother and father. One brother is twenty-two, the other twenty, and both were married a few months ago.

The soldiers killed both my brothers in front of me. They took the bodies away on a lorry. Then they shot my father. They raped my two cousins in the presence of my mother and then shot them. No one is left of my mother's or father's family. I also heard that all my other sisters, together with their families, were also dead.

I am like a living corpse, the only one left of my family. Six army men raped my little sister, who was fifteen. I watched her die. Before the military went away, they set fire to the house and took away the few valuables we had. They locked people in many houses in my village and then set them on fire.

I do not know how many men raped me. I was unconscious. When I opened my eyes all I could see was fire and smoke. With many others I came here to Bangladesh. To get here, we followed the river, walking for two nights. In the daytime we hid in the fields. To cross the border we had to pay a broker. He took 25,000 taka (£250) from every person just to cross the river. I didn't have enough money, so I was made to wait another night. Without money, the broker would not let us pass. The following night I got the money from selling my body to the broker for sex.

We all came here by night. A few days ago the people in the camp married me to someone staying here. I am with him now.

Anowar Sadiq

I am Anowar Sadiq, and I am eight-years-old.

The soldiers cut my mother's throat in front of me. Then they took her body away with them. They also killed my little sister and my big brother while I watched. My little sister was being shielded on my mother's lap. They picked her up and threw her outside. I came here on foot with my neighbour. We crossed the river by fishing-boat. The fisherman didn't ask me for any money. All the others had to pay.

I am not doing anything. When I am hungry, I ask people. If they give me anything I eat. Otherwise I stay hungry. I have been here for five days.

Latifa

I am Latifa, and I am ten years old. This is my sister, Shapnalata who is twelve. We live in Teknaf, Cox' Bazar. Our parents came from Myanmar a long time ago.

Our father's name was Mohammed Ullah. Eight years ago, he drowned in the sea, trying to go illegally to Malaysia. Many Rohingyas want to go to Malaysia, but many have drowned in the sea on the journey. Only two people came back alive after three months, and they told us everything that had happened.

Our mother's name is Yasmin. She is a beggar. She goes to Teknaf City and to the markets every day. Sometimes we go with her. Sometimes we go to the fish market to collect fish which we sell to people. Many bad people insult my elder sister Shapnalata. This makes her ashamed. I often find her at night crying alone. But we have no other choice.

We never went to school. I was two years old and my sister four when our father died. My mother is thinking of how she can get my sister married. She is looking for a husband for her, and she will soon be married.

Azimullah

My name is Azimullah. I am eight years old. A few days ago, Myanmar soldiers came to our village. They brought all the village people to an open space, and then started kicking and punching them. They selected some young girls, and took them with others, including my father, to their military camp. They shot down all the rest. Some people were hiding, but the Magh people found them and betrayed them to the military. The soldiers were taking any valuable things from people's houses. The next day we found my father's body near the river. His throat had been cut.

My mother was tortured and killed by the military.

My auntie brought me here with her. We were walking for five days from my village until we reached the Naf River. We crossed by fishing trawler. My auntie paid 10,000 *taka* per person.

Nobody helps us here. I am hungry from yesterday morning. We came to the camp two days ago. We are still not registered. My auntie is trying to register us, but so far no one has registered us: without that, we can get no relief. Last night I slept on the street in the camp with many other children.

8

THE END OF AN EPOCH

Casualties of moral welfare

The regimentation of children in homes and schools, charitable, local authority or private, reflected the disciplines of industrial society. Although these disciplines were relaxed in the
mid-twentieth century, this was slow to reach institutions for the
orphan, the delinquent and other young casualties of industrial
society. Rigid regimes persisted long after a softer nurture had
reached a majority of children. There is always a time lag in the
response to social change by sclerotic bureaucracies set up for
policies long decayed, but continuing through inertia. So it was
with children taken into care, particularly those of unmarried
young women, many of whom were cajoled or threatened into
giving up their babies under the waning influence of something
known as 'moral welfare', until the 1970s.

I was a social worker in 1969 with the School Care
Committees of the then Inner London Educational Authority.
These Committees, set up in 1908, were staffed by volunteers,
mainly upper middle-class women, who visited families and
guardians of school-children with social problems—non-attend-
ance, chronic sickness, malnutrition, lack of hygiene, long-term
parental unemployment.

Although use of volunteers was archaic by the 1960s, the tradition lingered. Care Committees worked under the direction of a professional organiser, but they absorbed the energy and commitment of women who chafed at their ornamental status as wives of business or professional men, and wanted to 'do something' for those less favoured than themselves.

The organiser in the office where I worked was unequivocally upper middle class. She wore tweeds and blouses, stout shoes, and a slight frown, constantly pained at the injustice of the world. High-minded and serious, she supervised work, not only of volunteers, but also of lower ranks of paid specialists, including Moral Welfare Workers. There were two of these in the office, known with amused detachment to the rest of the staff, as the Greater Moral and the Lesser Moral. Both—like many women employed in such posts—were unmarried. They were sensible, severe and dutiful. They spoke of their 'naughty girls': their principal task to ensure pregnant schoolgirls were whisked away to Mother and Baby Homes at the seaside, where they would be isolated from their peers to avoid the taint of example, but also to hush up the birth, and subsequent inevitable adoption, of the 'unwanted' child.

The truth was that the child frequently was wanted; desperately, obsessively. And although time was allowed for the young woman—and her family—to think over giving up the baby or keeping it, a majority were persuaded, as much by social custom as by any meaningful 'choice', to part with it; so they could start afresh, as though the moral lapse—as it was seen—could be erased, and she could resume, if not her studies, at least a respectable job in a factory or office, where only the long memory and loose tongues of neighbours might impair her prospects for a 'normal' married life.

Julia

Julia knew the stigma of the 'unwed mother'. She was born in Nottingham in 1946, where her father worked in the Players cigarette factory and her mother stayed at home

My mother was bored. Her only social contact was with her two sisters, who lived in walking distance. I couldn't have stood a life like that. I used to go out with friends, innocent stuff, milk-bar, dancing, youth club. It sounds pathetic today. I was still at school when I met Clive. He was a looker, dark hair and beautiful blue eyes, I fell for him, and the lies he told me. He worked on the buildings, the new estate near where we lived. We used to go onto the site after dark. It wasn't locked or anything. We would light a fire, and believe it or not, make tea and eat cake. We had sex. The first time, I was scared, I thought 'Oh no, I'll get pregnant'. I told him I didn't want to get into any trouble. But I didn't, and I got too confident. I thought Oh perhaps it won't happen to me. But it did.

The night I decided to tell him, he wasn't there. I think he sensed it even before I knew. On the site they had nobody of that name. He vanished without trace. I didn't even know who he was. It was like a phantom pregnancy, only he was the phantom. I wasn't. I'd never been to school much; and when you have a proper boyfriend, you look down on girls going off every day to sit in desks in front of some shrivelled up teacher, and you think 'Oh I know all about life, and they know nothing.'

The woman who dealt with me was a Moral Welfare Worker; actually it was immoral, it wasn't welfare and she didn't work. She came and talked to my parents. Their biggest concern was shame. They wouldn't throw me out, but they didn't want anything to do with illegitimacy. 'You've spoiled your life', they said. So they were happy to let Mrs Gibbons fix up the 'holiday', the birth and the adoption. It was never suggested I might want to keep the baby. I wasn't consulted. I knew from the neighbours, that if you got the father to marry you, a shotgun wedding they called it, it would be all right. You could keep the baby, and the neighbours counted on their fingers how many months you'd been married before it came, but you had done 'the right thing'.

It was near Hastings, the Home. The seaside was anonymous—a place where girls who've gone wrong learn how to get back onto the straight and narrow. There were eight or nine of us. We were given work, but none of it was practical, no instruction on looking after babies—it was assumed that you'd give the baby up. No teaching about relationships, nothing about emotions or even sex—they thought we knew too much about that already. Lots of polishing and cleaning, preparing food, good healthy walks. And prayers. They didn't push religion too much, but there was an understanding that you were fallen.

The minute I saw my baby I fell in love with him. Up to that point I just wanted to get it over and done with, I wasn't prepared for my own emotional reaction. I screamed and shouted. Then I went silent. I grieved for him. That also wasn't part of the programme. It seems so cruel now; but then 'It's all for the best'; 'what kind of life would he have with you?' 'He'll go where he's loved.' 'Yes but I love him.' 'What chance would he have?' I wanted Mum to let me keep him, but she wouldn't. She cared more about what other people thought. For years I missed him, thought about him all the time.

Between them, they made things worse. I got married at eighteen, and had three children. I love them to bits. But there's still a gap where my firstborn would have been. I have no idea what happened to him. I hoped he'd come to find me, after they made it easy for children to find their birth parents. But why should he? I used to lie awake, imagining him getting his birth certificate and tracing me. But he would have no memory of me. I'm the one with the memories and the feelings. I made an orphan of him; even if the best people on earth adopted him, they couldn't have given him the love I felt.

It is child abuse, twice over, separating a baby from his mother, because I was only a child myself. We were abused by those who thought they knew better. What makes it worse, it all changed so quickly. By the 1970s, girls had stopped being 'unwed mothers' and became 'single Mums'. It didn't matter. My parents felt bad about it later. They wouldn't talk about it; but by the time nobody cared about who was legitimate or illegitimate, it made all the shame redundant. I was sacrificed and so was he. I'm not a bitter person; but I feel regret. I think 'moral welfare' ought to have been more concerned with the quality of the relationship between mother and child, not the social reaction to what people did.

The lingering death of 'bastardy'

Julia was among the last generation of victims of laws concerning what used to be called bastardy (the last Bastardy Act was passed in 1923). Such children were a kind of dishonourable orphan, the fruits of sin; and as such to be scourged and punished, since the 'iniquity of the fathers [should be visited] upon the children unto the third and fourth [generation]'; and guilt had been scripturally assigned to their progeny.

The 1576 statute says:

> Concerning bastards begotten and born out of lawful matrimony (an offence against God's and man's laws) the said bastards now left to be kept at the charge of the parish where they were born, to be the great burden of the said parish, and in defrauding of the relief the impotent and aged poor of the same Parish, and to the evil example and the encouragement of the lewd life, it is ordered and enacted…

The child was to be supported by the putative father by a weekly sum, and by the mother's provision of 'needful sustenance.' Such a child could not inherit, and where the father was unidentified, was called *filius nullius*, nobody's child, a term that encouraged exploitation and mistreatment. An Act of 1609 enabled the mother of any child chargeable to secure the apprehension and even the imprisonment of the father until he should indemnify the parish. We have seen how such children were treated, both institutionally and socially, in the seventeenth and eighteenth centuries. In 1733, a woman pregnant with a bastard was required to declare the fact and to name the father. On the mother's oath, a man could be imprisoned or coerced into marriage; and although this gave women power (which they did not invariably use justly), it was abolished by the 1834 Poor Law Amendment Act, which found the Bastardy Acts 'unwise'. This was because the weekly payment from the parish was usually given directly to the mother; a position which placed her in the same position as a widow, and 'there can be no reason for giving to vice privileges which we deny to misfortune.' Bastardy was for centuries attributed principally to the 'lewdness' of women; and even after it became possible for them to 'swear to' a father of their child, they were still blamed for laws they never made. In the evidence taken by the Poor Law Commissioners in the 1834 report:

> At Exeter, an apprentice under eighteen years of age was recently committed to the house of correction for want of security. It was admitted that there was no chance of his absconding, but the overseers said he had been brought for punishment. The woman stated that she was only three months gone with child; and thus the boy is taken from his work, is confined five or six months among persons of all classes, and probably ruined for ever, on the oath of a person with whom he was not confronted, and with whom he denied having any intercourse.

After 1834, the law became more lenient to the putative father, but the unfairness of this was modified in 1845, when the mother was given a civil remedy against him, which would relieve the parish of involvement. In 1868, the right of the parish was restored to attach money from the father, and indeed to sue for it.

The milder designation of 'bastards' as 'illegitimate' did not lessen the stigma; and children continued to be punished for their birth outside of a matrimony the holiness of which diminished as the twentieth century progressed. The de-sacralisation of marriage made having children a matter of personal choice. But within living memory, before the social transformation of the past half century, treatment of the mother was harsh and the number of coercive adoptions high.

Apologies for history

Official apologies for history are now a familiar aspect of contemporary life. Penitence seems to have become a profession. In 2006 Tony Blair expressed his 'sorrow' over slavery. In 2010,

Cameron was 'profoundly sorry' for the Hillsborough cover-up, after the police falsified accounts of the deaths of Liverpool football fans in the Sheffield disaster of 1989. In 2013 Cameron said the 1919 Amritsar massacre in India was 'a deeply shameful event'. Regrets are now regularly expressed at the abuse and mis-treatment of orphans, unwanted and illegitimate children. Gordon Brown apologised for the Child Migrant Programme of the early and mid-twentieth century to former colonies. In 2013, the Church of England offered an 'unreserved apology' to victims of child abuse by Anglican priests, and admitted its own 'serious failure' to prevent it. Rotherham Council in 2013 apologised to the victims of child abuse in the town, who were 'let down' by 'systemic failure'. In 2015 the Roman Catholic Church in Scotland apologised to the McLellen Commission for abuse at Fort Augustus Abbey, a gaunt Gothic fortress that has the aspect of a medieval torture chamber rather than a school run by Benedictine monks.[1]

The Magdalene Laundries

Efforts to dissociate ourselves from an embarrassing past are not confined to Britain. In February 2008, Kevin Rudd, then Prime Minister of Australia made a formal apology to indigenous families, whose children had been forcibly removed from their care between 1910 and 1970. In 2013 the Irish Taoiseach, Enda Kenny, apologised to the women who had been detained and exploited in Ireland's Magdalene laundries. The nuns took in laundry from hotels, institutions and private families, and used the labour of orphaned and illegitimate girls for nothing: a penitential atonement for the faults of others, a regime of loveless, repetitive work as a prophylactic against the taint which, it was believed, could never be purged.

Nancy was left in a basket outside the Mount Orphanage in the 1930s.[2] At the age of ten or eleven she was transferred to a Magdalene laundry because the nuns said she was, 'a troublemaker.' She had been hit by one of the sisters, a blow that cut her so badly she had to go to hospital. She told the doctor 'the Sister did it', and her fate was sealed. Her name was changed: an identity, already fragile, further undermined by the invented character she was to become. Transferred to another laundry, her treatment was even worse. One day a girl died at her work. The nun said that they were now a worker short and the rest would have to make up for it. Nancy simply walked out one day, but with nowhere to go, slept in churches. Subsequently sent into service with a farmer who treated her with the same brutal contempt as the nuns, she slept in a barn with the cows; and found comfort only when she went to look after children in a private family.

The Magdalene laundries enacted punitive rituals upon children sent away for reasons unknown to them, often as a consequence of trauma and bereavement. There was no recognition that children had emotions. The girls were given a false identity, a new name. Their hair was cut off so they all shared an identical crop; an uncomfortable uniform, stiff frocks, itchy stockings and clog-like shoes. The staff, grim and unsmiling, gave no solace. They rose in the dark after sleep in unheated dormitories; washing was inadequate, often in cold water, no food until after Mass or morning worship, and then a diet devoid of taste and often of nutrients—lumpy porridge, greens, potatoes, bread and lard or margarine, watery cocoa, consumed out of unbreakable vessels. The atmosphere exuded disapproval of their very existence; beatings for small infringements of incomprehensible rules. Silence was imposed, not reflective or meditative, but a denial of communication with their peers to forestall particular friendships. After work from eight o'clock or eight-thirty until six o'clock and an insubstantial tea, there was needlework, making scapulars, toys or other objects for sale. Early bed was the rule, after prayers, said kneeling on cold floors; and a patrol of dormitories to ensure chastity; the loneliness of children untouched by loving hands and which they bear like stigma all their lives.

Menstruation occurred with no prior instruction from adults, which frightened the girls, who had to ask the nuns for sanitary towels, convent-made, bulky and obtrusive. There was a constant threat of being sent to an even worse place—the 'asylum'; and a lack of sympathy in sickness. Years of labour without pay created a sense of worthlessness. And this was deliberate policy. The long aftermath was an inability to express feeling, incomprehension in wounded adult relationships, insecurity and an inability to deal with elementary social relationships, no capacity for initiative and hesitancy in any form of self-expression. The wonder is, not that so many people perished or wound up in prisons or psychiatric hospitals, but that they survived, overcoming the erasure of self to which their orphaned or disgraced status added yet another layer of deprivation.

Surviving the orphanage

Bernadette Fahy went at the age of seven with her twin and younger brother to Goldenbridge 'Orphanage' in Dublin.[3] Their father had deserted the family, and although the judge asked the children to choose the parent they would prefer to live with, he 'committed' them to the orphanage anyway. It was an unhappy place. Many nuns saw elements of themselves they disliked in the children; as a result they thought it their duty to 'beat the devil' out of those in their custody. Lloyd de Mause describes this long rooted historical attitude towards children as a form of 'projection', whereby adults play out their own ambivalent feelings, beating their own sense of inferiority or wickedness in those they believe it their duty to correct.[4]

Bernadette Fahy describes mornings after breakfast as a particular ordeal:

> The children who had wet their beds, many of whom had already been punished by a staff member, were made to go and stand in one of the classrooms. I shall never forget the images I hold from these sessions. A large circle of children, boys and girls of all ages,

stood in a semicircle around the edges of the room. A nun would arrive and begin her ritual from a position on the rostrum, which was about 18 inches from the floor, but seemed very much higher to us at the time. We children, shaking in terror, and overwhelmed with fear and shame, would quake as she began her tirade of abuse, calling us at the very least, dirty, filthy and bad, as she shook a stick at us. It was inevitable that some of us were in for a severe battering. As she continued berating us, she would become red in the face. She seemed to us to work herself up into a frenzy. Then, suddenly, she would, literally, jump off the podium and pounce on any child in the circle within her reach. We were terrified of becoming the object of her frustrations. Our terror was nearly worse than the actual experience of being beaten by her…

I remember standing there as a child of seven or eight, thinking to myself: This is just crazy. What is the point? Children wet the bed when they are scared. They don't do it just to annoy the nuns and staff or just for a laugh. I remember rationalising that if they thought beating children would stop them wetting the bed, how come the same children were standing in front of them every day? It clearly wasn't working. But of course, that wasn't what the issue was about at all…Remember, we were the children of 'sinners', of incompetents who couldn't look after their own children, of social outcasts. We bore their shame, their sin. We 'deserved' to be punished.[5]

Orphan graveyards

A melancholy memorial to young lives lost in orphanages was uncovered in 2003, when scores of tiny graves in the St Mary's cemetery in Lanark were found to be those of orphan children who had died in the town's Smyllum orphanage; children tormented in an institution run by the Catholic Church. Children had been buried without ceremony, leaving no sign they ever existed. The orphanage was closed in the 1980s, but survivors testify to the coldness of the charity and the unkindness of staff. One man said that when a child died from disease, the nuns never spoke about it; but he had been forced to kiss the forehead of a dead nun at the start of her requiem Mass. The memorial to the children is a stone that bears the words, 'Sweet Jesus have mercy on the souls of the children of Smyllum.' The Sisters of Charity had no record of the children's names. The building has gone, like that of so many such institutions, replaced by flats and houses; another effacement of memory of those whose identity had already been erased by the time they were absorbed into a prison for innocents, guilty only of living.[6] An inquiry into institutional abuse of children in Catholic institutions in Scotland heard in 2017 that as many as 400 children may rest in unmarked graves in the grounds of the Orphanage.[7]

The state continues to make orphans

The making of orphans by state and charity did not end with the nineteenth century, in the sense that many children in institutional care, fostered or adopted, were bereft—if not bereaved—of all family attachments; a practice still widespread late into the twentieth century. Many still bear the scars of these affective amputations.

Ralph was born in 1966 to a woman in Salford. Taken soon after birth and placed in a Catholic orphanage, he was adopted at nine months by a white couple in Burnley. He was told nothing of his parentage, except that his birth mother was sick and unable to care for him. 'She couldn't cope and voluntarily put her children in care. It must have been a source of shame to her. She kept her youngest and oldest daughters. Transracial adoptions at the time were supposed to give children "a better life".'

Ralph was told his adoptive mother and father had been invited to select a child from the orphanage. They were pious people who gave him security and affection; but he keenly felt an absence of kin. 'It was the time of the Biafran war. There was much in the news about Biafran orphans; and although I am of Afro-Caribbean heritage, I think I must have been a beneficiary of publicity given to the children of Biafra.' Ralph found particular warmth and comfort from his mother's parents—the grandfather had been a miner and his grandmother in service: they had never seen a black person, but took great delight in their grandchild, telling him stories of the war, the mines and domestic service. This anchored him in the community in a way his adoptive parents could not:

> They did tell me that love was all that mattered, and that my mother giving me up was a 'sacrifice' she had made, for my sake. They tried to make the position more palatable to me, and I had compassion for her.

> When I came to trace her, it was a long, difficult search. I was told half-truths and given vague information. It appeared I had five siblings from different fathers. Of my mother's six children, four were adopted. My second sister was also adopted by a family in Burnley: she went to the girls' school in the same neighbourhood. I must have passed her, seen her frequently, but had no idea who she was, or even that she existed.

> I was never able to trace my father. I was told he was from Martinique. As a result of that my daughter made an effort to study French, because that might help us trace him. She hated French; and when it turned out that there was no connection—he was apparently from St Kitt's—I felt she had also been cheated by a lack of information about our past.

> I managed to contact three of my siblings. The oldest and the youngest sister lived with our mother. But my second sister and I felt we had been given away. My second sister was called Helen Margaret; and the same name had been given to the youngest. It is a very scary feeling to have a sister with exactly the same name. We have not been able to find them.

> Only in 2011 was I given access to 'the book of my life'—the dossier about my past. And even then, there was something missing. When the social worker presented it to me, I said 'But surely there was another sister?' And she said 'Was there? I'll go and look.' And she came back with some papers she said had got mislaid. It seemed that even then they didn't want me to know the whole story. My birth mother died four years ago.

My relationship with the others is still new—I contacted them only within the last year. We are still getting to know each other.

You feel you have no past. I think my adoptive mother must have known about my sister at least, because she knew the nun involved in placing both of us. When you discover those things, it drives a wedge even between those you trust and love. My adoptive mother is a remarkable woman. She was one of the first women to get a degree from the Open University. My father, whose family came from Dorset, traced his own ancestry, and when he shared it with me, I said 'Yes, that is all very well, but what has it got to do with me?' I think that hurt him.

The premise is that over time, maturity will remove these insecurities. But it doesn't. Self-doubt comes flooding back at moments of vulnerability. As a young adult, I saw people around me having children: to see a child unconditionally wanted was very poignant.

The family adopted three children, and then they had their own child. I never thought it made any difference, but it must have done. I adored my adoptive father. His attitude was 'You are my son and that's the way it is.' But they separated when I was sixteen and he remarried. He'd say 'You know where I am', but he became more distant, involved in a new relationship. I was angry with him. I suppose they had never really got on. My mother was strong, determined, committed to social justice. He was passive. I wanted to provoke a reaction from him—I wanted him to be upset or angry about things. Perhaps he was, but he didn't show it. She was very passionate.

The other side of it was that she was very controlling. She didn't like my research into my birth family. My father was submissive. Keith, their child, always took his mother's side. The other child they adopted is Anglo-Indian. She was slightly brain-damaged at birth, because they used forceps on her delivery. This held her back, and it was hard for the adoption agency to place her. But our mother took her on. I am close to her.

When I was growing up I was not myself. I had no reference point from the culture. Other black people, even if they were called names, discriminated against, at least they had each other and could gain support from them, learn to be proud of who they are.

I could have been exotically attractive as a young man. But I was too preoccupied with my own being in the world. Friends have said all the girls used to fancy me. I was afraid people would be disappointed when they found out I was only Burnley, nothing more exotic than that. It was also the 1970s and 80s. I was aloof, because there was always a danger of being attacked. I love cricket and was praised for being West Indian—they saw it in a positive way. But if I didn't do well, my Caribbean background was at fault. I was stubborn. I didn't listen.

I get a lot of love from my wife and children. But self-doubt never goes away. Observing other people's families shows you—as soon as my wife walks into her family house, there's not a shadow of doubt of who she is and where she belongs.

I was in a group that took issue with transracial adoptions, for all the reasons we now know. We were interviewed on TV, and the interviewers laid into us—called us ungrateful. They had no idea of the conflicts and anxieties.

It has taken a lot of work to bring my birth family together. It still isn't finished. It is an irony that the sister who grew up with my birth mother found the discovery harder than those who were adopted.

My birth mother was the youngest of twelve children from Ireland. The church played a big part in my adoption and upbringing. There is an irony in the story—my mother's mother had been married before she married my grandfather. Her first husband was from Barbados, and their first child, my auntie, was black. That must have been the 1930s, when such marriages were rare. When he died, she married and had eleven children with her second husband.

End of stigma

When divorce laws were liberalised, attitudes towards sex changed, diversity of human relationships was acknowledged, the stigma of illegitimacy decayed rapidly. Although enshrined in legislation, it was not originally a government initiative, since efforts to lift from children the unmerited shame of their parents were scarcely a novelty. Social change is mysterious: subtly and over time, in conjunction with other developments—affluence and social mobility, it works sometimes obscurely to restructure our perceptions of morality.

The transformation of attitudes to children has certainly been an aspect of greater economic well-being and the decay of the need for an archaic form of industrial discipline through the generations. Growing tolerance accompanied the greater security of the mid twentieth century; the rights of children recognised by an individualism which struck against the idea that childhood was an undifferentiated condition, in perpetual need of correction.

Whatever the cause, this threw into sharp relief the poignancy of people who had concealed their origins, lived down the public shame or hidden the circumstances of their own, or their children's, birth. It made cruelly absurd all the misery of illegitimacy and loss, and the energy spent in denial was a vast waste of human emotion. Such changes illuminate the arbitrary nature of values lately held to be unshakeable; but rarely can there have been so swift a disavowal of what were long held to be imperishable truths and their replacement by the opposite of everything previous generations had thought inviolable.

When it became possible for children adopted or in care to discover their birth families, this sets up other complex feelings. There was often a discovery of unsuspected affinities and late loving relationships developed; but remorse and disappointment awaited some. Sue Elliott tells of the reunion with her mother, Marjorie, who went to live with her for the last years of her life. She chronicles with love her discovery that she was not the only child 'given away' in the 1960s, that era of official prodigality with other people's children.[8]

When Jenny's birth mother opened the door to her for the first time, Jenny was in her forties. They recognised their kinship without words and simply fell into each other's arms. For others, unwilling to face their past, they slammed the door in their children's face; or the children themselves, injured and reproachful, heaped blame upon those who didn't deserve it, since they had acted under the coercion of others—parents, social workers, charitable or religious institutions.

Tracing birth parents

Anthony is seventy. He says:

My mother was twenty-one and working as a nurse. Her parents were missionaries. She had a sexual relationship with a doctor in Blackpool Hospital. They were not married, at least not to each other. The shame was socially overpowering, especially for a daughter of the church. She had to 'disappear' into the country-side, where she stayed with a relative, before giving birth in a hos-pital nearby. I don't know if she was persuaded to give me up for adoption or did so willingly. I was born in March 1947 and for-mally adopted at three months by Arnold and Nancy.

My adoptive mother was, by the end of the war, too old to have children and my adoptive father wanted a son. He had been in the army for six years and his wife was nine years older, so it was too late for another child. She was brought up in a workhouse: my grand-mother fell into poverty when her first husband, a small shopkeeper, died, leaving her alone with two young daughters. My mother was lucky one. Her mother was forced to choose which of her two daughters she would keep with her in the workhouse, since she was permitted to keep only one. She chose her younger, more vulnerable, daughter, my mother. My mother's sister was sent to an orphanage.

My mother later found her sister dying of TB in a sanatorium. My mother said she was able to talk with her sister, as she wheeled her around in a wheelchair in the clinic. Within a few months, she was dead. My mother never got over her sense of guilt that she was chosen over her sister, and her sister's death. Nor did she overcome the shame of the workhouse.

I discovered the truth about my adoption by accident. I'd been in hospital having my tonsils out—the first time I'd ever left my par-ents for more than a day. On the way back in our car I said to my dad 'Do you think I will ever be an author', as even then I wanted to write. He thought I said, 'Do you think I'll ever be an orphan?' to which he replied 'no, that was why we adopted you.'

This information coming so casually when I was nine shook me. I had never suspected I was not their natural son. It made me feel I had no real roots. This is one reason why I have been so committed—however flawed—to my own children, so I can at least create future branches of the tree even if I am without proper roots of my own.

It took fifty years to find the truth. I accepted what my parents—particularly my mother—told me about being chosen from a line of babies, and being adorable in the little red blanket that I was wrapped up in.

It was difficult at that time to trace my birth mother. I persisted, persuaded by my daughters. I had adoption counselling. From a self-help adoptees group I joined I discovered that while there were 'happy endings' many were not. The stories I heard were disturbing—a man who murdered his wife, received a life sentence and whose two young daughters were adopted. There were children who were the product of rape. These stories made me full of trepidation as to what I would discover.

For most young women of the 1940s, 1950s and 1960s it was that they were unmarried and the father either already married or disappeared. They were victims of the sanctimonious outrage of the age, doomed if they kept their children to a life of poverty and social ostracism. This forced them to give their children away, often under pressure from Christian charities.

I did trace my birth mother. The agency told me her husband did not want her to pursue this, since it was all too painful. I decided to send her a letter. It was brief and included a photo of me and my family. I said we were happy, had good lives. I would like to make contact, learn more about herself, my birth and my father. I bore no hatred for what she had done. I understood her situation at the time and the reasons why she gave me up.

Two weeks later the reply came. She said she was sending this brief reply to my questions. She was twenty-one when she gave birth.

She had met my father, a doctor, working in Blackpool. There were no details that would help me trace him, not even his name. She told me she was the daughter of South Seas missionaries. After giving birth, four years later she met her husband who was a solicitor. She told him nothing of my birth or the process of adoption. They subsequently went to Rhodesia, where she had three children. But the worst came at the end. She never wanted to see me or communicate with me again. She wanted my assurance that I would tell no one, including her family and my three siblings, as she never wanted anyone to know.

This second rejection was a heavy blow and hurt me more deeply and personally than having been given away as a baby.

I could never forgive or forget. I was unable to react as I should have done, and reproach her for her cold indifference to her own child. I was paralysed. I alternated between self pity and anger at the hurt she had inflicted on me. I wrote dozens of versions of a letter which I threw away. It was too late. She was old; she might be dead. The resentment and pain festered within me.

My mother and her husband retired to the North-East of England and lived in comfort. One of my daughters may decide to chase up that line of inquiry, but I never wanted to see her after that ice cold, self-centred, unloving, second rejection. I had always been loath to meet my siblings; but after that response I had no desire whatsoever to make their acquaintance.

A loving adoption

Deborah has no wish to know her birth-parents. It is not that she is without curiosity, because she is a successful businesswoman, in a long-term relationship with a man with whom she has two teenage children. Her love for her adoptive parents was, she says, so overwhelming that she would not want to jeopardise it by admitting into her life a needy or perhaps unhappy mother compelled to part with her more than forty years ago:

I was brought up in what might be called a lower-middle class family. I had an unfashionably happy childhood, and have no

memory of any other time. My parents—I should call them 'adoptive' but I won't—already had one little girl, but my mother was in
a car accident, which left her incapable of having a second child.
So they took me. They told me I was 'chosen', but whether or not
that was the case, it could not have worked out more happily.
People took my sister and me for twins, although there was no
particular resemblance between us. We had similar tastes, feelings
and even thoughts. And there was never the slightest distinction
between us. I don't think I ever felt unfairly treated. The worst
thing she ever found to say to me was, 'You're not my real sister';
and she was punished for it. Our mother said to us, 'You are both
my daughters.'

There was absolutely none of that sense of being on the look-out
to see what undesirable qualities I had inherited from my birth-
parents, which some of my adopted friends felt, a sort of 'what's
bred in the bone will out in the flesh'. Many adopted children are
taunted with that.

We were rather competitive as girls. I was slightly cleverer than
Janice at school, but she was prettier than I was. We mildly envied
the other's superiority, but not enough to spoil our relationship.
We were encouraged by our parents to stay on at school and go to
university, and we both went to the same one. We were not particularly gifted academically, but we fulfilled our parents' pride—
neither had the chance to continue education after they were
sixteen.

But we both had a flair for business. I have an independent flower
shop, and she has a hair and beauty salon. Nothing to do with
what we studied. I did Spanish and French and she did Media
Studies. We both wanted to get out into what we called 'the real
world', working and interacting with people. I should perhaps have
done Ecology or something because I always loved nature; and she
ought to have done Business rather than media. But you find your
own level.

Our father was an insurance company assessor. He hated it. I
remember him always being tired. He came home, looking grey
and exhausted, and we always rushed out to greet him, and he
would say, 'Another day another dollar'. But we were the light of

their lives. He died at sixty-seven. We share the care of our mother who still lives in her own house.

Strange to say Janice and I both have two children, and they are also very close. I never told them I was adopted. That was my life. They have their own lives. They don't need to be burdened with my history, since it doesn't burden me. I cannot imagine a better childhood than the one that was gifted to me; and because I have my own business, I am always afraid my kids are going to reproach me and say I wasn't there for them. I don't think I am as good a mother as mine was, even though I love them to bits.

The continuing legacy

However our understanding of children and their needs has evolved, older responses linger, especially towards the children of the poor, and of poor minorities in particular. We are always reacting against the last scandal that captured the headlines, and so busy forestalling another disaster like that of Jasmine Becker, Baby P or Victoria Climbié, that we scarcely notice the damage this obsession can cause. It was in the aftermath of the publication of the report on Victoria Climbié in 2003 that Kyle was born; unhappy timing for him and for his mother, Shania, who was only fifteen.

Within hours of giving birth, Shania was approached with the suggestion that she should give up Kyle for adoption. Still exhausted, she reacted angrily and refused. The baby was hers; she would not part with him under any circumstances.

Social services remained vigilant. Kyle proved accident-prone, which led to an inconclusive investigation into 'non-accidental injuries'. When the boy started school he proved inattentive, sensitive to criticism and unwilling to accept discipline. He was quickly stereotyped as an unruly black kid; a reputation which followed his two sisters. One teacher referred to them, in a cliché of the time, as 'feral'.

When he was eight, Kyle had a seizure, and only then did he receive serious medical attention. He fell from his bicycle and was taken to hospital. He was diagnosed with epilepsy, but for the next four years the prescribed drugs made no differences to the seizures, which became more and more frequent. The school continued to see his problems as behavioural. He could not always understand instructions, and when he became over-excited he was incoherent.

Social Services wanted the children to be taken into care, but this was fiercely resisted by their grandmother, Nadine. Fragmentation of responsibility—Social Services with its constant change of personnel, schools, the Housing Department, the police and the DHSS—created a Dickensian fog of unreliable information. Nadine felt that the state was doing its utmost to orphan her three grandchildren, and her insistence and force of personality resulted in custody being granted to her. Independent social workers attested that she was a loving and competent grandmother. The Family Court also reprimanded the Social Services Department for its obstructiveness.

Nadine tried to establish a regime of order and consistency in the children's lives. Hers has been a life of heroic self-denial; she gave up work to care for the children and found herself worse-off, but with more responsibilities than ever. She also demanded a more thorough examination of Kyle's condition. It was discovered that a brain cyst was the cause of disorders which teachers had confidently stated to be issues of conduct. The boy was clearly distressed and highly sensitive to any mention of his disability.

Nadine was re-housed in a neighbouring borough, where she was able to set up a special room for Kyle after he was referred to Great Ormond Street Hospital for Children. With the provision of a stable home and good nourishment, Kyle improved. The cyst shrank, and the highly dangerous operation which had been recommended was postponed, while the boy's progress had been further monitored.

The long tradition of separating the children of the poor from their parents—'philanthropic abduction'—lives on. State agencies sometimes fail to recognise the sometimes chaotic and wounding forms that love may take.

The great majority of children removed from parental custody have suffered, often heart-rending cruelty, abuse or neglect: Leanne, consistently beaten by her mother's boyfriend and suffering severe malnutrition; Belinda, abused by a family 'friend' for money; Darren who, at six, was left alone for a weekend with his two-year-old sister while their parents were 'partying'; Angel, who sat for three days by her mother's body when she died of an overdose. But as a result of social workers'—understandable—fear of media accusations of incompetence or neglect, the number of cared-for children had risen by March 2017 to 72,670; an increase of 20,000 or so over a period of twenty years. The vilification of social workers after the Climbié case and that of the seventeen month-old Baby P in 2007 has led to a 'defensive' approach to risk by many children's services; and a consequent increase in this highly contemporary, but also ancient, form of orphaning.

Parental orphans

Orphaned also are children whose parents depend upon them for care and protection. According to the 2011 census in Britain, more than 177,000 children under seventeen are 'carers' for their own parents, as a result of disability, sickness, psychiatric illness or other incapacity.[9] Some of these children are, the Children's Society says, between the ages of five and seven. Such a situation is familiar in Asia and Africa, where it is common to see a child leading a blind parent, and children regularly look after sick elders, younger children and animals as part of their daily domestic duties. Adult infirmity is one reason why children work for wages.

This is an 'acceptable' part of the 'natural' order of things in the developing world; but is rarely expected of the lives of children in rich Western countries. It shocks us to learn that many children's experience is shadowed by 'adult' responsibilities. It is astonishing how easily such a reversal of roles is accepted, when children become the 'parents' of those unable to care for them.

Sonia is sixteen. Her mother has suffered bouts of depression ever since she can remember. As a little girl she would wake up and wonder how her mother would be that day:

> If she was up and about when I got up, it was a good sign. If there was no sound in the house, I would make the tea and get my brother ready for school. When she was in that state I was ashamed of her. Her hair was all tangled and the dressing gown was grubby. She cried a lot. I used to ask her what was the matter, but she didn't know, and if she did, she couldn't tell me. I gradually took over looking after the house, and caring for her. Then there were times when she would be cheerful, and she would have a shower and get dressed and take me and Nigel out shopping or to the pictures. I loved those times. It showed how abnormal most of my life was, because after a few days she would sink back into despair. I think now it would be called bipolar, but then it was just 'depression'. She was on anti-depressants, but they didn't seem to make much difference—it was a cycle: it was as if she had gone away, and we waited for her to come back. I was in charge of the house. By twelve or thirteen I was that efficient, I could do the cleaning before school, shopping on my way home and get something to eat and then do my homework. Nobody knew. Neighbours sometimes asked if I was all right, but I dreaded teachers finding out, because I thought they might take her away. It is surprising what a kid can do when she has to. I work for a care company now. I never needed any training. From the first day, it was like going home.

In the long history of orphanage, what are now called 'feckless' parents have played a significant part. Those 'overburdened with children', without skills to provide sustenance, driven to despair, demoralised, incapable or ill-endowed, have always existed. Despite having been scourged, whipped, humiliated, imprisoned or deported, they remain in these best of all times. Nor is there any novelty in children fulfilling the role of absent or sick parents. Apart from this, temptations to place their own needs and desires above the care of dependants, people have turned to the ale-house, dram-shop or gin-palace, to the oblivion of laudanum or other opiates to deaden the pain of existence. Who knows how many of the street urchins of Victorian London left home because of mental illness, alcoholism or other addictions. Or indeed how many more, sage little girls in pinafores, went out to earn a living making matches or selling cresses on the street because of parental defect or incapacity?

Today's diagnoses of parents unable to perform their role show greater insight and understanding than their consignment to Bridewells, reformatories or exile in the past. But this still leaves thousands of children effectively orphaned of parents, if not by recognised disabilities, by the multiple distractions which call parents away from their purposes, just as they were in the eighteenth or nineteenth centuries, when all the poisonous consolations of yesterday seduced some of them from their expected role.

Child-parents

In a note on the history of orphans, Peter Laslett makes the comparison between parental deprivation now and in the past, he wrote, 'There were so many orphans and step-children present in the seventeenth and eighteenth century English communities that they may have equalled the proportion of children who have lost a parent by death, divorce or separation in England at the present time.' He could, perhaps, have added, that absentee parents do not have to desert the family in order to rob children of the nurture and protection they need.[10]

Sadie experienced an absence of parents, although she and her sister lived with the mother they had to care for. It is impossible to know for how many her testimony speaks, but they must be numerous.

Sadie's grandmother was an elective traveller in the 1960s. She moved around Britain in a wagon. She had seven children with six different men. The illusion of the time was that parents thought they were bestowing upon their children freedoms that set them apart from the rat-race, the demands of conformity and the proprieties of a hypocritically 'respectable' society.

She says:

My mother was born in 1972. The people she was with had lived like that for a long time. She was eighteen when I was born. The first few years we had a horse and cart, and went around Wales, Norfolk and other country areas. My father was married to some-one else. He had another family.

Eighteen months later, my sister was born. Her father was the man I called Dad. I had no schooling in the early years. I remember the wagon: there was a ledge in front, and as it went downhill I was very scared, the horses pushed back against the cart. We were once part of a film called Gipsy Fires: we provided material for a fictional story starring Edward Woodward.

My sister's Dad and my mother broke up. I knew my biological father and saw him sometimes, but I never liked him. I had no relationship with him at all.

Then we moved to Spain. A lot of English travellers settled there in the late 70s. It was a stupid move because she had no means of support. We had no money. We used to walk everywhere. Once we broke into a house in the mountains and squatted there. My mother cried a lot. I have clear memories of childhood. I was more aware of emotions than adults gave us credit for. They think you don't understand, but children have insights adults can't imagine.

After two years in Spain we came back to London. I say 'back', but we had never lived here. I was eight or nine. My mother met this guy, Des, bipolar and he drank a lot. He was slightly crazy, although he was lovely to us. When his ex-girl-friend got fired from a café where she was working, he took a baseball bat and smashed the place up. He went to the police and said he had killed us. The police came to check we were OK.

We lived with him in a one-bedroom flat. There was no space, it was hard to manage. We were there a year and I went to school for the first time, starting in year three. It was a strange experience because we had never been taught anything. I had no confidence. Nobody had the kind of background we did. It was hard. I didn't fit in. My mother would turn up drunk. It was a nice area, Primrose Hill, so we were even more out of our element.

I don't know how Des ended up. They said he killed himself. She doesn't think he did it on purpose. He took anti-depressants with alcohol and had a brain haemorrhage. We tried to get into the house. The key was in the door on the inside, and there was a pile of post on the floor. We saw the police come. I had a lot of friends in the block, and someone took us in. My mother found him, and she lost it.

There were practical problems. Although it was our home, they were not married or even officially living together, so we were homeless. My sister and I worried about her. We couldn't leave her. One or the other of us had always to be with her. She was very fragile, so we looked after her. We were ten and eight, perhaps even a bit younger. We were in effect her carers, parents in reverse. She was a victim. She has become bitter now, I always think of her as a kind of wild horse.

We were evicted. I remember sitting in Housing Offices in Camden. She marched us off to see Glenda Jackson who was the MP. We weren't entitled to a place because we were not residents. We were in short-term housing or hostels for a few years, and got a permanent place only when I was in Secondary School. Even that didn't exactly provide stability. She would stay away for days at a time. She took drugs and drank a lot and didn't seem to know that children were her responsibility. We spent a lot of time with the mother of a friend of my sister who lived next door to the school. It was not a haven—she was also crazy. Our permanent flat was in Gospel Oak; but because we had been in temporary accommodation, I didn't go to school. In year seven, when I was eleven or twelve, I had no schooling at all. I had no friends. Our mother was a nightmare. Other people's parents always seemed wonderful to us. At secondary school we were looked after by the parents of our friends.

I left at fourteen or fifteen. Things were so bad, there was physical violence between us. I was older and angry with her. She would have loud music on all night. If I asked her to keep it quiet she would turn it up louder. She was so selfish, other people's needs didn't register with her. Once she bit me badly. In the morning I showed her what she had done, and she said I'd done it myself.

She often didn't come home. At Christmas there would be nothing. My sister entered into a relationship with an older guy. She was only about thirteen or fourteen, he was in his twenties. I felt it was my fault, because I left her alone; but it was her way out of a terrible situation. When I look back, and think of what was happening, I wonder why nothing was ever done. Social Services were involved, but we were never taken into care. We had someone called a Travellers' Officer from Social Services, but that was it. The schools never picked up on anything.

When I left school I moved in with some very rich people in St Johns Wood. I met the daughter through a school friend. Things were so bad with my mother I went to live with them. The father of the family had died, and the mother didn't work, but she took a fancy to me. It lasted a year. It was horrible. I hated it. I was their project. I felt it was disgusting—buying me designer things, I felt it was manipulative. At their parties people would say, 'Oh we've heard so much about you', which meant they had boasted to them what they were doing for me. It was a mansion with a pool, and the woman would counsel me. Actually they had enough problems of their own. The brothers were like, 'Why is she here?'

Then I went to a hostel in Camden Road. That was also horrible in a different way. I tried to go home. My mother said 'Please come back.' I said to her 'I'll come if you stop drinking and [doing] drugs'. She just waved me away. No, no, she couldn't do that. I didn't stay long. One day they said, 'You've got three hours to move', because they were turning it into a hostel for families.

A woman from a centre for young people under twenty-five helped me, gave me money for clothes and helped me with benefit. I was sixteen. I think I dealt with it well. My feelings were, first, that it was better than home, and second, that it was quite nice to be independent. I had good friends at school. I smoked weed, and I bunked off with my friends. The school was not really interested; my form teacher gave me recipes to cook for myself. They had no idea. I learned to present myself well. I knew how to get on with other girls' parents. They liked me and I was good at it.

I was moved to Cricklewood. It had been the Montrose Hotel, but it was rented to the council. There were lots of rules, and no support from the hostel people. It was dreadful. You had to be in a certain time, the doors were shut at six. I thought, 'This is not going to work.' The mother of a friend who drove me there said, 'You're not staying here. You can come and live with me.' I was there for a long time. It was great. They were very laid back. The house was full of teenagers after school, smoking, plenty of food.

I was in the Sixth Form, when the school asked me to leave. I must have been sixteen. I didn't care. I hated school. In any case, I'm dyslexic, and I received no help. I got a job as a support worker in a school for autistic boys. I liked it, but some days I just wouldn't go. I found it hard to get there. It was rare if I did a whole week. They also asked me to leave.

My mother used to call me a lot. I felt angry towards her. She made me anxious all the time. I was subject to panic attacks. I couldn't go near the house. As a kid I used to hyperventilate a lot. I think I was jealous of my mother's boy-friends. I had tantrums and meltdowns. She would put me outside till I calmed down. I was an angry child, although I had good cause. I still feel angry. I would do a lot of punching walls, breaking windows, kicking down doors.

She still makes my blood boil in a way that nobody else does. She went to prison for bringing cocaine from Brazil. I was living with friends at the time. She called me saying 'I need you.' I went to Gospel Oak. As soon as I walked in, I knew it was something bad, I should get out. She was drunk. She got all this money out. She said, 'What I've done, I did it all for you.' Then she said if you don't hear from me you'll know what happened.'

I thought 'Fuck you,' and I left.

After two weeks I got a call from her friend. 'She's been caught.' It was not surprising. She was smoking crack in that flat, and all these weird men were around. It was a most horrible place to be. She was given seven years. I think she did four or five. I was eighteen then. I went to see her when she was on remand. She was so vulnerable. It seemed everything was stripped away. I felt compassion for her. I don't need her or love her, but I did go and see her.

She got home visits. She would go on a massive binge, drugs and drink. It's funny, they never tested her when she went back. She was hopelessly in debt. We had an electricity bill for £8,000.

I'm looking after children now. I was desperate to have a baby, something I could love. I became a nanny at sixteen, and the family I've been with are great. They had a late baby and called me back; and they have now recommended me to another family.

My mother had an abusive childhood, in communes, sexually open. She was exploited and abused. She is also a very angry woman. Her brothers and sisters are estranged from her. I think she felt unloved. She is now fifty-five, alcoholic, with very few teeth left. I think she was born with a sense of unfairness.

She loves me, although she has a funny way of showing it. She has always been jealous of me and my sister. When she came out of prison she never got a job. She has never worked except selling drugs. Her brothers and sisters are hippy types, not seriously into drugs. My grandfather went to prison in Morocco for a long time.

I am close to my sister now. She is also a nanny. I see it, in a way, as reliving my own childhood as I would have wished it to be. I love children, but I've been a nanny for ten years and I'm ready to move on.

When Sadie was asked what saved her from following the same path, she replied;

It hasn't been difficult for me not to be like that. My sister and I are positive happy people. My biological father has two other children, a few years older than I am. We met them now and again. Two years ago my half-brother died. He was on holiday, and got an infection in the pancreas. He was twenty-seven.

My father is now in Bristol. He had a brain aneurysm and is in a vegetative state. He has been like it for a year. You can talk to him, but he can't talk or eat. He is connected to tubes for intravenous feeding. He was in intensive care six months. He was refusing care at one point. I spent some time with my older sister, and we were looking at pictures of a happy family. I felt some jealousy and a sense of unfairness.

I don't think I ever craved attention until we thought he was going to die. He is in his late fifties, older than my mother. It was weird seeing him. This dying man is your Dad. Should I be sad? It forced me to look at my own situation. I would not change any of it.

I am at a crossroads though. I feel now I wish I'd been to school more and then to university. My friends are close to their parents. They give them advice and guidance. It is something I never had. That would have been helpful for me. My grandmother died when I was fifteen. Her dying words to my mum were, 'You're a waster.' She is always drunk. When my biological father had his aneurysm, we went to see her. It was all about her. It was very draining. She roused all my old anxieties again. I couldn't bear to be with her, even to be touched by her. Even asking how I was irritated me.

I lead her on, because I'm too soft. She says 'Let's meet up', and I say 'Yeah.' Then I don't turn up or phone to call it off. She is so vulnerable. I can't imagine anything worse than your child not wanting to be with you. I have written so many letters to her telling her how I feel, but I never sent them. I was constantly let down by her. Before she went to prison, she ran from man to man. I remember seeing and hearing all kinds of stuff you shouldn't know as a kid. When we were young, my sister and I used to creep into her room and steal twenty quid from the man she was with. We hated them.

My sister is very attractive, tall and slender. She continued her relationship with our mother until quite recently, but now she has turned away from her. She always lived rather in her own imagination. I used to think she was airy-fairy. She doesn't remember many of the things I did.

I've always been good at making friends. I'm now living in a house which belongs to the parents of my friend. There are five of us. I enjoy life very much. I am a happy person but a bit confused. I feel I have been healing myself through my work as a nanny. While she was in prison I lived with my boyfriend in the flat in Gospel Oak.

I often felt anxious then. When he was out, I thought would he come back? There are obviously aspects of your life as a child which, however well you think you have dealt with them, are always there.

I have worked with vulnerable women, but what I'd like is to work with younger people, teenagers. I have done a counselling course, but I don't want to be a counsellor. I have now seen what a loving family can be; and I am ready to move on.

PART THREE

ORPHANINGS OF MODERNITY

the proprieties of the hour has required more stringent correction than the behaviour of the children of power. This gained fresh impetus in the nineteenth century, when, no longer isolated in remote country parishes, the labouring poor were concentrated in slums and tenements of industrial cities.

There has always been a 'danger' that the young might stray from the orthodoxies of their elders, orthodoxies which are, in any case, mutable, and therefore the object of continuous vigilance. Arguments in favour of the separation, in one form or another, of children from their parents have usually been advocated as in the interests of the children themselves. Occasionally it has been for the benefit of parents or for the advantage of society. But the principal beneficiaries have been entities far more powerful than the objects of their attention—ecclesiastical, governmental, philanthropic, imperial or commercial. Unacknowledged orphanage has always been available to governing classes, whenever parents could not be trusted to bring up their own children according to the needs of the age as defined by ruling castes. Human affection might—indeed, often does—interfere with the inculcation of values approved by Authority.

Even the rich have not been exempt from the need to adapt their behaviour, usually for the sake of their own survival. The cultivation of insentience in upper class males in the imperial era, for example, in the cult of the stiff upper lip, suggests they, too, had to observe demands required for the retention of their own privilege. Did the stoicism inculcated into them inure them to their own sorrows, or render them impervious to sufferings they would inflict upon recalcitrant subjects of Empire—the famines, floggings, death sentences which they imposed as retribution to those who demanded freedom from colonial rule? In recent years, these values have been called into question. Prince Harry revealed in 2017 that his repressed grief at the loss of his mother for twenty years had disastrous results for his emotional and mental health. This recognises that such repression is now unnecessary. It might be asked why a twelve-year-old was ever left to make his own accommodation with bereavement: the day of emotional enlightenment evidently dawned late for the royal family.

Nicholas Orme notes that certain monastic orders—Dominicans and Franciscans in particular—were accused in the fourteenth century of abducting boys to be novices.[1] Although the official age was twelve, some boys were recruited younger in order to avoid parental control. Girls were occasionally 'gifted' to nunneries (Mary, daughter of Edward I, was veiled as a nun at the age of seven). It was principally the boys of nobles and the well-to-do who were placed in other households as pages or wards, partly so they would be instructed in the art of service, but also because more labour could be wrung from the children of strangers (however nobly connected) than would be possible where strong emotional attachments existed.

After the Reformation, it was necessary to prevent children from following the now outlandish, Popish practices of their parents; and the clergy took a greater interest in the education of children, particularly those of people of substance. National stability and religious orthodoxy were one, and it was vital that children accept that the reformed Church of England represented the true version of Christian teaching.[2] The raising of children could not be trusted to those brought up according to Catholic custom; and accordingly, sacerdotal intervention became significant in 'adjusting' the values of the young to new conditions. In the spiritual formation of children, parents came to occupy a precarious third place—after the Church and godparents—such significant figures in a child's life that he or she was often given the name of the principal godparent. (It might be said that parents are once more a distant third in the formation of the social sensibility of their children, subordinate to their fostering by the marriage of market and technology and the power of the peer-group.)

Cranmer's *First Book of Common Prayer* of 1549 provided a catechism to teach children the form and meaning of the Gospel;

they were also expected to master the Lord's Prayer and the Ten Commandments. Part of the function of the clergy was to ensure that parents did not transmit idolatrous practices. The custom of family worship in households of the nobility and the merchant class ensured that servants and those of lower station should also benefit from the revelations of the reformed Church.

Compulsory use of the English *Book of Common Payer* and obligatory attendance at church made 'recusancy' (which meant all disagreement with the tenets of the Anglican Church) an indictable offence. Ian Green points out 'the task of trying to move the bulk of the English population from an initial aware-ness of new teachings and practices to full comprehension of them, let alone active commitment to them, proved to require generations of effort.'[3]

Of course, there is always resistance to the spread of new orthodoxies. Puritans, in the later sixteenth and early seven-teenth centuries went further, with the Calvinist view that chil-dren were born in shame and sin. They were therefore, from infancy, in need of correction and coercion, and the salutary lesson that they should 'die in godliness', since die so many of them surely would. Infant models of holiness, with their lachry-mose exaltations and fear of hell, were regarded as prodigies, hallowed by their precocious understanding of the perilous nature of life and their risk of eternal damnation. James Hanaway cited 'Mary A, when she was between four and five-years-old, was greatly affected on hearing the word of God, and became very solicitous about her soul and everlasting condition, weeping bitterly to think what would become of her in another world.'[4] Such pressure would now be regarded as abusive; but this illustrates the changeability of appropriate instruction for the very young; and its vulnerability to abrupt discontinuities. What is considered a fitting formation for children in one gen-eration is seen as cruelty by the next. Even the progressiveness of our age has its shadows: the superior consciousness of poster-ity always contains its own hidden violence.

Grammar Schools founded by merchants' companies in the sixteenth century promoted classical authors, but were also profoundly inflected by Protestant theology. Learning, for those privileged to attend them, was intensive. Theoretical openness of such schools to the children of the poor remained, but they became articulated principally to education for the sons of clergy, gentry and the mercantile classes.

Forms of knowledge also changed as power evolved, and what seemed fitting for the young in consolidation of the norms of the Reformation had become archaic by the late seventeenth century. After the Restoration, French, Italian and mathematics took precedence over classical erudition. Children required practical skills to accommodate themselves to a world of mercantilism and scientific discovery. Nonconformists opened their own schools and colleges, offering natural sciences, history and geography as well as modern languages.

From these transformations of the childhood of the dominant classes, the children of the poor were largely excluded. Their destiny had been enshrined in the Elizabethan Poor Law and the Statute of Artificers: to labour was their lot, and to bow to their fate with cheerful obedience their expected response. Although children of poverty had always been in the eye of authority, particularly those unattached to families, the life of the poor was lived in a psychic place apart. Their beliefs depended upon a long oral tradition, compounded of traditional superstition, much of it a remnant of ancient animism, overlaid by Christian doctrine, feudal tradition and social disciplines imposed by their betters. It has always been difficult to impose upon them the ideology of ruling castes. Punished, re-settled, incarcerated, hanged, transported, exiled, excoriated, whether as 'valiant beggars', rogues, anyone 'able to give no reckoning how he doth lawfully get his living', as criminal classes, as profligate, vicious and idle, as an 'underclass' in the modern world, as 'spongers,' scroungers and parasites in our more instructed age, they nevertheless remain. The poor must be pursued and punished, but not to the point of extinction. Although nothing would be easier in the late industrial age than to abolish poverty, the poor are too valuable a foil to the creators of wealth to be dispensed with. More effort is concentrated on preserving the poor than on any other threatened species; for their survival embodies the need for economic growth into perpetuity.

It is not surprising that 'idleness' of the poor, especially of energetic young men, should be a recurring fear of ruling classes. For 'idleness' has historically been reserved for the rich, whose availability for governing the country, fighting wars and controlling their subordinates, has never been so pressing that they didn't have ample time to attend to their estates. 'Leisure'— as it became known when applied to those of superior station— only added to their prestige and wealth, and dazzled the people with their extravagant way of life. No wonder they resented any claim by the poor to the gilded absence of occupation that was of such importance to them: it was encroachment on their privilege, and dealt with accordingly.

Poverty, first of all as a virtue, later as a burden to be borne with fortitude was overtaken with time by poverty as disaffection and indiscipline. Poor children became the object of attention of the Charity School Movement at the beginning of the eighteenth century, and the Anglican Society for Promoting Christian Knowledge. This, despite its religious foundation, represented the beginning of centuries of systematic colonising the poor; for Britain's spectacular imperial conquests began, like its sometimes grudging charity, at home. The importance of charity schools should not be exaggerated. The labour of children remained for most parents of greater usefulness than learning, even if orphans and their companions, the offspring of vice, would later provide a rich field for the exertions of those whose business was with pacifying the dangerous classes in Britain.

The education of children of the labouring poor and those without families consisted primarily in providing them with basic skills required for agricultural work, service or such crafts as it befitted their station. This came together with an effort to prevent such instruction from encouraging them to question the station in life to which Providence had called them. Such a benevolent, but intricate, intention was supplemented by the Sunday School movement from the 1780s, designed to sequester a new generation, not merely from their slothful parents, but also from dangerously radical ideas and from disaffection from an increasingly negligent established church.

The 'setting on work' of the children of the poor was intended to raise them to habits of industry and obedience ever since this had been formulated by the Elizabethan Poor Law. The subordination of such children was perceived as their 'natural' condition. But Hugh Cunningham observes ensuring the 'natural' state occupied by the poor was achieved only with a great deal of elaborate contrivance by those who maintained them there.[5] And there is indeed an astonishing quantity of exhortation and advice—to employers, pedagogues, parliamentarians and authority in general—as to the necessity of imposing forcefully upon them a sense of their lowly place in the world. It's backed up by ecclesiastical rhetoric, stemming from the Catechism of 1549, which becomes punitive in the late seventeenth and early eighteenth centuries and then milder towards the end of the eighteenth century, before degenerating into coercive brutality in the years of early industrialism.

During the radical social disruptions of the industrial era, it was essential that the children of the poor should not grow up to be part of any 'mob, mutinous or revolutionary. Children were essentially 'colonised' by reformers, in much the same way that the 'children' of Empire were exposed to the civilising influence of missionaries, by means of both spiritual and highly material force.[6] This mission of 'refining', 'reforming' or even 'taming' (with its undertones of 'livestock') fresh generations of the multitudinous poor was present long before the industrial revolution; but it took on new urgency from the beginning of the nineteenth century, when the making of Joanna Penglase's 'orphans of the living' was at its height. Among the products for which Britain was celebrated at that time as workshop of the world, the manufacture of orphans rarely figures.[7] Yet they played an indispensable role, both in sustaining the ideology of the family and in the peopling of Empire.[8]

This may be traced through the publications of all who, seeing an increasing population of the impoverished, feared their children were potentially 'uncontrollable.' Mrs Sarah Trimmer in 1801 declared:

> The education of the children of the poor therefore should not be left to their ignorant and corrupted parents; it is a public concern, and should be regarded as public business, so far as is consistent with that freedom which it would be an injury to the community to infringe...The poor might probably resist in these times of licentious freedom, that authority which would force them to give up their children entirely to the state; but they are, in general, glad to accept that eleemosynary education for them; and the bounty of the rich cannot be better employed than in providing it.[9]

The reasons for isolating the poor in the first half of the nineteenth century are plain in the words of E. C. Tufnell, Assistant Poor Law Commissioner. Writing to members of the Commission in 1839, he said:[10]

> Under the old system of poor laws, it is well known how frequently a family which once became pauperised remained so ever after: pauper parents reared pauper children; and thus habits of dependence on the poor-rates seemed to descend, as part of their natures, from generation to generation. To stop this *hereditary taint* would be to annihilate the greater part of the pauperism of the country; and this may be done in that the children thus situated may be so brought up to make it a moral certainty that they shall never in afterlife become dependent on the rates, but always remain respectable and independent stations may, I think be proved by demonstration.

When poverty had been established as the fruit of wilfulness and moral deficiency, the idea of removing children from the surroundings that produced the evil, gained ready acceptance. Lord Shaftesbury referred to street children in the 1840s as, 'tribes of lawless freebooters, bound by no obligation and utterly ignorant or utterly regardless of social duties.'[11] Saving children from moral pollution of the communities that bore them had greater urgency than avoiding the material degradation in which they lived.

The epoch which left the deepest stain upon the character of the people was the violent imposition of industrial society upon a wasting feudalism and the decaying tradition of agriculture and rural life. More recently, the removal of those disciplines, once essential for the productive power of manufacturing, has opened the way to an apparently more lenient shaping of the popular temper. Yet there is also a sense of loss, since labour is now no longer fashioned for the making of useful and necessary things. The consequences of this are among the most intractable problems of our time.

It seems some times that each epoch has been a kind of masquerade, in which people don the livery of the service they are called upon to perform at any given time. The tragedy is that they become so attached to the garments they are required to put on, that they mistake them, like the characters in a fairy story, for their own skin; and setting them aside feels, less like the necessities of progress, than injuries to flesh and blood.

Subtly wrought orphanings have become more systematic in our own time, partly as a consequence of the intense penetration of people's lives by the communications industries. Orphans may be counted not only among the personally bereaved, but also among the culturally orphaned, those disinherited by the dissolution of manufacturing industry.

wants have been artfully placed within their consciousness by the contrivance of others.

It is one thing to observe the profound reversal of the way we treat the young; harder, perhaps to understand it. Children, the best hope of whom, until the day before yesterday, was that they might go about their business seen but unheard, unobtrusively fulfilling roles attributed to 'childhood', have been subject to a prodigious transformation. Always harbingers of better tomorrows, children have become prophets and seers, since they will live to see the only afterlife in which a majority now believe, namely, that of a wholly terrestrial future of limitless expansion and opportunity. This endows them with semi-magical qualities.

The energy invested in this change might, perhaps, alert us to the treacherous nature of appearances, especially in a society obsessed with image, surface and presentation. The narrative of our growing sympathy for the child, and the fading, as the twentieth century advanced, of the conviction that adults knew best, may be less of a journey of progress than it seems. That it was appropriate for parents and guardians to choose on behalf of children their dress, their food, their times of sleeping and waking, to direct their play and even their relationships with their friends, has given way to its opposite. Those older certainties have been replaced by fretful consultation with children, not only about their choice of what they eat and wear, but how the family budget should be spent, where they would like to go on holiday, what treats and toys they prefer; what is needed for their pacification and contentment. Adults entreat their children to tell them what they most long for, that they may fulfil their every desire. There has never been greater anxiety among parents, even though children are more likely to grow safely to maturity than ever before. Their raising seems to require safe passage through the danger-infested landscapes of infancy and childhood, where ill-wishers, abusers are everywhere, malevolent abductors lie in wait in the most innocent places, and keeping children from harm requires constant Argus-eyed watchfulness. Such a world is as beset by superstition as one where evil spirits lurked everywhere, waiting to take possession of the souls of the young and vulnerable. Indeed, it sometimes seems that we are living, despite the trappings of a perpetually intensifying technological capacity, in a reconstitution of the medieval world, with its children's crusades, its spiritual fervours and fears of the powers of darkness. Does this represent a culmination of the wisdom of the ages, or is it yet another mutation of Dr Barnardo's 'philanthropic abduction?'

Childhood is now a major generator of industries that serve it—indeed, it seems scarcely necessary to rehearse the range of profit-producing commodities, services, sensations, entertainments, distractions required in order to fit children for the contemporary world. In 2016 the Centre for Economic and Business Research estimated the average cost of raising a child until the age of twenty-one in Britain was £231,843; clearly the greatest 'investment' of people's lives, apart, perhaps, from their property, an aspect of which children have historically been a part.[1]

Does this change of heart represent progress, a deeper understanding of the true nature of childhood? Does it serve some other purpose than altruistic concern with what is best for the young? Perhaps our virtuous present, which seeks to extend its solicitude to *all* children, is calculated to conceal the busy work, not only of government reform and social change, but also that of other forces. A hyperactive market, for instance, which knows how to wring from their well-being extravagant prizes for the entities who have built business empires (and business is the only area in which imperial ambitions are still conceded) upon catering to their needs, sustenance, contentment and even their whims?

What lies behind this sudden overthrow of all we knew—or thought we knew—about the nature of childhood? Children have become a different order of human being from that which they were believed to be in a past associated now with ignorance, superstition and darkness, just as the 'children' of Empire were belatedly accorded adult status. There is, surely, in the penitence society now shows for its former failure to answer their needs and afford them adequate protection against predators, a strong sense of guilt. How could we, for such ages, sought to have stifled and oppressed those the nineteenth century German writer Adalbert Stifter, graphically if sentimentally referred to as 'Knospen der Menchheit', buds of humanity? If it is hard now to comprehend our clouded apprehension of the experience of the child, and our traditional celebration of adult power over the young, our efforts to compensate for these wrongs are scarcely less extreme. Children of today did not suffer the evils of previous generations. Why would making them the beneficiaries of adult atonement be to their advantage, any more than such repentance can make good the fate of the numberless perished children of want? The effusiveness of our altered response suggests something more than the zeal of recent converts. Perhaps our remorse at historical mistreatment of children is also a displacement of regret—or at least uncertainty—over more recent, even present-day, failings and betrayals.

Sexualisation

There are many aspects of the social development of children which prompt the politics of repentance. Among the most prominent of these is the much commented sexualisation of society; a process from which children are not exempt. There is much in Neil Postman's assertion that, just as pre-literate society had few secrets from the young—since they were exposed to the realities of animal sexuality and proximity to the activities of mature adults—so the ubiquitous technological power of post-literate communications industries, especially its diffusion of images, make it hard to keep from the young what are sometimes called the facts of life, and, perhaps even more damagingly, some of its more beguiling fictions.[2]

In the exposure of children to early consciousness of sexuality, it is not sober pedagogues who have been their instructors.

It is a mixture of the pornography industry and fables propagated by peer-group folklore. If the effects of this have dispelled ignorance, they may also have impaired innocence; or perhaps it is more true to say, engendered new forms of ignorance appropriate to a supremely knowing age. Preoccupation with body-shape, aspirations to perfection and supremacy, particularly those exhibited by celebrities, the appropriation of 'role-models' by the media which diffuse them among the most impressionable, create radical dissatisfactions, feelings of unworthiness and incapacity. The more so, since it is now regarded as a realistic ambition for children to distinguish themselves competitively from their peers by fame, money, stardom or other publicly marketable characteristics; a tendency reinforced by parents, whose moral teachings are increasingly in keeping with the imperatives of a culture which urges the young 'to live the dream', to 'go for it', to let nothing and nobody stand in the way of the realisation of a self which is not necessarily autonomous. Role-models are no longer the loved but fallible flesh and blood of kindred; they are shadows and images, projections of media conglomerates and market-driven success. This is perhaps why 'fantasy'—an industrialised form of the imagination—is a preferred mode of juvenile entertainment. Wish fulfilment, and forms of infantile omnipotence are enshrined in stories of superhuman achievement and transcendence of the here and now, daily life, the local, humdrum reality and all the rest of the dreary necessities to which elders have long ago—perhaps reluctantly—resigned themselves.

The sexualisation of childhood may also explain why the paedophile has become such a potent figure in the contemporary world, an ugly phenomenon no doubt, but raised to the level of universal menace in our time. Here is another focus for the politics of penitence: for many years, sexual abuse of children went unremarked in state institutions, in care homes, in charities, in revered social activities—army cadets, football coaching, schools, youth clubs, the BBC, NHS, philanthropic and religious establishments. It is not only that such practices were overlooked by those in authority over children, but treated with what can only be described as a knowing indifference. The worst affected were, naturally, the unattached and orphaned children of the poor, the undefended and unprotected. Nobody (that is to say nobody who mattered) knew, or chose to know, anything about it, even though it may have been an open secret.

Such negligence only intensifies a remorse that must expiate its own guilt by the fury with which it hunts down perpetrators. Whenever the powerful are shamed, they inevitably deflect blame from their own failings and weaknesses. This is why the crusade against child abuse has their sanction; so that paedophiles now rank with mass murderers and terrorists as the curse of our age. That is even though out of the exploitation of sexuality—including that of children—large fortunes have been made, profits carefully garnered and cleansed; and now appear in the innocent guise of real estate, luxury goods and all the other iconography of wealth, while the abused wait for justice. The intensive use of sex to open up markets for just about everything has consequences which those advantaged by it are anxious to disavow.

A new tabula rasa

The most recent refashioning of the psyche of the people begins, as it always has done, with children. But this time, characteristics associated with the world of social function, community, culture and identity, have to be, not simply modified in order to receive the new versions of truth propagated by their betters, but unlearned, forgotten, excised from memory. When John Locke wrote that children were 'tabula rasa', he meant that they were blank spaces on which society could impress its ideas, habits of morality, industry and obedience.[3] 'Whence has [the mind] all the materials of reason and knowledge? To this I answer in a word, from EXPERIENCE.' What he could scarcely have intended was anything resembling our contemporary erasure of all heritable and transmitted cultural features, in order that children should be reschooled, not as the workers of this or that locality, not as social beings, but as captives of the market and vassals of technology. In this way, all our children—including those only lately brought within the embrace of a system which now values them so highly—are subject, to some degree, to a benign and collusive detachment from the preoccupations of parents, kindred, and even of those whose official function lies in teaching and instruction; archaic professions, since their purpose is now to facilitate education of a kind quite at odds with the pedagogy with which they are nominally entrusted.

These are some of the orphanings of modernity. New generations must be removed once more socially from the values and customs of parents, forebears, ancestors. This does not, of course, mean that parents love their children less, any more than Philippe Aries' medieval parents regarded their offspring with an indifference which some have read into their stoical sorrow in the presence of loss and bereavement.[4] But it suggests that the social beings children become are created elsewhere than in the loving transmission of treasured beliefs and cherished tradition. They are the products (by a strange inversion of a human tendency to anthropomorphism) of a market-determined culture, increasingly mechanistic, technological, money-driven.

In a culture where belief in life after death is fading, children become the only conceivable posterity. This role makes of them ambassadors from the future, whose purpose is to instruct, indeed educate, their elders in the spirit of the time to come. The fumbling fingers of the elderly, the slowing eye-hand coordination, their puzzlement in the presence of the most recent items of technological empowerment, and the amused or irritable tolerance of their defects by children, are familiar aspects of the contemporary social landscape. Such manipulation—of both young and old—is presented as freedom, despite having been confected in the distant laboratories of the knowledge-industries, communications conglomerates, a vast incoherence created by merchants of the transitory and the unmemorable. It represents in effect continuity—a more efficient one too—with the less adroit alterations in the psyche and sensibility of the people in the past. The child-snatchers of modernity enlist the complicity of children themselves. This is inevitable, since the young have been shielded against alternatives: choice, so highly prized in consumer society, is in this respect, absent.

The ruling castes of the world have acquired considerable expertise from their constant intervention into the lives of the people. It has been a perpetual reworking of malleable human material: from serfdom into peasantry; from Catholic into Protestant; from peasant to manufacturing labour; from a people governed by the natural world and the rhythm of the seasons to those who dance to the music of money and the harmonies of profit; from clodhopping parochials into jingoistic wider-still-and-wider enthusiasts of Empire; from workers in a dissolving industrial base into a gilded technological servitude. It is unnecessary to send delegations of anthropologists to South Sea islands to discover the strange rites and curious customs of which humanity is capable; for these are conspicuous within our own society and its culture. Our vaunted traditions and timeless customs are only flags of convenience which conceal extraordinary shifts in the mentality and psyche, as people are remade again and again in whatever image is demanded by wealth and power. Even these are far from immutable: different forces arise and prosper, eclipse established elites or are absorbed by them, and take on the mantle of rulers. New energies are released which demand recognition; and then fade and disappear as they yield to more potent players. Yet throughout, the spectral magic of wealth continues to surround its possessors. Strategies deployed to sustain it alter over time, assume different shapes, and appear from one era to another with the renewed vigour of novelty and progress.

The greatest pressures in these perpetual transformations have been applied to the reluctant and the refractory, to coerce them into the form required by betters, rulers or masters. This remaking of new generations has often required the assistance, not only of the coercive machinery of the state, but also of private entities, charities, philanthropic institutions. There have been arrangements for instruction in whatever 'new ways' are required; forms of 're-education' more usually associated with dissenters in Stalinist Russia than in evolving democracies like Britain or the USA. One of the many scare-stories advanced to shock and appal during the era of Soviet power was the tale of children encouraged by the state to denounce their parents if they failed to exhibit a suitably intense revolutionary zeal. Soviet Communism, it was alleged, divided families and set the generations against each other; a description now serenely accepted as part of the natural order of things in our own society and safe from scrutiny now that the aberration of Communism has been dissolved in the corrosive acid of universal capital.

There is an important difference in the re-forming of the identity of children in our time from the clumsy manipulations of the past. When children were being schooled to the new religion in the sixtenth and seventeenth centuries, or being set on work, brought up to 'principles of thrift and industry', shaped to be the grateful recipients of charity or citizens of Empire, they were being endowed with specific characteristics. These defining features which they brought to the world (not always successfully) were meant to be a kind of armoury against the existential desolation that the absence of such norms might have induced in them. In recent generations, rather than acquire fresh attributes, children are encouraged to shed those already inherited or transmitted. This is until they are left only with the most irreducible—ethnicity, gender, sexual orientation, religion perhaps—in order to create space, in this great clearance of the psyche, for the prodigious goods, services and sensations provided for them by a global plenty unequalled in human history. (Or perhaps not: the Kwakiutl of the Pacific Coast lived with such abundance of natural resources they destroyed the wealth they had within reach by conspicuous and competitive demonstrations of their power to squander it without purpose.)[5]

Children of the market

It has long been observable (although rather more rarely, observed,) that the social formation of the young has been pro-foundly penetrated (a sadly apposite word) by their relationship with the market, which whispers its seductive lullabies into their ears from earliest infancy. Indeed, upbringing has become, increasingly, an aspect of its ubiquitous presence: the principal influences on receptive and unformed minds are now the imperatives of commerce. The freedom of markets is one thing; the bonding of children to *that* freedom quite another.

This far from benign project involves an orphaning without parallel. There is a long-established tradition of re-moulding the psyche, an 'engineering of human souls', a function attributed by Stalin to writers. But in spite of considerable efforts to dis-mantle and re-make the sensibility of the people, E. P. Thompson showed how people were rarely passive recipients of the changes demanded of them, but reaffirmed their own priorities and needs, asserted their autonomy against everything imposed by the powerful.[6] Similarly, there is in our time a growing critical appre-ciation of the machinations of the market, and a desire to distin-guish between human need and economic necessity, although programmes for practical action are slower to materialise.

Whatever the response, there has never been on the scale we now witness, so consistent and systematic an interruption of the way in which children are raised, insofar as the values, beliefs and traditions of parenting have been taken over, subverted or replaced by intensive commercial enterprises designed to re-make children in the image, not of society, but of market and technology. That this has called forth less resistance than, for instance, the creation of an industrial labour force, is due, in large measure, to the fact that it occurred at a period of une-qualled prosperity, and was therefore, unlike the assault on the human personality that would reduce people to 'hands' of this or that factory, largely uncontested. The longer term consequences of this apparently benign transformation will prove—indeed already are proving—less favourable than immediate, highly tangible, rewards suggest.

At least two generations have now grown, formed within, by and for the market rather than by and for society. 'Free markets' are the slogan of certain libertarians. Some of the baleful phenomena that come in their wake are dissociated from source, ascribed instead to 'society' (that shrunken realm, the very existence of which was denied by Margaret Thatcher) or to 'human nature', which has become a toxic dump for systemic evils, including poverty, crime and addiction. But the multiple addictions of our age are, to a degree as yet undetermined, by-products of childhoods conceived under the extra-zodiacal sign of the Market—drugs, alcohol, gambling, sex, or to the most dangerous substance on earth, money. There is also the cult of celebrity, or violence—both external, in the form of knife and gun-crime, or its inner-directed form of self-harm, self-hatred. Beyond this there are the consolations of industrialised fantasy which have colonised the imagination, waves of anger and cruelty that swirl around cyberspace, bullying, abuse of power, the infantilisation of adults and the adulteration of childhood. That which has captured the heart and imagination of the young (and our obsession with 'hearts and minds' abroad might be more usefully directed to the alienations of 'home') is a peer-driven, reductive market culture. This now stands as a primary determinant of identity, far from any rootedness in place, social function or purpose, which offered some (perhaps small) consolation for the privations of the industrial era.

The elevation of the market

The market exists in all cultures and societies, where it has been embedded in, and subordinate to, a wider system of values.

Only in our time, the market has been wrenched out of social context and set up as an end in itself. It is now of such commanding majesty that to say 'there is no market' for any service, commodity or experience is to consign that faulty item to oblivion, to non-existence.

There is good reason for this. Our revulsion against state power—reinforced in the twentieth century by the grisly workings of Fascism and Communism through institutions and agencies of the state—has led us to seek refuge in what appears the opposite of all that over-mighty governments are capable of. In doing so, we scarcely paused to reflect that there may be other roads to serfdom than the broad highway of an omnipotent state; and that the sinuous, blossom-strewn pathways of the market may also be dead ends.

Those who have undertaken crusades to 'shrink the state', to get government off the backs of the people, to cut red tape, make celebratory bonfires of controls, tear up rules and regulations and release what are sometimes referred to the 'animal spirits' of the free market, have, not for the first time in human history, seen liberation in processes which have consequences scarcely less damaging to humanity than the elevation of the state in the recent past. Concentration and labour camps, exile, denial of citizenship, sequestrating dissidents in carceral institutions or 'liquidating' them altogether, have legitimised yielding to the freedom of markets, even though these may be as capable of subjugating society as armies of secret police and the unblinking watchfulness of state bureaucrats. Indeed the ravages of uninhibited markets were plain in the early industrial era: 'market forces' evoke a menacing, almost militaristic, idea. Their impersonality has an abstract appeal, so that no one can be held culpable for those who perish as a result of their dematerialised workings.

Some early enthusiasts of the free market were less squeamish in what they saw as its advantages. Joseph Townsend in 1786 extolled its agentless violence when he wrote:

...legal constraint [of labour] is attended with too much violence, trouble and noise...whereas hunger is not only a peaceable, silent and unremitting pressure, but as the most natural motive to industry it calls forth the most powerful exertions. Hunger will tame the fiercest animals, it will teach decency and civility, obedience and subjection to the most brutish, the most obstinate, the most perverse.[7]

It was only a short step from this celebration of violence which found both home and hiding place in the iron 'laws' of economics and which assimilated one powerful social and economic system to Nature itself; which received fresh impetus in the mid nineteenth century from Darwin, and the principle of 'natural selection' and 'the survival of the fittest.' Whether this represented the imposition of economics upon biology or applied evolutionary theory to an economic system, may be a matter for debate; but the outcome was to reinforce the idea that capitalism was an emanation of the natural world; a superstition from which it has been difficult to dissuade even today's partisans of Kipling's 'law of the jungle' and Tennyson's 'Nature red in tooth and claw', 'dog eat dog' and all the other wisdom of exploitation and cruelty. The most sophisticated version of this 'knowledge' ascribes to 'human nature' all the disagreeable consequences of economic necessity: in a competitive natural world, from which reciprocity, symbiosis and co-operation have been gratuitously excluded, human nature readily fuses with the nature of capitalism.

The state has reverted to a kind of laissez-faire in the *social* sphere, clearing spaces for the invasive entity sanctified as the free market; so that the raising of children has become primarily another aspect of marketing. Parents—who love their children with a passion in no way diminished and perhaps intensified by the loosening grip over their social identity—perceive their waning power, since they have been bypassed by markets which appeal over their heads directly to the young. 'Parenting' has come to mean, increasingly, supplying the money to provide children, not only with all the good things for which publicists know how to kindle instant desire, but also for the satisfaction of hunger, thirst, need for knowledge, information, the capacity to amuse and entertain. Fast-food outlets provide nurture and thirst is slaked by companies that have captured water from its sylvan springs, created fizzy drinks from nature-identical chemicals or from addictive recipes known only, not to wise grandmothers, but the keepers of secrets of international drinks conglomerates. Meanwhile similar entities offer them such information as they need in order to function socially; and, no longer able to divert and delight one another out of their own native store of ingenuity and imagination, they turn to the phantasms emanating from the minds of 'creatives' employed by an industrialised entertainment industry. And even the care and welfare provide for those who need it must now be furnished by approved 'care-providers', whose resemblance to the contracted-out management of paupers of the eighteenth century becomes daily more conspicuous. This generation of predestined orphans is fostered by commerce and technology, whose primary purpose lies elsewhere than in the welfare of those in thrall to their compulsions.

Orphans of commerce

One consequence of this depowering of parents is an anxiety that their children might be 'groomed' for sexual purposes, subject to 'cyber-bullying', seduced by spectral online friendships, or 'radicalised' for malign political ends by social media and websites set up for these purposes. Child victims of such influences are often described, by parents, social workers and police as 'impressionable', 'vulnerable' or 'susceptible'; a state which lays them open to the most baleful of predators.

But that condition of receptiveness is no chance characteristic. It is a situation carefully cultivated by a market which must ensure that its present and future customers remain suggestible. They must be available for whatever new product, experience, novelty or must-have item will sweep through their unencumbered consciousness, a tinder-dry undergrowth to be kindled into bush-fires of desire by the next object of intensive promotion. To know what they want, but not why they want it, nor how that want is answered, is the essence of the instruction children receive from consumer society. To remain undefiled by disturbing ideas is a form of virginity which, like sexual continence in the past, must be jealously guarded against the assault of those who would disseminate troubling forms of consciousness. In other words, the adoptive parents of these children who were never boarded out or fostered are profoundly protective of them; so that they will not stray into undesirable (and critical) company.

It is in the light of this that efforts by government, its agencies and sources of 'intelligence' to counter attempts to 'radicalise' young Muslims, to 'groom' children or to forestall cyber-bullying should be understood. Not for the first time, the instrument promoted as the agent of universal liberation—the free market—proves to be in subversive alliance with the forces of social breakdown, violence and disintegration. That is to say, governments which have made a virtue of removing themselves from the arena of socialisation, are now trying to undo some of the effects of those freedoms, either disingenuously, or without fully understanding the true scope of the forces they have helped set free in the world, and with little idea of the mechanisms required to halt an 'extremism' to which they have themselves contributed by a perverse commitment to conditions that promote it.

The idea of 'consumerism' is not an abstraction invented by intellectuals to disparage the dreams of the people. It is an ideology, knowing and baleful, which seeks to leave fallow the fields of popular creative imagination and critical curiosity, and turn the populations of the whole planet into 'customers', 'clients', 'consumers', 'dependants', even 'addicts.'

In another age, many individuals died of consumption. Now this same erosion of the tissue of life threatens the fabric of whole societies, and indeed, the planet. If this really is 'our way of life', its champions and defenders have become allies of the most destructive of forces. The freedom of markets has less to do with human liberty than with pressing us into the service of their invasive need to expand and grow at the expense of our own self-reliance and autonomy. They break down resistance, undermine our capacity to make and do things for ourselves and others; above all leave a pliant, tractable state of mind, not for the diktats of government, but for the reception of the manufactured, contrived—and often highly desirable—wonders of the world.

It is certainly correct to call 'abusive' the activities of radical-isers or groomers of the young. But their ability to accomplish their malignant objectives depends upon an anterior and legiti-mate form of abuse, which does not take place in the shadows. It is not committed by villainous exploiters who lurk in dark-ness, but occurs in the broadest of daylight. The perpetrators do not break surreptitiously into our homes. They are not stran-gers who offer sweets or rides in cars. Quite the opposite. They are actually invited into virtually every domestic sanctuary in the land, where they work their mischief unchallenged. These are the tillers of internal landscapes, preparing fertile spaces for the yield of strange harvests by the farmers of desire and the refined cultivators of wants that still lie slumbering in the minds of children. It should not astonish us if, among the approved beneficiaries of these developments are also to be found the peddlers of destructive ideologies, with their ruinous exalta-tions, their promises of a better hereafter, or seductive promises of affection to loveless and excluded young people.

The infinite market imposes itself upon Locke's assertion that children are a blank slate upon which society will inscribe val-ues, beliefs and opinions written by experience. Yet that experi-ence has already been pre-selected, and whispers into their infant ears its mysterious cradlesongs of desire; so that the earli-est signs of intelligence which the world detects are the magic

words 'I want'; words which have taken on the sound of command to parents and guardians, for whom, obeying the dicta-
torship of the market, feel themselves unfit or unworthy if they
are unable to fulfil the desires implanted in what William Leiss
called the 'culture of wanting'.[8] Indeed, there is nothing else to
do in a world of showy and conspicuous abundance than to
want: a verb that implies at the same time the absence of something vital and the desire to secure it. There is certainly no
urgency to change a world which was brought to such a high
degree of perfection long before today's children were born that
there can be no conceivable requirement to alter it; and to heap
up its treasures is the only consolation for having been born so
late; and into a world which has so little clearly defined function
to offer them.

Identity is now to be chosen in market abundance to orna-
ment an orphaned status, which has forfeited all features except
the most irreducible—of gender, ethnicity, sexual orientation
and faith. These are viewed as troublesome survivals, which act,
in certain devout or extreme individuals, as an impediment to
the construction of the market-created personality of the
orphans it has produced.

The market usurps society; and in the process, produces
strange phenomena, responsibility for which, in general it man-
ages to avoid by means of its insistence upon its caring cherishing
of its adoptees. It sings its wares incessantly in an unceasing and
rapturous psalmody to the commodities and sensations it offers.
The air is alive with hymns and praise to the shining desirability
of everything it offers; a strident publicity which, apart from
entreating the people to buy, also serves as a constant distraction
from any perception that its imperatives might also lie at the root
of many disagreeable aspects of contemporary life.

There has always been a certain lack of comprehension
between generations: the young are clearly going to inhabit a
different social landscape—the future—from that of their
elders. But the intervention, not only of major conglomerates

who have struck much of the power to provide the necessities of life from the hands of parents, but also of technology which swiftly outpaces the capacity of the previous generation to keep pace, adds a fresh impetus to the estrangement between them. Parents humble—even humiliate—themselves before their children, in order to retrieve some sense of social function, begging them to choose this or that delicacy, consulting them as oracles before any major expenditure. They struggle on the edge of their children's lives, trying to find a way in; urging them on from the touchline, giving free rein to their talents, exhorting them to fulfil themselves, realise their fantasies as they wait for the result of the audition, the trial-run, the interview, the test. They pace up and down, not always metaphorically, outside the door of their children's rooms, to which access is forbidden, while their young, supplied with the mysterious necessities which make up a complete and full childhood, wondering who they are contacting on line, who are the shadowy seven hundred virtual friends, marvelling at the manual dexterity with which they play computer games or text their peers. They do not know into what eerie twilight they are straying and what prompts the unaccountable elations and sudden outbursts of tears, the anxieties over their body, their abilities, their impenetrable relationship with food, their desire for fame or wealth, the need to 'be somebody', to 'show them' by distinguishing themselves. Their inner world is peopled with who can say what insubstantial ghostly creatures emanating from vast transnational companies dedicated to their perpetual distraction, diversion and entertainment. Parents no longer even blame 'the people they mix with', because these are unknown and have only a phantasmal existence through social media or random acquaintance in networks of affinity and attachment which hold them in thrall.

We might also ask who is advantaged by the state of gilded inutility which is considered the proper condition for children in our own time. Is it simply a reaction against excessive labour, when infants were sent into the corn to pick stones or to lift mangelwurzels from frozen fields; were consigned to trackless seas and infinite prairies or shipped to the mills of the North from the London workhouses? Is it so they may devote their early years to the acquisition of learning and knowledge that will provide them with a secure and satisfying livelihood? Or does it also have some other purpose? For it also deprives them of any sense of social function, of any contribution to the work of construction and creation in the world, robs them of an identity of doing by means of arduous effort and application, in favour of a more passive identity of the adventitious features of simply being? In this void some of the pathologies of our time luxuriate.

This social detachment of children does not mean, as it might have at an earlier time, that they have been abandoned. For they have been fostered, 'taken in'—in more than one sense—by the caring institution that is consumer capitalism, with its limitless technological capacity to provide amusement, information, distraction, friendship, love, on condition that the individual has the money to pay for it, or on the promise of future payment—indebtedness—if not. All children, in an echo of the Elizabethan Poor Law, are 'indentured' to the market and its addictive technologies, apprenticeships that have the advantage of being prolonged indefinitely, and lucratively, far into adult life. Concerns for the 'mental health' of the young, the prevalence of eating disorders, depression, bullying, obesity and loneliness, the misty quality of 'friends' on social media (can it be true, as the Office for National Statistics affirms, that almost five million people in Britain say they 'have no real friends'?), seek to locate within individuals disorders which are generated externally, and not even by 'society', which increasingly serves as a usefully decorative mask for the ubiquitous, inescapable market.[9]

These social developments are not, of course, confined to children, but reach out to modify the psychic structures of a whole society. In presence of the power of individualist ideology, many parents are also called away by having their own lives to lead. The absence of belief in any hereafter means that we must fill the brief space of our too-short lives with as many of the experiences, pleasures, materials and *stuff* that beckon to us from the capitalist cornucopia. In the process, the fissures that appear in neighbourhood and community also infiltrate the sanctuary of kinship and family. It isn't simply that families break and are scattered and that new sets of semi-kin appear. Even within families apparently socially intact, adults are sometimes seduced into placing their own desires above those of their children; and parenting—always fallible, anxious and imperfect—is also undermined by the separate pathways followed internally by those responsible for the lives of a new generation. There have always been neglectful and exploitative parents—as abandoned infants and wasted youth of both rural England and the landscapes of industrialism testify—but there can never have been so many diversions, delights and solicitations to beguile even those who most loudly proclaim their devotion to giving their children the best of everything; a best that often means hunting in the bazaars of capitalism, not only for *things*, but gathering accomplishments, achievements and advantages that will not only enable them to stand out from the crowd, but will also satisfy their own sense that they have done all that is *humanly possible* for their young. Is there any spectacle more affecting than the constant unquiet delivery of children by parents to extra-curricular tuitions, to classes for ballet, karate, playing the violin or clarinet, drama, horse-riding, educational outings and travels that will provide them with all arts of living and give them a head-start in what we still guilelessly refer to as the competitive 'rat-race'.

Freedom and (economic) necessity

Social and moral wrongs often go unnoticed because unnamed. This is not the first time we have sought salvation in the very source of the evil we perceive. It was said, for instance, in the struggle against slavery, that captivity in the Americas represented a better life for those trafficked—but baptised—people stolen from the malarial heathenish shores of Africa. It was believed that child labour—whether the rural monotony of straw-plaiting and rush-gathering by six-year olds, or infants cleaning the dust and lint from under the still-moving looms in cotton mills was a 'wholesome and necessary discipline.' The Puritans thought that children, as bearers of original sin, should be scourged and whipped into righteousness for the sake of their immortal soul. All these horrors duly passed away; but whether we entered the realm of light may be questioned.

Perhaps some of the serenely accepted 'norms' of our own society will one day come under a scrutiny similar to that which we now bring to our examination of past wrongs. Shall we one day come to question how we parked our children in the nurseries of desire, sparkling grottoes of the market, just as we park our cars outside the supermarket? Will it come to seem aberrant and bizarre that the greatest skills with which we equipped our children was a preoccupation with their own desires in the presence of the showy displays in the existential hypermarket? Shall we wonder whether this is an enfeoffment no less damaging than that of feudalism or of an agrarian world, in which ragged children shooed away birds from growing corn or walked barefoot on the frozen earth, or than a labour market to which starvelings of the nineteenth century were tied, as their clogs rang out at dawn on the cobbles and the mill gates closed against them for poor timekeeping?

If this seems unlikely at this moment, well, so did the reforms which agitated the conscience of Victorian England. That we are expected to find a meaning in life in the accumulation of goods, services and sensations, in the technology of limitless communication, independently of the content of what is transmitted in the sunny souks, bazaars and exchanges of a cosmic capitalism, is, surely, an inadequate account of human aspiration. It is as unworthy, as the fate of those condemned to scraping a spare subsistence in the stony pastures of industrial Britain. The roads to servitude do not pass solely through the louring canyons of overweening state power, but may also snake tortuously through the sacred groves of the free market.

Orphans of the earth

There is another, perhaps even more destructive effect in the world of children of the market; for the dilation of appetites, omnivorous and insatiable, only intensifies the assault on the waning resources of the world. Economic growth works through the hungers of a humanity robbed of its own resources, since it must fill and fulfil an inner emptiness contrived by the very entities that claim to heal it. The devouring of the substance of the earth is an inescapable response to the using up of human powers, diminished and disgraced as they are by technological perfection and the materialised dreams of utopian fantasy. In other words, children are raised so that their fulfilment (and the even more essential accomplishment of the purposes of the market) depends upon gutting the earth of its treasures, just as they have been eviscerated of their own capacity to do, make, create and share for the sake of their own survival.

These melancholy orphanings subordinate children—and the adults they will become—to the power, not of their parents, but of the 'providers', not only for their basic needs, but of their ambitions, hopes and dreams. In the process, this creates dependency upon an economic system, which, for its constant growth and expansion, assaults and demolishes the human habitat and its capacity to sustain them and future generations. It is one thing to live in the present; but when the present uses up in advance the necessities of the future, it becomes something more than hedonism: we are in the realm of cultural myth which devours its own children.

Orphaned of the capacity for self-provisioning in any significant way, we are at the mercy of those by whose grace we are

provided for. This is no longer those who, by reason of parentage, are closest to us, but distant entities that have continued the
ancient practice of enclosure, and have appropriated the nourishment of the earth, its water and forests and treasures mined
and processed, ostensibly for our comfort and ease, but primarily for their own enrichment, while the resource-base of the
planet wastes and shrinks, as fresh populations bring to the
depletion of the world the same waxing desires which privilege
and wealth increasingly command. Hope inhabits the dynamic
system which appropriates and monopolises human resources,
and leaves an emptiness that requires ever greater compensa-
tions from a dwindling world in order to make good the exhaustion within. That this form of growth is destructive and
pathological is scarcely a secret; but where is liberation to be
found from its compulsions?[10]

Adult discomfort with the knowledge acquired by children
through the technological receptors of powerful corporations
mimics the ancient lament that generations are divided: they
always have been, but rarely by the intensity with which the
instruments of communication remove them from all that has
gone before. There has been much comment on the consequences for children of dependency upon—or addiction to—the
technological toys of our time, but this has been directed principally at their physical and psychological effects. The much-
quoted Kaiser Foundation study in 2010 (which already seems
like pre-history) that elementary schoolchildren spend seven and
a half hours a day with entertainment technology, that
75 per cent have TV in the bedroom and that in 50 per cent of
US households TV plays all day, warns of the dangers to young
children of attention deficit, delay in development, speech
impairment, anxiety, stress, sleep loss in the sedentary but chaotic and incoherent stream of sounds and images that assail their
senses.[10] It is a necessary argument, whether the advantages to
children of dexterity and speed of reaction, as well as facilitation
of certain kinds of learning, outweigh the baleful effects of other

forms of deprivation associated with an inescapable technology.
But a more disquieting result of this baptism by total immersion
in the Lethe of technology, is that they become more deeply
installed in a technosphere that is ever further removed from the
natural world; a natural world on which its dependency is para-
sitic and possibly destructive. The charity Plantlife revealed in
2017 that 80 per cent of people in Britain did not know the
common violet and less than half of young people could name
a bluebell—redundant knowledge for those attuned to the
urgencies of technological communication, but vital in the safeguarding of species in a world already robbed, not only of its
treasures, but also of some of the elements required to sustain
certain forms of life, including that of humanity.[11] In 2016, the
Royal Botanic Gardens in Kew reported that one-fifth of the
world's plants are threatened with extinction.[12] The International
Union for the Conservation of Nature estimates one in eight
birds are threatened, one in four mammals; while 75 per cent of
the genetic diversity in agricultural crops has been lost, and three
quarters of the world's fisheries are over-fished.[13] A culture that
encourages its children to live in a sphere in which these extinc-
tions have no part is preparing orphanings of future generations
which we can scarcely imagine.

In this development, we can see how privilege, once the jealous preserve of ruling castes of aristocracy and the nobility,
colonised the professional and upper middle class, spreading in
the nineteenth century to the lower middle class, and the more
highly skilled ranks of the artisan and working class, reaching
the mass of the people only in the years since 1945, and excluding only the very poor until the present. Recent concern for the
poorest children suggests that even these must also be included
within a totalising culture of constant growth; even as a whole
world mimics the same pathology. In other words, it is taken for
granted that no part of humanity will remain untouched by the
ever-expanding market; and human desire has been yoked like
a beast of draught to a 'demand' for more that will ensure, for

the time being, if not in perpetuity, growth and expansion of an economy becoming global.

We are living through a different kind of orphaning, estrangements unprecedented, whereby children are voluntarily surrendered from the tender encirclement of loving arms, and passed, fondly and trustingly, to the baleful surrogate parenting of the baby-farmers of market and technology; a fostering that knows nothing of the precious resourcefulness of people, and sets no limits upon the promises with which it lulls its dependants; so that the day when humanity must learn to live within its own resources, and not those borrowed from a future used up in advance, recedes for a season, and expands to occupy the already colonised inner spaces of generations yet to be born. The orphaned and disadvantaged, no longer living in a culture apart, join with the privileged and entitled, as they pass into a world which promises forms of transcendence borrowed from a discarded religious sensibility.

This menaces the integrity of what more 'primitive' cultures referred to as mother earth or mother nature, and the particular soil that gave them sustenance as mother- or father-lands (even if these ideas were abused by the rhetoric of savage nationalisms), the bestowing of parental characteristics upon rivers, mountains, forests which sustained life and guaranteed perpetuity. Often these were elevated to the status of divinities, which made even more certain a solemnity of respect for the elements that sustain all life. The systematic ruin of these in the name of 'growth' and 'development' mocks humanity and threatens us with the most melancholy—because elective and avoidable—orphaning of all; and at the same time gives fresh poignancy to the centuries of alternating piety and punishment towards orphans.

NOTES

1. ORPHANS

1. Senior, Jayne, *Broken and Betrayed*, Pan Macmillan, 2016.
2. Laslett, Peter, *The World We Have Lost*, Methuen, 1965.
3. Seabrook, Jeremy, *Working Class Childhood*, Gollancz, 1982.
4. Simpson, Eileen, *Orphans: Real and Imaginary*, Weidenfeld and Nicholson, 1987.
5. Interview with Anna Mottram, 2017.
6. Simpson, op. cit.
7. Nixon, Cheryl, *The Orphan in Eighteenth-Century Law and Literature: Estate, Blood, and Body*, Ashgate, 2011.
8. Similar feelings also govern attitudes towards widows—another category of the 'deserving'. It is never wise to take official pieties at face value. Ancient gravestones in Britain are often carved with the word 'relict', (Old French *relicte*, Latin *relicta*, from *relinquere* to relinquish), meaning one left behind, or surviving from an earlier age. There is in this a hint of censoriousness—one who lingers when her husband has gone—presumably to a higher place or better world. In some cultures, notably traditional Hinduism, the practice of *sati*, self-immolation by widows—was erased with difficulty. It was revived, shockingly, by a woman called Roop Kanwar in Rajasthan in 1987 in the fortieth case since India's Independence. She became an object of veneration to Hindu fundamentalists. And the streets of Vrindavan in Uttar Pradesh are full of widows from all over India, who have made a final pilgrimage to the birthplace of Krishna; their white robes flutter in the breeze as they do

penance for their longevity. Even in the West, avoidance of bereaved women is common, particularly when couples, former friends, do not want to be reminded of the loss that also lies in wait for them. We know from our own past that widows, or other elderly women living alone, were also in danger of accusations of witchcraft, and so they remain in many parts of the world.

2. THE CARE OF ORPHANS

1. Hindle, Steve, *On the Parish? The Micro-Politics of Poor Relief in Rural England circa 1550–1775*, Clarendon Press, 2004.
2. Stubbs, Philip, *The Anatomie of Abuses*, Richard Jones, 1583.
3. Laslett, Peter, *The World We Have Lost*, Methuen, 1965.
4. Hoggart, Richard, *The Uses of Literacy: Aspects of Working Class Life*, Penguin Classics, first published 1957, most recent edition 2009.
5. Johnson, Alan, *This Boy*, Transworld Publishers, 2014.
6. Wordsworth, Dorothy, *The Greens of Grasmere: A Narrative Concerning George and Sarah Green of the Parish of Grasmere, addressed to a Friend*, first written 1808, Oxford University Press, 1936.
7. 'Fast-acting paramedic rescues baby from submerged SUV in Illinois lake', *Chicago Tribune*, 17 March, 2017.

3. ORPHANS OF THE RICH

1. Jones, Norman, *Governing by Virtue: Lord Burleigh and the Management of Elizabethan England*, Oxford University Press, 2015.
2. Hale, Matthew, *History of the Common Law*, 1713.
3. Pinchbeck, Ivy and Margaret Hewitt, *Children in English Society: From Tudor Times to the Eighteenth Century*, Routledge and Kegan Paul, 1969.
4. Carlton, Charles, *Court of Orphans*, Leicester University, 1974.
5. www.british-history.ac.uk/no-series/index-remembrancia
6. Ibid.
7. Ibid.
8. Carlton, Charles, op. cit.
9. *Reports of Cases Argued and Determined in the High Court of Chancery, and of some Special cases adjudged by the Court of the King's Bench*, collected by William Peere Williams, 1749.
10. www.cruttendenfamily.talktalk.net/historical/90677.html

11. Vesey, Francis, *Reports of Cases Argued and Determined in the High Court of Chancery 1789–1817*, Vol. IX, 65.

12. Lamb, Charles, 'On Coleridge', *New Monthly Magazine*, November 1834.

13. Roosevelt, Eleanor, *Autobiography*, Da Capo Press, 1992.

14. Ibid.

15. Russell, Bertrand, *Autobiography*, Routledge, 2014.

16. Poe, Edgar Allan, *The Premature Burial*, 1844.

17. Stanley, Henry Morton, *The Autobiography of Sir Henry Morton Stanley: The Making of a Nineteenth-Century Explorer*, Stackpole Books, 2001.

18. Hecht, Ben, Joshua Green and Marilyn Monroe, *My Story*, Stein and Day, 1974.

19. Milnes, Monckton, *Keats: Life, Letters and Remains of John Keats*, Edward Moxon, 1843.

20. Williams, Peter, *J S Bach: A Musical Biography*, Cambridge University Press, 2004.

21. Birukoff, Paul, *Leo Tolstoy, His Life and Work: Autographical Memoirs, Letters and Biographical Material*, 1906.

22. Bernstein, Nina, 'Ward of the State; The Gap in Ella Fitzgerald's Life', *New York Times*, 23 June 1996, https://www.nytimes.com/1996/06/23/weekinreview/ward-of-the-state-the-gap-in-ella-fitzgerald-s-life.html

23. *Memoirs of the Life, Character and Writings of Philip Doddridge*, 1766, https://archive.org/details/memoirslifechar00ortogoog

24. Baird, Julia, *Imagine: Growing Up with John Lennon*, Hodder, 2007.

25. Vasili, Philip, *Colouring over the White Line: The History of Black Footballers in Britain*, Mainstream Publishers, 2000.

4. THE POOR LAW, 1601–1834

1. Anon., *An Ease for the Overseers of the Poor*, Cambridge, 1601.

2. Trubner, N. & Co, *Early English Text Society*, Paternoster Row, 1871.

3. Webb, Sidney and Beatrice, *English Poor Law Policy*, Longmans, Green and Co., 1910.

4. Pelling, Margaret, *The Common Lot: Sickness, Medical Occupations and the Urban Poor in Early Modern England*, Longmans, 1998.

5. Hindle, Steve, *On the Parish? The Micro-Politics of Poor Relief in Rural England circa 1550—1775*, Clarendon Press, 2004.

6. Pinchbeck, Ivy and Margaret Hewitt, *Children in English Society*, Routledge and Kegan Paul, 1969.
7. Wilson, John Iliff, *A Brief History of Christ's Hospital*, 1809.
8. Coleridge, S. T., *Table Talk*, John Murray, 1886.
9. Act of the Privy Council of James I, London 1925, Vol. 2.
10. Coldham, Peter Wilson, *Emigrants in Chains*, Sutton Pub, 1992.
11. Stone, Lawrence, *The Family, Sex and Marriage in England 1500–1800*, Weidenfeld and Nicholson, 1977.
12. Beier, A. L., *Masterless Men: The Vagrancy Problem in England 1560–1640*, Methuen, 1985.
13. Ibid.
14. David Keys, 'Skeletons of Scottish prisoners proved evidence of child soldiers in Britain's civil wars', *The Independent*, 2 September 2015, https://www.independent.co.uk/news/science/archaeology/skeletons-of-scottish-prisoners-provide-evidence-of-child-soldiers-in-english-civil-war-10482793.html
15. Tawney, R. H., *Religion and the Rise of Capitalism*, Penguin, 1990.
16. Cunningham, Andrew, *Health Care and Poor Relief in Protestant Europe, 1500–1700*, Routledge, 2002
17. Ibid.
18. Cary, John, *An Account of the Proceedings of the Corporation of Bristol in Execution of the Act of Parliament for the Better Employing and Maintaining the Poor of the City*, 1700.
19. Ibid.
20. Cunningham, *The Invention of Childhood*, BBC Books, 2006.
21. Addison, Joseph, *The Guardian*, Volume the Second, 1713.
22. Fildes, Valerie, *Women as Mothers in Pre-Industrial England*, Routledge, 2014.
23. *A Particular and Exact Account of the Trial of Mary Compton*, 1693, London.
24. Burg, B. R., *Boys at Sea*, Palgrave Macmillan, 2007.
25. Ibid.
26. Coldham, Peter Wilson, *Emigrants in Chains*, Sutton Pub, Ltd, 1992
27. Detroisier, Rowland, 'A Lecture Delivered to the New Mechanics' Institute, Manchester … on the Necessity of Moral and Political Instruction Among the Working Classes'.
28. Fildes, op. cit.

29. Bowers, Toni, *Politics of Motherhood in British Writing and Culture 1680—1760*, Cambridge University Press, 1996.

30. Evans, Tanya, *Unfortunate Objects: Lone Mothers in Eighteenth Century London*, Palgrave, 2005.

31. Hitchcock, Tom, *Down and Out in Georgian London*, Hambledon, 2004.

32. Hitchcock, op. cit.

33. Anon., *The Annals of Crime and New Newgate Calendar*, Issues 1–53, Berger, Holywell Ct, London.

34. *The Guardian*, November, 2000.

35. Wagner, Gillian, *Thomas Coram, Gent.*, Baydell Press, 2004.

36. Jonathan Kaiman, 'Chinese city suspends baby hatch after it is overwhelmed by unwanted children', *The Guardian*, 17 March 2014, https://www.theguardian.com/world/2014/mar/17/china-baby-hatch-suspended-parents-abandon-infants

37. Allin, D. S., *The Early Years of the Foundling Hospital 1739/41–1773*.

38. Pugh, John, *Remarkable Occurrences in the Life of Jonas Hanway Esq* third edition, London, 1798.

39. Hanway, Jonas, *An Earnest Appeal for Mercy to the Children of the Poor*, London, 1766.

40. Hanway, Jonas, *A Sentimental History of Chimney Sweeps in London and Westminster*, edn. Cambridge University Press, 2013.

41. Scott, John, *Observations on the Present State of the Parochial and Vagrant Poor*, London, 1773.

42. Potter, R, *Observation on the Poor Law, or the Present State of the Poor and on Houses of Industry*, London, 1775.

43. Trimmer, Mrs Sarah, *The Oeconomy of Charity*, London, 1801.

44. Higginbotham, Peter 'London Orphan Asylum, East London/ Watford, Hertfordshire', www.childrenshomes.org.uk

45. Seabrook, Jeremy, *Working Class Childhood*, Gollancz, 1982.

46. 'John Hudson. Theft: Burglary', The Proceedings of the Old Bailey 1674—1913, 10 December 1783, https://www.oldbaileyonline.org

47. https://www.oldbaileyonline. org

48. *The Philanthropist or Repository for Hints and Suggestions Calculated to promote the Comfort and Happiness of Man*, Vol. IV, London, 1814.

49. Pennant, William, *Some Accounts of London*, 5th edn., London, 1814.

50. *The Newgate Calendar*, 1767.
51. Byng, The Honourable John, *Diaries, A Tour in the Midlands 1790*, Manchester Archives and Local Studies.
52. Lynd, Sylvia, *English Children*, William Collins, 1942.
53. Brown, John, *A Memoir of Robert Blincoe, An Orphan Boy*, J. Docherty, 1832.
54. Brown, op. cit.
55. Honeyman, Katrina, *Child Workers in England, Parish Apprentices and the Making of the Early Industrial Labour Force*, Ashgate, 2007.
56. Honeyman, Katrina, *Child Workers in England 1780–1820: Parish Apprentices and the Making of the Early Industrial Labour Force*, Routledge, 2007, p. 104.
57. Lane, Joan, *Apprenticeship in England 1600—1914*, Taylor and Francis 1996.
58. Webb, Sidney and Beatrice Webb, English Poor Law Policy, Longmans, Green and Co., 1910
59. *Westminster Review*, January 1837.
60. Fawcett, Henry, *Pauperism and its Causes and Remedies*, Macmillan, 1871.
61. Walvin, James, *Black Ivory: A History of British Slavery*, Howard University Press, 1994.
62. Equiano, Olaudah, *Interesting Narrative of the Life of Olaudah Equiano, or Gustavus Vasu the African*, 1789, edn. Dawson, 1969.
63. Thomas, Hugh, *The Slave Trade*, Simon and Schuster, 1999.

5. AFTER 1834

1. *Report of Commissioners on the Poor Laws*, Appendix A, Wylde's Report, 1834.
2. Frierson, Cathy and Vilenski Semen Samuilovitch, *Children of the Gulag*, Yale University Press, 2010.
3. Ibid.
4. General Orders issued by the Poor Law Commissioners 1841, 1842 and since the passing of the 7 and 8 Vict. C. 101, London, 1845.
5. Martineau, Harriet, *Poor Laws and Paupers Illustrated, Society for the Diffusion of Useful Knowledge*, 1834.
6. Barlee, Ellen, *Friendless and Helpless*, Emily Faithfull London, 1868.
7. Pelling, Margaret, *The Common Lot—Sickness, Medical Occupations and the Urban Poor in Early Modern England*, Longmans, 1998.

8. Doran, Susan, Norman Jones (eds), *The Elizabethan World*, Routledge, 2011.

9. Davenport-Hall, Florence, *Children of the State*, Macmillan and Company, 1899.

10. Pennant, William, *Some Accounts of London, Fifth edition*, London, 1814.

11. Crabbe, George, *The Village, The Parish Register and Other Poems*, William and Robert Chambers, 1838.

12. Cunningham, Hugh, *The Children of the Poor*, Blackwell, 1971.

13. Dickens, Charles, 'The Paradise at Tooting', *The Examiner*, 20 January 1849.

14. Thomas, Amanda J., *Cholera: The Victorian Plague*, Pen and Sword, 2015.

15. Nick Hopkins, '"We have to deliver justice": the man who fought for the survivors of Shirley Oaks', *The Guardian*, 8 October 2016, https://www.theguardian.com/society/2016/oct/21/we-have-to-deliver-justice-the-man-who-fought-for-the-survivors-of-shirley-oaks

16. Thomas Wontner, London, 1833.

17. Baxter, G. R.W., *Book of the Bastiles*, London, 1841.

18. Ibid.

19. Mayhew, Henry, *London Labour and the London Poor*, 1851.

20. Ibid.

21. Scott, John, *Observations on the Present State of the Parochial and Vagrant Poor*, London, 1773.

22. Rose, Lionel, *Massacre of the Innocents: Infanticide in Britain 1800—1939*, Routledge, 2015.

23. 'Muller Orphan Home, Ashley Down' www.childrenshomes.org.uk

24. Vale, Allison, *The Woman Who Murdered Babies for Money*, Carlton Books, 2011.

25. Cobbe, Frances Rowe, 'Friendless Girls and How to Help Them', Social Science Congress in Dublin, 1861.

26. Barlee, Ellen, *Friendless and Helpless*, Emily Faithfull London, 1868.

27. Ibid.

28. Davenport-Hill, Florence, *Children of the State*, Macmillan and Company, 1868.

29. Seabrook, *Children of Other Worlds*, Pluto Press, 2001.

30. Carpenter, Mary. *Reformatory Schools for the Children of the Perishing and Dangerous Classes for Juvenile Offenders*, C. Gilpin, London, 1851.
31. Tuckwell, Gertrude, *The State and Its Children*.
32. 'The Barnardo Story: The First Home', www.childrenshomes. org.uk/DB/firsthome.shtml
33. Murdoch, Lydia, *Imagined Orphans*, Rutgers University Press, 2006.
34. 'Steep decline in international adoptions to the US', Pew Research Center, 2017, pewresearch.orgfact-tank

6. PHILANTHROPIC ABDUCTION

1. Murdoch, Lydia, *Imagined Orphans*, Rutgers University Press, 2006.
2. Barnardo, Dr, *Taken out of the Gutter*, London, 1871.
3. Tuckwell, Gertrude, *The State and Its Children*, Methuen and Company, 1894.
4. Murdoch, op. cit.
5. Barlee, Ellen, *Friendless and Helpless*, Emily Faithfull, London, 1868.
6. Tuckwell, op. cit.
7. Clarke Hall, W., *The State and the Child*, London, 1917.
8. Tuckwell, op. cit.
9. Tuckwell, op. cit.
10. Fawcett, Henry, *Pauperism and its Causes and Remedies*, Macmillan, 1871.
11. 'Fire at Industrial School', *Northampton Mercury* 1 January 1890.
12. Pinchbeck, Ivy and Margaret Hewitt, *Children in English Society*, Routledge and Kegan Paul, 1969.
13. 'Annie Macpherson and the Gutter Children', www.spitalfield-slife.com/2015/11/25annie-macpherson-the-gutter-children
14. Bean, Philip and Joy Melville, *Lost Children of the Empire*, Unwin Hyman, 1989.
15. Bean and Melville, op. cit.
16. Crane, Denis, *John Bull's Surplus Children*, H. Marshall, 2015.
17. Bean and Melville, op. cit.
18. Penglase Joanna, *Orphans of the Living*, Curtin University Books, Fremantle, 2005.
19. Cunningham Hugh, *The Children of the Poor*, Blackwell, 1971.
20. Penglase, op. cit.
21. Simpson, op. cit.

22. Hendrick, Harry, *Child Welfare*, Policy Press, 2003.
23. 'The National Children's Home Story: The Curtis Report', www. childrenshomes.org.uk/NCH/Curtis.shtml
24. Simpson, op. cit.

7. WAR AND THE ORPHANS OF STRIFE

1. Brent, Leslie, *Sunday's Child? A Memoir*, Bank House Books, 2009.
2. Hiroshima Peace Culture Foundation, *Eyewitness Testimonies: Appeals from the A-Bomb Survivors*, 1990.
3. Interviews by Iqbal Hossein, Italy, 2016.
4. Interviews conducted in Cox's Bazar, Bangladesh, by Iqbal Hossein, 2016.

8. THE END OF AN EPOCH

1. Pockington, David, 'Safeguarding in Scotland: The McLellan Commission Report', *Law and Religion UK*, 19 August 2015.
2. O'Riordan, Steve, *Whispering Hope, The True Story of the Magdalene Laundries*, Orion Publishing Group, 2016.
3. Fahy, Bernardette, *Freedom of Angels*, O'Brien Press, 1999.
4. De Mause, Lloyd, 'The Evolution of Childhood', *History of Childhood Quarterly, The Journal of Psychohistory*, Vol. 1, No. 3, 1974.
5. Fahy, op. cit.
6. 'Forgotten Orphans of Smyllum laid to rest by nuns in unmarked graves,' *The Scotsman on Sunday*, 14 September 2003, https://www.scotsman.com/news/forgotten-orphans-of-smyllum-laid-to-rest-by-nuns-in-umarked-graves-1-1293737
7. Owen Boycott, 'Hundreds of Scottish orphanage children allegedly buried in mass grave', *The Guardian*, 10 September 2017, https://www.theguardian.com/uk-news/2017/sep/10/smyllum-park-lanark-orphanage-catholic-nuns-children-mass-grave-allegedly
8. Elliott, Sue, *Love Child*, Ebury Press, 2006.
9. Ben Quinn, 'Thousands of children as young as five act as family carers, figures show', *The Guardian*, 16 May 2013, https://www.the-guardian.com/society/2013/may/16/thousands-children-caregivers-family-data

10. Laslett, Peter, 'Parental Deprivation in the Past. A note on the history of orphans in England', *Local Population Studies*, 1974.

9. SOCIAL FOSTERINGS

1. Orme, Nicholas, *Medieval Children*, Yale University Press, 2001.
2. Pinchbeck, Ivy and Margaret Hewitt, *Children in English Society*, Routledge and Kegan Paul, 1969.
3. Green, Ian, *Humanism and Protestantism in Early Modern English Education*, Ashgate, 2009.
4. Hanaway, James, *A Token for Children*, 1670.
5. Cunningham, Hugh, *The Children of the Poor*, Blackwell, 1971.
6. Ibid.
7. Penglase Joanna, *Orphans of the Living*, Curtin University Books, Fremantle, 2005.
8. Peters, Laura, *Orphan Texts: Victorian Orphans, Culture and Empire*, Manchester University Press, 2000.
9. Trimmer, op. cit.
10. Tufnell, E. C. 'Letter to the Poor Law Commissioners', Report on the Education of Pauper Children, 1839.
11. Parliamentary speech by Lord Shaftesbury, quoted in Murdoch, Lydia, *Imagined Orphans*, Rutgers University Press, 2006.

10. A MILLENNIAL RESTRUCTURING

1. Patrick Collinson, 'Cost of raising children in UK higher than ever', *The Guardian*, 16 February 2016, https://www.theguardian.com/lifeandstyle/2016/feb/16/cost-of-raising-children-in-uk-higher-than-ever
2. Postman, Neil, *The Disappearance of Childhood*, Delacorte Press, 1982.
3. Locke, John, *Essay Concerning Human Understanding*, 1689.
4. Aries, Philippe, *Centuries of Childhood: A Social History of Family Life*, transl. 1960, Jonathan Cape, 1962.
5. Benedict, Ruth, *Patterns of Culture*, Mentor Books, 1946.
6. Thompson, E P, *The Making of the English Working Class*, Gollancz, 1962.
7. Townsend, Joseph, *Dissertation on the Poor Laws*, 1786.
8. Leiss, William, *The Limits to Satisfaction: An Essay on the Problems of Needs and Commodities*, University of Toronto Press, 1976.

9. *Daily Telegraph*, Office for National Statistics, 12 August 2014.
10. Sparks, Glenn, Media Effects Research, Cengage Learning 2012.
11. Plantlife, Salisbury, Wiltshire, 2017.
12. Royal Botanic Gardens, Kew, State of the World's Plants, 2016.
13. Damian Carrington, 'Forest giraffe on the brink of extinction, red list warns', *The Guardian*, 26 November 2013, https://www.the-guardian.com/environment/2013/nov/26/iucn-red-list-endangered-species-extinction

INDEX

animism, 293
Anne, Queen of Great Britain
    and Ireland, 104, 123
Annual Register of all Parish
    Poor Infants (1762), 124
anthropomorphism, 305
Apollo Theatre, Harlem, 76
apologies for history, 223,
    260–61
Apothecaries' Hall, London, 73
Appleby, Mary, 132
apprenticeships
    chimney sweeps, 125–6, 139
    in factories, 125, 145–50
    marine service, 107, 112,
        121, 124
    parish, 35–6, 49, 86–8,
        95–101, 106, 124, 125,
        129, 150, 153–4
    Poor Laws, 83, 84, 85, 86–7,
        100, 101, 112
    rich orphans, 49
    Viginia Colony, 90
    and workhouses, 129, 145–6,
        147, 149
Arabs, 85
arbeit, 8
arbha, 8
arbya, 8
Aries, Philippe, 305
asylums, 28, 197, 204, 227,
    231, 233, 263
    London Orphan Asylum,
        130–33
    Reedham Asylum for Father-
        less Children, 15, 20–21,
        28, 133, 134–8

atheism, 56, 58, 67
Atkinson, Richard, 116
Auschwitz concentration camp,
    17, 240
Australia, 15, 24, 142, 219, 223,
    261
Auxiliary Territorial Service,
    137–8

baby farming, 106–7, 125,
    190–92
Baby P (Peter Connelly), 274,
    276
Bach, Johann Sebastian, 64, 66,
    73–4
Baghdad, Iraq, 19
Baltimore, Maryland, 66
Bangladesh, 85, 106, 147,
    200–204, 213, 220, 249, 250
Barbados, 90, 164, 268
Barbara, Maria, 74
Barisal, Bangladesh, 201
Barkingside Girls' Village
    Homes, 209
Barlee, Ellen, 176, 197–8, 214
Barnardo, Thomas John, 202,
    208–9, 210, 211–14, 221,
    301
Barnardo's, 1, 114, 208–9, 210,
    211–14, 230, 301
    emigration programme, 221
    fostering, 230
    Home for Destitute Boys,
        Stepney, 208, 212–14
Barnburgh Hall, Yorkshire, 46
bastardy, 84, 99, 106, 191, 230,
    259–60

INDEX

motor neurone disease, 12
Mottram, Anna, 3
Muller's Orphan House, Bristol, 192
Mumbai, India, 213
Murdoch, Lydia, 3
Murphy, Margaret, 160
Myanmar, 3, 244, 248–53

Nagasaki atomic bombing (1945), 242
Naisong Zawmadat, Myanmar, 249
Nancy, 90–91
Napoleonic Wars (1803–1815), 113, 130, 248
National Children's Homes, 209
National Health Service (NHS), 59, 168, 303
national orphans, 11
National Society for the Prevention of Cruelty to Children, 230
Nazi Germany (1933–45), 12, 17, 123, 237–41
New York State Training School for Girls, Hudson, 75
Newgate Calendar, The, 119
Newgate Prison, London, 118, 144
Nicholas Orme, 291
Nigeria, 13–14, 265
Nixon, Cheryl, 22
Nobel Prize, 240
Nonconformism, 47, 293
Norfolk Island, 142

Northampton Mercury, 218
Northampton Town F.C., 78, 79
Northamptonshire, England, 77, 78, 79, 133
Northern Ireland, 109–10
Northern Star, 184
Norway, 247
Norwich, Norfolk, 87, 177
Nottinghamshire, England, 146
Noy, William, 47
Nun's Story, The, 59
Nurjehan, 154–62
Nyerere, Julius, 40

O'Brien, James Bronterre, 184
O'Neill, Dennis, 228–9
oakum-picking, 207
Observations on the Poor Laws (Potter), 128
Observations on the Present State of the Parochial and Vagrant Poor (Scott), 127
Oeconomy of Charity, The (Trimmer), 130
Office for National Statistics, 317
Old Bailey, 20, 90, 139, 142, 144
Old Bailey Experience, 182
Old Church Slavonic, 8
Oliver Twist (Dickens), 23
Omsk, Russia, 172
On the Parish (Hindle), 3, 32
Once a Little Vagrant, Now a Little Workman (Barnardo), 209
Open University, 267

Transportation Act (1718), 110
transportation, 1, 89–91, 107–
  15, 139–42, 184, 219–24,
  261, 296
  and abuse, 108–9
  to American colonies, 89–91,
    107, 110, 111, 118
  to Australia, 24, 219, 223
  to Canada, 220, 221, 222
  George III's commution of
    death penalty (1789), 141
  to Rhodesia, 223
  to South Africa, 223
travellers, 278–83
Treaty of Utrecht (1713), 104,
  116
Trimmer, Sarah, 130, 296
*Trip from St James' to the Royal
  Exchange*, 138
tuberculosis, 17, 29, 33, 68, 270
Tuckwell, Gertrude, 206, 213,
  215–16
Tufnell, E. C., 296
Tull, Walter, 78–9
Turkey, 166, 244–5, 246, 247,
  248
Turn of the Screw, The (James), 26
Tyburn, Middlesex, 118, 143,
  183
typhus, 25, 43, 172

Ukraine, 173
Uncle Tom's Cabin (Stowe), 164–5
unemployment, 228, 237, 244,
  255
Unfortunate Objects (Evans), 117
United Nations, 244

Children's Fund (UNICEF),
  209
United States, 36–7, 90, 244
  Chicago orphans case (2017),
    36–7
  Declaration of Independence
    (1776), 90
  Fitzgerald, 64, 68, 75–6
  Monroe, 64, 66, 71–2
  Poe, 64, 66, 68
  Roosevelt, 64, 66–7
University of East Anglia, 60
University of Nottingham, 60
University of Oxford, 47, 53,
  56
Uses of Literacy, The (Hoggart),
  33

Vagabonds Act
  1547 84
  1572 84
  1609 259
vagrancy, 83–7, 98–100
Vardine, Katherine, 87
Venables, Jon, 120
Vilenski, Semen Samuilovich,
  172
violence, 309
Virginia, 90–91, 107, 110
voluntary separation, 49, 88,
  166–9, 225, 244, 265

Wade, Mary, 140–42
Waifs and Strays Society, 209
Wales, 59
Walker, Clarissa, 132
Walvin, James, 164

Wandsworth, London, 141
war, 1, 12, 68, 166, 171,
  235–55
  Battle of Palashi (1757), 55
  Black Hole of Calcutta
    (1756), 55
  Boer War (1899–1902), 33,
    228, 236
  English Civil War (1642–51),
    47, 100–101
  Napoleonic Wars (1803–
    1815), 113, 130, 248
  Syrian Civil War (2011–),
    244–7
  World War I (1914–18),
    78–9, 221, 235–7, 248
  World War II (1939–45), 12,
    14, 17, 63, 123, 137–8,
    237–44
  Yemeni Civil War (2015–),
    244
wards of the state, *see* cared for
  children
wardships, 45–6
Warsaw, Poland, 17
Waters, Margaret, 192
Watford, Hertfordshire, 133
Way, Albert, 177
Weare, HMP, 113
Webb, Sidney and Beatrice, 86,
  147, 153–4, 190
Webb, William Henry 'Chick',
  76
welfare state, 28, 29, 34, 163,
  167–9, 174, 185, 217, 293
Welles, Orson, 64
Wesley, John, 206

Wesleyanism, 69, 78, 149
West, Anne, 46
West, George, 46
Westbrook, Eliza, 57
Westbrook, Harriet, 56–7
de Westhall, Agnes, 50
Whigs, 174
Whiting, Jane, 140
Wilcke, Anna Magdalena, 74
William III & II, King of Eng-
  land, Scotland and Ireland,
  55
Williams, Kenneth, 58
Williamson, Peter, 111–12
Windscale nuclear reactor,
  Cumberland, 58
witchcraft, 29, 47, 84, 99
Wollstonecraft, Mary, 56
Wonham Manor, Brockham,
  214
Woodward, Edward, 279
Worcestershire, England, 154
Wordsworth, Dorothy, 35
Wordsworth, William, 35, 64
Workhouse Visiting Society, 207
workhouses, 2, 13, 35, 43, 84,
  102–4, 119, 127–9, 171–80,
  196–9, 204–5
  and apprenticeships, 129,
    145–6, 147, 149
  Barlee on, 176, 197–8
  Cobbe on, 196–7
  Drouet's Establishment, 172,
    178–80, 205
  Hartismere Union, 184
  and Knatchbull's Act (1723),
    127